THE INTERNATIONAL RELATIONS OF JAPAN

Also by Kathleen Newland

THE SISTERHOOD OF MAN

The International Relations of Japan

Edited by
Kathleen Newland
Department of International Relations
London School of Economics

MACMILLAN in association with
Millennium: Journal of International Studies

First published 1990

Published by
MACMILLAN ACADEMIC AND PROFESSIONAL LTD
Houndmills, Basingstoke, Hampshire RG21 2XS
and London
Companies and representatives
throughout the world

Typeset by Latimer Trend & Company Ltd
Plymouth

Printed in Great Britain by Billing & Sons Ltd, Worcester

British Library Cataloguing in Publication Data
International relations of Japan.
1. Japan. Foreign relations. Policies of government
I. Newland, Kathleen
327.52

ISBN 0–333–53456–5 (hardcover)
ISBN 0–333–53457–3 (paperback)

To Caroline Martin
whose knowledge of Japan
grew with mine
and will soon surpass it

Contents

Notes on the Contributors   x
Acknowledgements   xi

1 **Introduction**   1
Kathleen Newland

2 **Where Does Japan Fit In?**   5
Robert Gilpin

    The Japanese Challenge   6
    The Lessons of the Past   9
    Japan's Economic Strategy   15
    Conclusion   21

3 **Money and Influence: Japanese Power in the International Monetary and Financial System**   23
Eric Helleiner

    Japan as Creditor to the World   23
    State Control of External Assets   27
    Importance of the Internationalisation Process   33
    Implications for Japanese Power: Structural Power   36
    Conclusion   38

4 **The Japanese Industrial Presence in America: Same Bed, Different Dreams**   45
Michael Hodges

    Japanese Investment in the United States: Emollient or Irritant?   46
    Japan's FDI in Perspective   49
    The Changing Nature of Japanese FDI in the United States   53
    US Policy toward Inward Investment: A Case of Benign Neglect   54
    Competition between the States for Japanese Investment   60
    Anti-Trust as Industrial Policy   64
    Trojan Horse or Scapegoat? The Future of Japanese FDI in the United States   65

5 **The Third World in Japanese Foreign Policy** 71
William Nester

Japan's Foreign Policy and the Third World 71
Japan's Political and Economic Ties with the Third
World 75
Bilateral and Multilateral Relations 78
Conclusion 96

6 **Japan's Aid Diplomacy: Economic, Political or Strategic?** 100
Juichi Inada

Japan's Aid: Becoming More Political? 103
Aid Policy Making: The Facts behind Political Input 109
Commercial Interests: Myth or Reality? 113
Conclusion 117

7 **Political and Economic Influences in Japan's Relations
with China since 1978** 121
Walter Arnold

Hirschman's Trade and Investment Influence Effect
Theory 122
Political and Economic Characteristics of Sino–Japanese
Relations 124
The Influence Effect in Sino–Japanese Relations 126
Political Determinants of Sino–Japanese Economic
Relations 132
Political and Economic Conflict 133
Crisis Management through Political and Economic
Accommodation 138
Conclusion 140

8 **Japan's Security Policy after US Hegemony** 147
Tsuneo Akaha

The Decline of US Hegemony 147
Japan's Perceptions of US Power 149
US Military Presence and Security Commitments in the
Asia–Pacific Region 155
Perceptions of Security Threats to Japan 156
Broadening US–Japan Security Co-operation and Burden
Sharing 158

Troubling Defence–Trade Linkages 164
Conclusion 165

9 Stuck in a Mould: The Relationship between Japan and the Soviet Union **174**
Wolf Mendl

The Legacy of History 174
Issues in the Post-1945 Relationship 178
The Gorbachev Phenomenon 194
Conclusion 195

10 Four Japanese Scenarios for the Future **206**
Takashi Inoguchi

Japan's External Role: Opinion Poll Results 208
Four Scenarios 210
Requirements for the Four Scenarios 217
The Four Scenarios Reconsidered 219
Conclusion 222

Index 227

Notes on the Contributors

Tsuneo Akaha is Associate Professor of International Policy Studies at the Monterey Institute of International Studies, Monterey, California.

Walter Arnold is Associate Professor of Political Science at Miami University, Oxford, Ohio.

Robert Gilpin is Professor of International Affairs at the Woodrow Wilson School of Public and International Affairs, Princeton University, Princeton, New Jersey.

Eric Helleiner is a doctoral candidate in International Relations at the London School of Economics.

Michael Hodges is Senior Lecturer in International Relations at the London School of Economics.

Juichi Inada is a Research Fellow at the Japan Institute of International Affairs, Tokyo.

Takashi Inoguchi is Professor of Political Science in the Institute of Oriental Culture, University of Tokyo.

Wolf Mendl is Reader in the Department of War Studies, King's College, University of London.

William Nester is Assistant Professor in the Department of Government and Politics, St John's University, Jamaica, New York.

Kathleen Newland is a lecturer in International Relations, London School of Economics.

Acknowledgements

This volume has its origin in a special issue of *Millennium: Journal of International Studies*, which is published from the Department of International Relations at the London School of Economics. The special issue was very much a group effort. Michael Singer, then a deputy editor of *Millennium*, conceived the idea of a special issue on this subject in 1988, and brought it closer to fruition by proposing to the International Studies Assosciation that *Millennium* sponsor a panel on the international relations of Japan at the Convention of the ISA and the British International Studies Association in London in 1989. A number of the contributors to this volume participated in that panel, as did my co-editor at *Millennium*, Charles Armstrong. Other contributors were in the audience and took part in the discussion that later evolved into this book.

The entire editorial team of vol. 18 (1989) of *Millennium* contributed to producing the special issue. Book Reviews Editors Joan Dea and Ian Rowlands; Deputy Editors Scott Lichtman and Arne Wasmuth; Associate Editors Rebecca Grant, Fred Halliday, David Long and John Vincent; Business Manager Priya Mukherjee; and my co-editor Charles Armstrong. Of these, Rebecca, Ian and Charles were particularly closely involved. Spyros Economides and Hugh Dyer pitched in with much-needed help at crucial moments of the production process. Malory Greene, John Hannaford, Richard Jerram, Janet LeNoble and Sophia Okpala helped with proofreading.

I am especially grateful to the authors in this volume, who produced their chapters on a very tight timetable and in a marvellous spirit of co-operation without any of the usual inducements to such an endeavour: no foundation grants, no expense-paid trips, no honoraria. Both their work and the work of the *Millennium* editorial team was entirely voluntary. The resources expended on this project consist solely of the time and dedication of the participants and the support given to them by their home institutions, along with the institutional support in kind provided to *Millennium* by the London School of Economics, in particular its Department of International Relations.

I would also like to express thanks to Tim Farmiloe and Clare Wace at the publishers, who encouraged us to turn the special issue of *Millennium* into a book. Thanks also to the Royal Institute of International Affairs for permission to reprint the article by Takashi

Inoguchi (Chapter 10), which first appeared in the Institute's journal, *International Affairs*. As ever, Jurek Martin helped in ways too numerous to mention.

1 Introduction
Kathleen Newland

The extraordinarily rapid rise to economic prominence of Japan has cast a spotlight on its relations with the rest of the world and its place in the international system. There is little doubt that the country has the capacity to exert a profound influence in international affairs. It is, indeed, beginning to do so. In the late 1980s, the indicators of its emerging status as a major power accumulated: Japan became the world's largest creditor and its largest aid donor. Tokyo became one of the Big Three global financial centres, and Japanese institutions came to dominate international capital flows: nine of the world's ten largest banks and the top twenty-one financial institutions were, by the beginning of the 1990s, Japanese.

In the late 1980s, Japan broke through both quantitative and qualitative constraints on military spending. It has the world's third largest defence budget, of the same order of magnitude as Britain's or West Germany's, though still small relative to Japanese GNP. Its weapons capabilities are highly sophisticated, though its forces are strictly defensive in nature and barred from any use of nuclear components. Unusually, perhaps uniquely for an advanced industrial power, Japan does not export weapons.

Cautiously, Japan has begun to exert itself diplomatically as a member of the community of advanced industrial democracies, moving beyond the preoccupations of its immediate Asian neighbourhood. In the 1980s, it became the second largest contributor to the United Nations, and began to take a more active role in multilateral organisations such as the International Monetary Fund and the World Bank. It stepped into the front rank of both public and private sector efforts to rebuild market economies in Eastern Europe, not an area traditionally of interest to Japan.

No one would argue, yet, that Japan's international role matches its capacity. Many constraints, both internal and external, inhibit sharp growth in independent activism in international relations, ranging from the bitter historical memories of its neighbours to the paucity of Japanese nationals who speak foreign languages. But there are signs of change in a number of different dimensions.

The importance of Japan as an increasingly powerful and active

1

force in the international system is sufficient justification for an exploration of its international relations. The need for such an exploration has some urgency, because so much discussion of Japan's international role is one-dimensional, concentrating on its commercial relations as a trading nation. To the extent that political and military factors are brought in, the discussion is most often focused on the bilateral relationship between Japan and the United States.

This volume is an attempt to contribute to a more rounded view. The nine chapters that follow examine some of the less thoroughly explored aspects of the international relations of Japan, both in its bilateral and multilateral partnerships with other states and as the home country to important non-state actors in the international system. There are, of course, far more aspects of the international relations of Japan than one volume can hope to cover.

Robert Gilpin (Chapter 2) begins by addressing a question that has been at the forefront of speculation about Japan's rise: the relativity of power in a hegemonic international system. He asks whether the exceptional speed of Japan's emergence as a powerful national actor threatens the stability of the post-war international order. Can the other national actors – and particularly the dominant one, the United States – adjust peacefully to a new division of global responsibilities and capabilities?

Eric Helleiner (Chapter 3) looks more closely at Japan's newly acquired financial power. He argues that it derives from two separate, though interconnected, developments: Japan's emergence as a creditor and the internationalisation of the Japanese financial system. While the former has given Japan a certain degree of power in relation to other nations (most notably the United States), the latter has endowed it with a deeper and possibly longer-lasting structural power – in other words, a degree of influence over the terms on which financial and monetary relations are conducted.

Although Japan's economic success is most commonly pictured in terms of exports, foreign direct investment (FDI) is an increasingly prominent and controversial element of its international economic relations. Japanese multinational corporations use FDI in the pursuit of business expansion and as a way of avoiding protectionist barriers. The United States, with few regulations and with an undervalued dollar making US purchases relative bargains, has been their favourite destination for direct investment. In the US, Japanese FDI is welcomed by some and deplored by others. Michael Hodges (Chapter 4) explores the discrepancies between Japanese and American expectations attached to FDI, and the political tensions that result.

In contrast to relations with the United States, which sometimes seem almost suffocatingly close, post-war Japan has avoided deep involvement in the Third World. It does, however, have an important stake in Third World trade, both as an importer of raw materials and a supplier of manufactured goods. In addition, relations with Third World countries have an impact on Japan's standing within the community of nations. William Nester (Chapter 5) traces the web of Japanese interests in Asia, Africa, the Middle East and Latin America and argues that both the government and private sector have skilfully pursued Japanese interests at relatively low cost, under the rubric of 'comprehensive security'.

Juichi Inada (Chapter 6) looks specifically at Japan's official development assistance (ODA) programme, which has grown dramatically in recent years. The Japanese government has consciously used aid to promote stability in areas of strategic importance to the West, in part as a way of compensating for its relatively low military spending. It has in addition made offers of aid a part of its bilateral diplomacy in the Third World. Inada discusses the terms on which Japanese development assistance is offered, and the influence of Japanese companies on the aid programme. He concludes that Japan's aid policy clearly reflects Japanese national interests.

In the context of Third World relations, Japan's most important bilateral relationship is undoubtedly that with China. Walter Arnold (Chapter 7) demonstrates that, particularly since the signing of the Long-Term Trade Agreement (LTTA) in 1978, China has become an important market and raw-material supplier for Japan as well as a major aid recipient and a potential destination for foreign investment. But political tensions between the two countries have erupted regularly, and have been manipulated with skill by China in an effort to counterbalance a growing economic dependence on Japan.

The most distinctive feature of Japan's international posture in the post-war period has been its strictly limited military role, imposed and made possible by its relationship with the United States. This feature is increasingly problematical as the United States reduces military commitments in the Asia–Pacific region and increases pressure on Japan to raise military spending and take a more active role in regional security. According to Tsuneo Akaha (Chapter 8), a debate about the future of the military relationship between the United States and Japan has been set in motion, encouraged by the widely discussed hypothesis that the United States as a global power is in decline. He argues that internal and external political sensitivities prevent Japan from enlarging its direct military responsibilities in the region. Japan is instead making greater economic contributions to the military partnership with the United States, and expanding its overseas development assistance.

Wolf Mendl (Chapter 9) examines the relationship between Japan and the superpower that is its near neighbour to the northwest, the Soviet Union, finding very little development in relations during the post-war period. The bilateral issues that topped the diplomatic agenda in 1945 still dominate it today. Mendl analyses the current status of the territorial dispute over the Northern islands, economic relations, security concerns and public perceptions as well as the possible effects of new directions in Soviet policies in the 1990s.

Finally, Takashi Inoguchi (Chapter 10) speculates on Japan's international role in the future, sketching out four possible scenarios involving different degrees of independence from the United States. He assesses the feasibility and desirability of each scenario against the background of public opinion on foreign policy alternatives, and identifies three factors that are likely to influence the direction of Japan's role. He foresees continuing close co-operation with the United States evolving slowly toward a more multipolar system in which Japan is an important actor.

Taken together, these nine chapters reveal the complex, many-faceted nature of the international relations of Japan. Those who persist in a one-dimensional view of Japan in the international system – whether as an export machine willing to subordinate all other goals to global market share, or the permanent junior partner of the United States – are unlikely to understand or foresee accurately the evolution of an international system in which Japan is bound to exert considerable influence. Whether and for what purposes Japan will use that influence is a central question for international relations in the 1990s.

2 Where Does Japan Fit In?

Robert Gilpin

To maintain its stability, an international system must be able to absorb and respond to rapidly changing economic and military power. The sudden emergence of a new and powerful national actor triggers a process of economic and political displacement that profoundly affects the interests and status of other nations – sometimes beneficially, but more frequently detrimentally. Some states will obviously gain as a rising power stakes out its position in the game of nations; for example, at least in the medium term, the emergence of a strong and unified China gave an advantage to the United States in its confrontation with the Soviet Union. However, as power and status are by definition relative, some formerly dominant and secure states will necessarily decline and their interests will be adversely affected. Thus, the existence of an independent, industrialised China has greatly undermined the security of the Soviet Union and transformed the international politics of East Asia.

Many scholars of international relations consider this process of status displacement, or what A. F. K. Organski has called the 'power transition' problem, to have been an important source of the great conflagrations of world history.[1] As the rising state attempts to assert a claim to a higher status in the international hierarchy commensurate with its expanding power and wealth, its ambitions are resisted by the potential losers. In the absence of an effective method of 'peaceful change', or a solution to what economists call the 'adjustment problem', there is a danger that the issue will be resolved by a great war. Thus, the rapid development of German power in the late nineteenth century and the failure of Europe to make a successful adjustment to this shift in the balance of military and economic power laid the basis for the two great wars of this century.

The astounding rise of Japan in the latter decades of this century has brought to the fore the crucial issue of power transition and economic adjustment. Is peaceful adjustment to the new power equation possible? What may be the consequences of this significant displacement of established global relationships? Will we repeat the terrible mistakes of the past, or is there reason to hope that a process of peaceful change

5

will bring about a new and stable international economic and political order?

Obviously, some important and striking differences exist between the contemporary situation and the past. The advent of nuclear weapons has made the great powers significantly less willing to settle their quarrels by the direct use of armed conflict. The rapid growth of economic interdependence and the benefits of international commerce have created a mutual interest in maintaining the stability of the world economy. Furthermore, 'the Japanese challenge' to the system arises, at least for the moment, from its economic dimension and a desire for a higher status in the international system. There is not a wholesale attack on the foundations of the international economic and political order such as that which occurred in Wilhelmian/Nazi Germany and pre-war Japan. Nonetheless, it would be overly sanguine to conclude that Japan, if its ambitions were frustrated and discriminated against by the United States and Western Europe, would not revert to extreme nationalistic and militaristic policies.

Thus far, the 'Japanese challenge' to the international economic status quo has appeared in two basic forms. In the early 1970s, as a consequence of the revolution in world energy prices, the Japanese made a radical shift in their foreign economic policy. Having accomplished the post-war reconstruction of their economy, they restrained domestic economic growth and shifted to an aggressive policy of export-led economic growth. In the early 1980s, due to the revaluation of the yen, foreign pressures to reduce their massive trade surplus, and the rise of foreign protectionism, Japan modified its overwhelming emphasis on exports and began to take full advantage of its newly achieved status as the world's foremost creditor nation.

THE JAPANESE CHALLENGE

The economic and political consequences of the rise of new industrial and trading powers such as Japan over the past two decades are powerfully affected by the speed with which this change takes place. How long does it take for the rising challenger to take a significant share of world markets? In the modern world, four nations have captured substantial shares of international trade in manufacturing in relatively brief periods and thereby upset the international status quo. After the Napoleonic Wars and continuing late into the nineteenth century, Great Britain became the first successful challenger. The second was Germany between 1890 and 1913, and the third was the United States, also beginning in 1890 and greatly accelerating its challenge in the twentieth century.[2] Since 1964 Japan has risen spectacularly as an industrial and trading power. In each case, the impact of the resultant export drives and of the dislocations caused to other economies generated strong resistance and economic conflict.

As Arthur Lewis points out, the process that we are observing was well understood by David Hume in the mid-eighteenth century: 'Manufacturers gradually shift their places, leaving those countries and provinces which they have already enriched, and flying to others, whither they are allured by the cheapness of provisions and labour'.[3] As this occurs, technological imitation and the creation of similar industrial structures lead to a global over-capacity in particular sectors.[4] Invariably, the result has been an intensification of economic rivalries.

Although advanced countries do trade with one another more than with non-industrialised countries and thus, over the long term, benefit from the spread of economic growth, in the short term the creation of highly similar industrial structures and export patterns does cause commercial conflict in a number of manufacturing sectors.[5] As Gautam Sen argues: 'The reproduction of similar structures of production introduces a secular tendency towards the creation of surplus capacity in substantial areas of manufacturing since internal and external economies of scale compel a level of production which most countries cannot sustain through domestic consumption alone.[6] The result is intensified competition.

Japan's failure or unwillingness to limit its trade surplus sufficiently, and the equal failure of other industrial powers to adjust their economies to the structural transformation of the world economy, threaten the stability of the international system. Each of the three major centres of the international economy – the United States, Western Europe, and Japan – are protecting their basic industries and, through various forms of state interventionism, are attempting to establish themselves as leaders in those high technology industries that are becoming the 'commanding heights' of the emerging world economy. In this struggle for industrial supremacy and world markets, the Japanese are seen, correctly, to be rapidly outdistancing their American and European rivals.

Until the 1980s, the Japanese challenge was limited to the realm of international trade. Then, in the mid-1980s, a new and politically more significant Japanese economic challenge began to take shape as Japan became the world's largest creditor nation. The emerging role of Japan as a financial power and capital exporter has magnified the seriousness of the Japanese threat for many American and West European observers. It has given Japan the capacity to penetrate and influence other economies, much as Great Britain and the United States were able to do at those earlier periods when they each succeeded in converting their growing trade surpluses into the instruments of financial power.

This transformation of Japan's trading and financial status has made the question of where an expanding and dynamic Japan fits into the world's economic and political system increasingly urgent. In the United States, this issue has become one of the most important on the political agenda. For many politicians and the professional Japan-bashers, the 'Japan question' and the perceived threat posed by Japan to the American economy have even superseded concerns over the Soviet Union and international communism. Others regard Japan as America's helpmate, a partner which will share the financial burden of maintaining the international status quo and use its wealth to solve the problems of the world economy.

West Europeans, on the other hand, appear to be less equivocal regarding the Japanese challenge; they take a very different position from that prevalent in the United States. Whereas the potential US–Japan economic conflict is leavened somewhat by shared political and security concerns in East Asia, no such compensating influence exists in European–Japanese relations. An extensive array of alliances among US and Japanese corporations, as well as the remarkable expansion of production by Japanese firms in the United States, moderate US antagonism toward the Japanese. In addition, after several painful experiences, citizens of the United States have discovered that they need the Japanese to help finance the US economy, to supply high quality components for their industry and, increasingly, to obtain the most advanced technology for their civilian economy and armed forces. On the other hand, West Europeans, at least judged by their past behaviour and the policies associated with the implementation of the Single European Act, appear to want to keep the Japanese as far away as conceivably possible.

A partial answer to the question of where Japan may fit into the changing world economy may be found by considering the experiences of Great Britain and the United States as rising trading and financial powers. What are the similarities and, perhaps of greater significance, the differences? Does the behaviour of other creditor nations suggest that Japan could or would fill the gap created by the relative decline of

US power and perform the supporting role envisioned by many Americans? Or, as some Americans and West Europeans fear, does Japanese economic expansionism pose a potential danger that must be stopped before it is too late?

THE LESSONS OF THE PAST

It is desirable to study British and US experiences to find lessons that can be distilled for the Japanese as the emergent economic leader. What clues do the British and American eras of international finance give the forthcoming era of Japanese finance? What are the implications for the sharing of burdens and power by the United States and Japan? What are the prospects that the Japanese will assume the 'global responsibilities' expected of them and use their capital to promote the public good of global economic development? Several generalisations derived from the historical experience of international finance will be discussed, along with their possible implications for Japan as a capital exporter.

Political, military, and financial dominance have tended to accompany and reinforce one another in the modern international system. Both Great Britain and the United States, especially, employed their financial power to advance their perceived national interests. While the British interests were mainly commercial, their trade and overseas investment also strengthened their global military and political position, at least until very late in the nineteenth century.[7] In the era of US dominance, strategic interests have played an even greater role in financial affairs. From the Marshall Plan (1947) to the present, successive US administrations have used foreign aid and influenced financial flows to support US foreign policy objectives. Both dominant nations have also used military and other forms of power to protect their overseas investments and their larger commercial interests. When British and American power waned, their overseas investments and economic interests became increasingly vulnerable.

The historical connection among these aspects of national power suggest that it will be very difficult to achieve a division of labour between Japan as financial leader and the United States as political/military leader. An arrangement in which the Japanese, like the British and Americans before them, used their financial power to advance their commercial interests while the Americans continued to pay the major share of the costs of maintaining the security of the international system would not be very satisfactory from the latter's point of view.

Nor would the Japanese feel secure that the United States would use its influence to protect their overseas commercial interests. Reconciling the divergent interests of the two nations in such a division of labour would tax political ingenuity.

The financial and monetary systems have also been intimately linked in the past. In the nineteenth and twentieth centuries, the currency of the dominant financial power served along with gold as the principal reserve and transaction currency, and this in turn reinforced the political and military position of the dominant power. For example, the role of the dollar as the basis of the monetary system since the Second World War has given the United States what Charles de Gaulle called an 'exorbitant privilege'. It has enabled the United States to pursue its policies with little concern for its balance of payments. The decline of the United States to the status of net debtor over the past several years has undermined the international role of the dollar and in turn has affected the overall power of the United States. The reasons why this change in the status of the dollar has not yet significantly affected the international position of the United States will be discussed below.

How the Japanese will use their financial power to shape the international monetary system is a crucial question. Will they continue to support the dollar as the basis of the system, or will they want the yen to play a much larger role? Thus far, they have financed the continuing importance of the dollar, but there are many reasons why this policy could change. It is doubtful, for example, that Japan would continue to support the dollar if it were substantially devalued in order to help the United States achieve a trade and current account surplus to repay its huge accumulated foreign debt.

The present situation of divided responsibility for the international financial and monetary systems surely cannot last indefinitely. While the dollar continues to be the basis of the monetary system and the currency in which the American debt to the Japanese is denominated, the exchange rate risk is transferred to the Japanese. In these circumstances, the Japanese have a powerful short-term incentive to influence the value of the dollar and an equally powerful long-term incentive to displace the dollar with the yen in the international monetary order, at least to some extent. Although this latter development would mean the loss of the 'exorbitant privilege' of the United States, it would also have beneficial effects for the American economy. The costs and benefits of such a change in the international role of the dollar, however, will not be pursued here. The point is rather that any discussion of Japan's responsibilities as a leading creditor nation must also take into account the role of Japan and the yen in the international monetary system and its implications for American power and domestic prosperity.

Huge capital flows such as those that took place in the British and American eras can occur only in a stable and predictable international environment. Particular economic and political conditions have in the past encouraged creditors to lend vast sums to foreigners. The first has been the military supremacy of the dominant financial power and its consequent capacity to protect the investment. In the oft-quoted couplet of Hilaire Belloc, 'Whatever happens we have got/the maxim gun and they have not'. The second condition has been the relative stability of the international monetary system and the absence of exchange rate risk. British and American foreign investment, with the important exception of the 1970s, took place in a system of fixed exchange rates based on the gold standard and the dollar standard, respectively. The third condition has been the stability of international prices, as in the late nineteenth century. While international bankers failed to heed the dangers of inflation in the 1970s, the guarantee of a low rate of global inflation has undoubtedly become once again a prerequisite for a renewal of a massive flow of development capital to the world's developing economies.

It is also important to recognise that almost all of the exported capital in the British and American eras went to economies located within the larger European cultural and political framework. Although one can cite important exceptions, the borrowing countries tended to be overseas colonies populated by European emigrants ('lands of recent settlement'), other European countries and, as in the case today of the so-called East Asian NICs, economies in the creditor's sphere of influence. In other words, foreign investment has tended to take place in other capitalist economies or in political dependencies. The borrowers could be trusted in part because they shared a similar set of values or were politically subordinated. But they also could be and frequently were pressured by the use of the creditors' economic and military power. In general, the capital went to economies that could use it to produce exports with which the borrowers could repay the debt.

These lessons from the nineteenth century were largely forgotten in the 1970s, when capital flowed much too freely to economies that could not employ it effectively. A substantial portion of investment went to East European and less developed countries with strong traditions of inefficient state interventionism and histories of subsidising consumption. The more recent and cautious behaviour of international investors suggests that these lessons have now been relearned as a result of the global debt crisis and the confiscation of foreign investments by nationalistic governments.

At the present, these three prerequisites for a massive flow of Japanese capital to developing countries simply do not exist. As James Dale Davidson and Sir William Rees-Mogg argue in their insightful albeit overly dramatic book *Blood in the Street* – whose subtitle is 'Investment Profits in a World Gone Mad' – the security of foreign investment has greatly decreased as a result of the decline of American power and of Western capitalism more generally, relative to Third World countries with histories of interventionist and nationalistic policies.[8] While one would not want a return to the gunboat diplomacy of the past, the debt crisis and the confiscation of foreign investments reveal the impotence of creditors. Secondly, the shift from fixed to flexible exchange rates has greatly increased the exchange-rate risk inherent in foreign investment. And, thirdly, the jittery behaviour of the global financial community suggests that it fears a return to the high inflation of the 1970s.

Under these extremely uncertain conditions, it may be unrealistic to expect that the Japanese will loan vast sums to the developing world for economic development. At the least, the Japanese will require the establishment of international policies and institutions that protect such an investment, i.e. policies and institutions over which they can exercise greater influence. All of the existing international economic institutions such as the World Bank and the International Monetary Fund are controlled by the United States and Western Europe. Recent experience suggests that neither is willing to see its influence diminish in order to accommodate Japanese demands for a larger role in the leadership of these organisations. The Japanese have stressed their unwillingness to place large amounts of their capital in the World Bank and other multilateral institutions unless they have a greater say about its use. Japanese initiatives for increasing the flow of capital to developing countries in fact include the requirement that Japan's influence be increased over existing international financial institutions. They have also proposed the establishment of new organisations over which they would exercise control. Japan's increasing importance as a creditor nation will surely have significant implications for the management of the world economy and its institutions.

This last point brings us to another important lesson from the eras of British and American financial leadership. Other nations acquiesced in the role that these economic powers came to play in the international economic system in part because they were unable to prevent it. The rise of these two countries to the status of pre-eminent creditor nations, which meant acquiring a powerful influence over other economies, occurred in a highly conducive environment. Other nations were unable to thwart the export drives that provided the basis of British and then of American accumulation of capital. Moreover, the process of capital accumulation for both Great Britain and the United States took place slowly and during a period in which the overall rate of global economic growth was generally high (except for periodic recessions and the Great Depression of the 1930s): approximately from 1820 to 1900, and from 1920 to sometime in the 1970s, respectively. As a consequence, other nations had a greater opportunity to adjust to the changes in the structure of world trade forced upon them by the trade offensives of the expanding British and American economies.

Of equal significance, the international division of labour that resulted from these developments, at least for the temperate zone economies, was based largely on manufacturing. Although other nations had to respond to the structural changes caused by the rise of Great Britain and the United States as trading and, subsequently, financial powers, the fact that these economies were major importers of the manufactured products of other countries mitigated, at least to some extent, potential international economic conflicts. Both nations in fact ran deficits in manufactured goods at the height of their rise as financial powers. Therefore, despite the expressions of alarm in many countries over British and American exports, the continued existence of the manufacturing base in other economies was never really threatened.

Japan's emergence as a creditor nation is taking place in a decidedly different manner and in a much less favourable environment. Its remarkably rapid rise as a trading and financial power has imposed a large adjustment burden on other advanced countries. In addition, the slowdown in the global rate of economic growth and the peculiar structure of the Japanese economy and Japanese trade accentuate this adjustment problem. As an importer of raw materials and an exporter of manufactured products, Japan has a relatively low propensity to import the manufactured goods of other countries. As a creditor nation, Japan should be expected to import more manufactured goods from other developed and developing countries. If it fails to assume this particular 'global responsibility', its rise to the status of creditor nation could have a distorting and negative effect on international trade and economic development.

Thus far, Japan has not followed the course set by Great Britain and the United States during their ascendancy. Instead of using its capital to foster global economic development, Japan has chosen to use its capital to strengthen further its global financial position, to establish manufacturing subsidiaries abroad, and to solidify its political ties to the United States. In part, Japan's unwillingness to invest in the developing world is due to the global debt crisis, the low absorptive capacity of most LDCs, and the political risks involved. But, as will be argued below, the preference for investing in the United States and a few other countries is also a consequence of Japan's basic economic strategy. In section 3, I shall return to this subject.

Whereas Great Britain and the United States were able to surmount the political opposition to their rise as trading and creditor nations, Japan is in a much weaker position. As Japan has moved rapidly up the technological ladder and increased its competitiveness in one sector after another, powerful economic interests in the United States and in Western Europe have become more and more hostile. The West Europeans have become particularly resistant to what they perceive as Japan's economic threat in manufacturing and in finance. Whatever the ultimate success of Western Europe's plans to create a unified common economy by 1993, the motive in part is to counter the growing challenge of the Japanese in trade and in financial services.[9]

It is also important to consider the implications for US–West European relations and, more generally, for the global international economic and political system if the United States were to enter into a significant 'burden-sharing/power-sharing' arrangement with the Japanese, as some Americans propose. It is highly unlikely that the West Europeans would accept graciously such a shift in American foreign policy and its consequences for the international distribution of economic power. A US choice between Atlantic and Pacific allies would be an exceptionally important development with major political and military ramifications. Thus, in evaluating Japan's new role as a powerful economic actor, the potential implications of this development for the Western alliance and other global political relations should not be neglected.

Will Western Europe, or even the United States for that matter, accept Japan's emergent role as the world's dominant economy? Rising protectionist pressures in the United States and Western Europe reveal that influential forces in these economies will oppose the international division of labour implied by the growth of Japanese trading and financial power. Western Europe has already taken strong actions to protect its industrial base and even more stringent measures appear to be in the offing. In the United States, the implications of ongoing developments are increasingly resented by many groups and feared by public officials on both the left and the right.

The descent of the United States to net debtor status during the Reagan years has already begun to raise a number of pressing problems in American–Japanese relations. For example, the United States will have to achieve an export surplus some day to repay its vast accumulated foreign debt. This in turn could necessitate that the Japanese run a trade deficit and reverse, or at least slow, their transformation into the world's dominant financial power. The Japanese have only just begun to make the necessary domestic and international adjustments to their new economic position.

The available evidence indicates that a deceleration of the rate of Japanese capital accumulation has in fact begun. The rise of the yen and the slowdown in global economic growth are forcing the Japanese to increase their emphasis on domestic-led economic growth. This shift is occurring in accordance with the so-called Maekawa Report of 1986, whose title, *Report of the Advisory Group on Economic Structural Adjustment for International Harmony*, suggests that the Japanese appreciate the increasing intolerance of other countries toward their huge trade surplus. However, it is doubtful that the Japanese will ever willingly accept a trade deficit, or follow the British and American examples as creditor nations of becoming net importers of manufactured goods. Yet, if Japan does not assume such a global responsibility, its new role as a creditor nation will become an increasingly important cause of friction between Japan and other countries.

JAPAN'S ECONOMIC STRATEGY

It should not be surprising to learn that Japan, like Great Britain and the United States before it, has taken advantage of the opportunities provided by its new role as the world's foremost financial power to advance its perceived national interests. However, these interests and the environment within which Japan has thus far pursued these interests set Japan's situation quite apart from Great Britain and the United States as creditor nations. These differences have profound implications for the role that Japan may be expected to play as a capital exporter and for its relations with the United States and the rest of the world.

A label for Japan's strategy as a creditor has already been provided by the distinguished economist Kiyoshi Kojima. Contrasting Japan's foreign direct investment with that of the United States, Kojima argues that Japanese foreign direct investment attempts to be 'trade-creating', whereas American foreign direct investment has been 'trade-destroying'.[10] Japanese foreign direct investment has sought to increase, or at least maintain, Japanese exports; US foreign direct investment, on the other hand, has tended to replace US exports by establishing production facilities abroad to serve the US or world markets. Although Kojima was referring specifically to direct investment by Japanese corporations, his characterisation is applicable to almost all Japanese foreign investment.

The fundamental purpose of Japanese investment policy has been to further the strategic objectives of Japan. Through its economic policies and influence over foreign investment, Japan has sought to further its own economic development, national security, and political autonomy. The pursuit of these objectives has entailed the preservation of Japan's protective alliance with the United States and the continual strengthening of the Japanese industrial base. Although Japan, in the name of 'comprehensive security', has given substantial official foreign assistance to several key countries such as Pakistan and the Philippines, the Japanese, like the British, have identified their national interest primarily in commercial terms. Unlike the British and more like the Americans, however, security and economic interests have always been closely linked for the Japanese.

Initially, the Japanese strongly resisted the idea of foreign investment because they feared the weakening of their manufacturing base and preferred exporting from domestic plants. For example, they eschewed foreign direct investment in manufacturing and preferred short-term contracts to procure commodities from overseas suppliers. With the rise of labour costs in Japan and the appreciation of the yen in the 1970s, they began to invest in the developing countries of East Asia and to automate domestic production. Of equal importance, the threat of protectionism in other advanced countries as well as the rising value of the yen have more recently caused the Japanese to accelerate their investments in the United States and Western Europe. Despite this significant reorientation of their economic policies, their strategic objectives of strengthening their domestic economic base and increasing national autonomy have not really changed. Only the tactics have changed.

The most conspicuous aspect of this change in Japanese economic policies is the establishment of a manufacturing and economic base in the United States and Western Europe and the consequent jumping of trade barriers. The rapid expansion of Japanese manufacturing subsidiaries, distribution networks and, more recently, financial institutions in the United States is the most impressive manifestation of this fundamental shift in Japanese policies. These overseas subsidiaries continue to be closely linked to their home industries and to serve the latter's interests in 'trade-creation'. For example, it has been estimated that approximately 40 per cent of Japanese exports to the United States are of component parts, a substantial fraction of which go to Japan's own subsidiaries or to joint ventures with American firms.

Although the differential rate of return on capital in Japan and the United States is the most important explanation of the massive flow of capital from the former to the latter in the 1980s, the political and economic links that developed between Japan and the United States during the Reagan presidency are also of considerable importance. A close symbiotic relationship, which *The Economist* has called the 'Nichibei economy', has been created.[11] The term 'Nichibei' amalgamates portions of the Japanese characters for 'Japan' and 'United States', and thus symbolises the fact that Japanese investment in the United States is rapidly integrating these two economies in one sector after another and is undermining the earlier primacy for the United States of trans-Atlantic economic and political relationships.

The special American–Japanese financial relationship was codified in the May, 1984 report of the Japan–US Yen–Dollar Committee, which resulted from pressures by the Reagan Administration on Japan to liberalise and internationalise the Japanese financial system.[12] Although the details of this agreement lie outside the scope of this chapter, its effect was to open the door to massive exports of Japanese capital to the United States. It also increased the international role of the yen and thus may have accelerated a movement toward a tripartite monetary system based on the dollar, the yen, and the Deutsche Mark.

As Peter Drucker has pointed out, the subsequent development of American–Japanese economic relations has been extraordinary. The key element is that the United States has been borrowing its own currency from the Japanese. The scale and significance of this situation are unprecedented in international finance. 'For the first time in history a debtor nation stands to benefit both on its capital account and on its trading account from devaluing its own currency.'[13] Although Japanese capital has flowed into many sectors of the American economy, one of its most important functions has been to finance the huge American budget deficit.

Since the early 1980s, the Japanese have been the most important purchasers of notes and bonds issued by the United States Treasury to finance the American budget deficit. In effect, during the Reagan Administration the Japanese began to underwrite the American defence buildup and domestic prosperity. Japanese capital flows to the United States have tripled, from an annual rate of $20 billion in 1982 to $60 billion in 1987.[14] The Japanese, having found a ready market for the output of their factories, are thus loaning the United States the money to sustain their own export strategy, to maintain a high level of domestic employment, and to help finance the American military power upon which the security of Japan rests.

The Japanese, by loaning dollars back to the United States, have sought to maintain their most valuable export market and to prevent unemployment in Japan, where approximately 15 per cent of the jobs are tied to exports. Although domestic demand has recently become more important for Japanese industry, the loss of the American market would result in high unemployment and severe repercussions in those heavy and high-technology industries committed to the concept of lifetime employment. Again, in Drucker's words, 'the Japanese policy maker prefers the almost certain but future losses on the loans made to the US government to the political and social – and immediate – risks of massive unemployment at home'. It should be noted that due to the devaluation of the dollar since 1985, Japanese investors have probably lost billions in dollar-denominated securities and are now investing more in real assets.

Perhaps the most important and questionable aspect of this new American–Japanese relationship is in the area of international monetary affairs. Whereas the Reagan Administration has depended on Japanese capital to finance its budget deficit, the Japanese have desired a stable dollar pegged at a level sufficiently high to maintain the American market for Japanese exports. An implicit understanding appears to exist between the two countries that the Japanese will continue to finance the American budget deficit as long as the exchange rate of the dollar and the yen is satisfactory to the Japanese. As Lawrence B. Krause has argued, the Baker–Miyazawa Agreement of October 1986, and the subsequent Louvre Agreement of February 1987, were at least in part attempts by the United States to placate the Japanese by stabilising the exchange rate of the dollar and preventing its further decline.[15] In Krause's opinion, although these agreements met the interests of Japanese exporters and investors, the value of the dollar was set too high, so that it has been detrimental to the interests of

American industry. The continuing huge trade deficit of the American economy lends credence to Krause's argument.

The coincidence of interests between the American and the Japanese governments has become quite remarkable. The former needs Japanese capital to compensate for the inadequacy of American savings, to finance its budget deficit and to keep American interest rates low. Without Japanese capital the budget deficit would cause American interest rates to soar and economic growth to slow considerably. The Japanese have been willing to export capital to finance the budget deficit, uphold the value of the dollar, and help their American ally. Thus, the Japanese are exploiting their new role as a creditor nation in pursuit of their perceived national interests.

Despite the short-term benefits of this seemingly mutually beneficial American–Japanese relationship, its long-term prospects are problematic. Although the basic problem is ultimately the American budget deficit, many American economists and others believe that the overvalued dollar, which is supported largely by Japanese capital, is harmful to important sectors of American industry and encourages the spread of protectionism. Critics of the relationship have become concerned over the increasing influence of Japanese finance in the American economy. Others take note of the fact that a growing segment of American securities, real estate, and other tangible assets are in Japanese hands.

The long-term problem for the United States, and for the rest of the trading world as well, is the repayment of the vast accumulated US debt – which is rapidly approaching one trillion dollars – to the Japanese and to other foreign creditors. To accomplish this task, the United States will have to devalue the dollar even more substantially than it has already and achieve a trade surplus.

The problems that such an American turnaround in trade and finance would cause for other nations can only be described as formidable. It would certainly require a substantial appreciation of the yen and Japanese importation of huge quantities of foreign products. The Japanese as well as the West Europeans and the NICs could be expected to resist strongly any large appreciations of their currencies because of the consequences for domestic employment. Changes in exchange rates would most certainly require considerable international co-operation over macroeconomic policy among the United States, Western Europe and Japan in order to avoid a devastating mercantilistic conflict over trade.

Doubts also exist on the Japanese side of the US–Japan special relationship. In the short run, Japan is buying time and adjusting its domestic economic base and policies to a world in which the US economic and military roles will be substantially diminished. In anticipation of this era of post-hegemonic America, Japanese political and economic leaders have begun to ask if it is in the long-term interest of Japan to finance US prosperity and an international leadership whose primary concerns are not always complementary to those of Japan. Few Japanese are prepared to jettison their economic and security ties to the United States; however, the Japanese sense US decline and are aware that the United States too frequently has proved to be an unreliable partner, given to quixotic changes in its policies. Surely, the Japanese must ask themselves whether they can use their new role as a capital exporter to increase their overall security and political independence.

For many Japanese, the possibility that they could use their economic and financial power to strengthen Japan's leadership position in the Pacific and in East Asia is an increasingly appealing idea. Through the export of capital to Asian countries and the creation of new markets in this most rapidly growing region of the world economy, Japan would be able to decrease its over-dependence on the United States. This possibility was suggested in a 1986 report by the influential Nomura Research Institute. In response to the question what the role of the Tokyo international financial centre should be, the report replied that 'Tokyo should be the core international financial center for the Western Pacific region, channelling globally traded funds into regional markets'.[16] In such a fashion, Japan could establish itself as the financial hegemon of the fastest growing region in the world and move closer toward its strategic objectives of economic security and political autonomy.

If Japan continues to perform as it has in the past and Tokyo does become the principal financial centre in the world, a number of questions arise about how it would use the power that accompanies this role. What would its relations be with the two other financial centres in London and New York? Would Japan continue to support the dollar, or would it encourage a greater use of the yen, thus transforming the international monetary system? In an era of global capital shortage, would the Japanese use their financial resources to acquire leadership of the debt-ridden Third World, to strengthen their ties with other advanced economies or, as the Nomura Research Institute implies, to carve an economic sphere of influence in the Pacific? Would they

Robert Gilpin 21

finance the development of China or Soviet Siberia? Perhaps they would, after all, choose the option of greater 'burden-sharing' with the United States. As this chapter has attempted to argue, in deciding whether or not this American–Japanese partnership is really a sound and feasible idea, a number of political as well as economic and technical issues need to be addressed.

CONCLUSION

A principal issue posed for the contemporary world economy is whether conditions are ripe in the late twentieth century for Japan to repeat the earlier British and American experiences as the leading economic and creditor nation. In setting forth this question, this chapter assumes that it is necessary for a particular nation to play a leadership role, especially by exporting huge amounts of its capital to other nations and thereby providing the collective good of economic development. If Japan does not follow the British and American examples, one must still ask the question: where does an economically powerful and dynamic Japan fit into the emergent international economy?

Notes and References

1. A. F. K. Organski, *World Politics* (New York: Alfred A. Knopf, 1968).
2. W. Arthur Lewis, 'International Competition in Manufactures', *American Economic Review*, 47 (1957) p. 579.
3. Lewis, 'International Competition', p. 582.
4. Gautam Sen, *The Military Origins of Industrialization and International Trade Rivalry* (New York: St Martin's Press, 1984).
5. Sen, *The Military Origins.*
6. Sen, *The Military Origins*, p. 158.
7. Paul M. Kennedy, 'Strategy versus Finance in Twentieth-Century Great Britain', *The International History Review* (January 1981) pp. 44–61.
8. James Dale Davidson and William Rees-Mogg, *Blood in the Streets* (New York: Summit Books, 1987).
9. Richard W. Wright and Gunter A. Pauli, *The Second Wave: Japan's Global Assault on Financial Services* (New York: St Martin's Press, 1987).
10. Kiyoshi Kojima, *Foreign Direct Investment: A Japanese Model of Multinational Business Operations* (London: Croom Helm, 1978).
11. *The Economist* (7 December 1985) Survey Japan, p. 17.
12. Jeffrey A. Frankel, *The Yen–Dollar Agreement: Liberating Japanese*

Capital Markets (Washington: Institute for International Economics, 1984).

13. Peter F. Drucker, 'American–Japanese Realities', *Wall Street Journal* (11 October 1985) p. 28.
14. William Branson, 'Capital Flows from Japan to the US: Economic and Political Realities' (unpublished 1987).
15. Lawrence Krause, 'The Challenge of Japan's Financial Reach for the US Economy' (unpublished and undated).
16. Nomura Research Institute, *The World Economy and Financial Markets in 1995: Japan's Role and Challenges* (Tokyo: Nomura, 1986) p. 338.

3 Money and Influence: Japanese Power in the International Monetary and Financial System

Eric Helleiner

In the past few years, much attention has been paid to the growing power of Japan in the international monetary and financial system. At the end of the day, however, opinions vary considerably about the degree of this power. Robert Gilpin, to provide one example, portrays Japan as the dominant financial power of today.[1] Susan Strange, on the other hand, asserts that Japanese power in the international economy is still quite limited.[2] This chapter argues that the confusion might stem in part from the fact that Japan's growing influence in the international monetary and financial system is derived from two separate although interconnected developments: Japan's emergence as a creditor nation and the internationalisation of the Japanese financial system. Each of these can be seen to have brought a different kind of power to the Japanese state. Creditor status can be seen to have given Japan a certain amount of 'relational power' – defined by Strange as 'the power of A to get B to do something that they would not otherwise do' – while internationalisation has allowed Japan to acquire a degree of 'structural power', which in Strange's terms is the power to 'change the range of choices open to others'.[3] In what follows, each of these phenomena is outlined in turn and analysed in terms of its impact on the influence of the Japanese state in the international monetary and financial system.

JAPAN AS CREDITOR TO THE WORLD

In most people's minds, the rising power of the Japanese state in the international monetary and financial system is connected with Japan's emergence as a major creditor in the 1980s. A short summary of this development is in order before proceeding to analyse its implications for Japanese power.

From the end of the Second World War until the 1980s, Japan had been, with the exception of a few periods, a net borrower of funds from the world. After 1981, this pattern was suddenly and dramatically reversed. Between 1981 and 1988, Japan's net external assets rose from $10 billion to $291.7 billion. In comparative terms, this growth in its net external asset position turned Japan into the world's largest net creditor, a rank it has now held for the past four years consecutively.[4] It is because the vast bulk of this investment abroad has been in the form of portfolio investment, rather than foreign direct investment, that observers have come to talk of Japan's new 'financial power' arising from its creditor status.[5]

What is the explanation for Japan's rapid emergence as a major creditor to the world? Some have concluded that capital outflows from Japan are simply a natural byproduct of its growing wealth. In particular, it is often suggested that Japan is merely following a common historical path of growth in which a country moves through a number of phases from 'young debtor' status to that of 'mature creditor'.[6] This explanation, however, is weakened somewhat by the fact that, as Douglass North points out, few nations have in reality followed this path: 'There is not a normal sequence through which an economy must move from young debtor to mature creditor over a given span of time. The notion that such a sequence exists was drawn from U.S. experience, but it fits few other countries'.[7]

In place of this explanation, a more satisfactory account is one which focuses on the changing balance between savings and investment within Japan. Throughout the post-war era, Japan had promoted a high rate of savings in order that there would be a ready source of funds for large-scale corporate investment. With the slowdown in economic growth in the early 1970s, however, corporate demand for funds decreased while the rate of savings remained high. The 'excess' savings which emerged were absorbed initially by rapidly growing government deficits. By the late 1970s, however, considerable political resistance to these government deficits had emerged. The opposition came principally from the Ministry of Finance (which feared a departure from the post-war norm of balanced budgets) and from the corporate lobby (which worried that future tax increases would fall largely on big business).[8] After the failure – owing to widespread political resistance – of an attempted tax reform in 1979 which would have provided a wider base of revenue from which to fund government spending, these two groups began to push successfully for reduced government spending. The government's deficit as a proportion of GNP consequently dropped substantially from its peak in 1978 of 5.5 per cent to 0.8 per cent by 1985.[9]

It is in this context that the massive capital exports from Japan grew in the 1980s. As government borrowing fell, the 'excess' savings previously absorbed by the government were released, exerting a downward pressure on the interest rate. This was further reinforced by an easing of monetary policy. In these circumstances, Japanese investors with large excess funds began to look abroad for better investment opportunities. They found these primarily in the United States, where an expanding government deficit and tight monetary policy pushed up local interest rates.

The Japanese capital outflows that emerged were thus largely a product of domestic imbalances. These in turn can be traced to domestic political trends and decisions. Not only did Japan continue to promote a high savings rate after its post-war growth boom had begun to taper off but, more importantly, it has been unable politically to absorb the 'excess' savings which have emerged. This has been, first, because of political resistance to tax reform, and second, because of an unwillingness to engage in deficit-financed public investment. Gilpin's parallel to late nineteenth century analyses of European imperialism seems apt: 'Unwilling to make the needed domestic reforms, Japanese capitalism therefore required a "colony" to rid itself of these financial surpluses. The Japanese found this "vent for surplus" in an America experimenting with Reaganomics'.[10]

Does this enormous build-up of external assets give power to the Japanese state? It is commonly assumed that the Japan must have acquired a significant degree of power in the international monetary and financial system through its status as a major creditor. If we look to some examples of past creditors, however, we can see that it is necessary to be cautious before reaching such a conclusion. In some cases, such as that of the United States after the Second World War, considerable power has accrued to a creditor state. In others, such as Saudi Arabia after 1973, it has not. In order to determine the degree of power that the Japanese state has acquired, insight may be gained by comparing its experience to that of these two contrasting examples. Three variables emerge out of this comparative approach as important in determining whether creditor status brings power: (1) the duration and size of the financial flows, (2) the degree of the creditor's vulnerability to its major debtors, and (3) the degree of state control over the financial flows.

First of all, the length of time during which a country is a creditor and the size of its foreign assets will play some role in determining how much power will accrue to the creditor state. In the case of Saudi Arabia, it could be argued that its status as a major creditor was too short-lived and involved too small a sum of funds for it to be able to build up sufficient leverage over its debtors or to establish institutions which might have translated its creditor status into power. By contrast, the greater relative significance and longer duration of US financial exports to Europe and Japan after the Second World War enabled the United States to exert a larger and more consistent influence over its debtors during this period.

Judging the Japanese case with respect to this variable is difficult because we are uncertain as to the duration or future size of its capital exports. In quantity terms, it is worth noting that Japan has already reached a creditor status roughly equal to that of OPEC as a whole at its peak. In terms of duration, however, the situation is less certain. Bill Emmott suggests that Japan's creditor status could disappear as early as 1995. In his opinion, this is too short a time for Japan to acquire significant power within the international monetary and financial system.[11]

A second variable influencing the degree of power that can be derived from creditor status is the overall vulnerability of the creditor to its debtors. In the case of Saudi Arabia, military and economic vulnerability to the West left it with less leverage than it might otherwise have had. Saudi Arabia's economic vulnerability was two-fold, operating not only through its heavy dependence on the West as a market for oil, but also through the fact that its assets were held primarily in the currency of its major debtor, the United States. Moreover, Saudi Arabia had little military might to counter a possible freezing of its assets by one of its debtors. By contrast, the low level of US economic and military vulnerability to Europe and Japan after the Second World War largely freed it from these constraints.

Japan's vulnerability to its major debtor in the 1980s – the United States, probably lies closer to the case of Saudi Arabia after 1973 than to that of the US after 1945. Japan, like Saudi Arabia, has been lending and holding most of its external assets in US dollars, leaving it vulnerable to American manipulation of the value of the dollar. Moreover, the United States is its major export market. The military dependence of Japan on the United States also considerably increases the risks involved in flexing its newfound creditor power.

While these two factors – duration of creditor status and vul-nerability – can tell us a significant amount about whether a creditor state will acquire power, there is a third equally important factor which has tended to receive less attention: the degree of the creditor state's control over its nation's external assets. The higher the degree of control, the greater the power of the creditor state. If, for example, the creditor state is unable to exercise control over the nation's external assets, it will be less able to direct their use to serve its own ends.

With respect to this third variable, there was a difference again between the cases of Saudi Arabia and the United States which may go some way in accounting for their respective power as creditors. In the US case, its power as a creditor was augmented by the fact that the US government was directly involved in the external lending process. US funds flowed abroad either in the form of direct government-to-government loans or through international institutions over which the US exerted a large degree of control. Although the Saudi Arabian government directed the vast majority of Saudi Arabian funds abroad through the Saudi Arabian Monetary Agency,[12] its decision to place a large portion of these funds with Western banks meant that its overall degree of control was weakened. With a large part of its surplus being recycled via private intermediaries over which it had little direct influence, the Saudi Arabian government lost the ability to specify who ultimately would receive its funds, and for what purposes they would be used.

There is considerable controversy over the degree to which the Japanese government has been involved in the export of Japanese funds in the 1980s. This is particularly true of the most important segment of these exports – the massive investments in the US. On the one side are those who claim that the Japanese government has exerted a great deal of control over the Japanese-based private financial intermediaries (insurance companies, trust banks and commercial banks) which have invested Japanese funds in US securities and equities. The opposing view sees little control involved, and portrays Japanese financial investment in the US in the 1980s as entirely a market-driven phenomenon. In what follows, these two extreme positions are laid out and their respective interpretations of recent patterns of Japanese investment are described.

STATE CONTROL OF EXTERNAL ASSETS

Let us begin with the view which sees a high degree of state control. Those who believe that the Japanese government has been actively involved in controlling Japanese financial investment in the US point above all to the high degree of informal influence – or 'discretionary power'[13] – which the Japanese Ministry of Finance (MoF) is alleged to exert over Japanese financial institutions. This influence is said to come from a variety of factors. First, financial institutions are said to be wary of disobeying MoF suggestions because of its extensive regulatory powers.[14] Second, it is suggested that both historical experience and the 'elite' status of MoF officials have brought into being a strong tradition of deference towards the Ministry among Japanese financial institutions.[15] Third, interaction between the state and financial institutions is said to be encouraged both by regular meetings and by the *amakudari* system, whereby ex-MoF officials customarily retire into important positions within leading financial institutions. A dramatic example of the effectiveness of the former occurred in Spring 1987, when the MoF called in the chief executives of more than twenty leading Japanese banks, ten securities companies and ten life and casualty insurance companies to ask them to refrain from speculative foreign exchange transactions. As a result, foreign exchange trading volume was down by one half during the following week.[16] Finally, it is pointed out that co-ordination between the state and financial institutions is facilitated by the small number of important firms involved.[17]

Those subscribing to this 'realist' account of the role of Japanese financial institutions in the world economy see a strong political hand behind the Japanese financial investment in the US since 1981. To provide a flavour of their argument, we can look at three trends in Japanese financial flows since 1985 which have been commonly cited by this school to back up the point that 'politics' rather than markets best explain the pattern of Japanese capital exports.

The most common piece of evidence cited by realist accounts is the fact that Japanese financial institutions continued to invest in the US even after they began to receive large exchange rate losses on their US investments, beginning in 1985 with the dollar's fall. Between February 1985 and the middle of 1986, for example, currency losses wiped out 38 per cent of the cumulative value of Japanese overseas investments in yen terms.[18] That the Japanese kept investing in the face of such massive losses is cited as evidence that this was not a market process. Rather, it is concluded, some coercion from the Japanese state must have been involved. In Gilpin's words: 'The Japanese, having found a ready market for the output of their factories, have in effect lent the US money to sustain Japan's strategy of export-led growth, to maintain a high level of domestic employment, and to help finance the domestic military buildup on which the security of Japan rests'.[19]

A second episode which can be cited by those of a realist persuasion was the retreat from the US economy by Japanese investors beginning in mid-1987. Net long-term capital outflows fell from $19.2 billion in June to $2.3 billion in September. In October of the same year, the Japanese sold more foreign bonds than they bought for the first time since 1983 (although they were still net buyers of equities). Including short-term capital flows, Japan was actually a net importer of capital in August and September.[20] Because this reversal had the effect of unsettling the US financial scene and ultimately providing an important trigger for the stock market crash in October[21] it might appear as a deliberately organised demonstration of Japan's financial muscle by the Japanese government. Evidence for this portrayal of a new assertiveness on the part of the Japanese government could be found in Japanese Prime Minister Nakasone's statement soon after the beginning of the crash that the major economic powers should not meet to discuss the collapsing stock prices and uncertain dollar until after the US had first acted to cut its budget deficit. Moreover, the fact that the MoF did *not* instruct its huge investors to participate in the important early November auction of US government debt, in contrast to its traditionally activist role during financial crises, could be interpreted as a further piece of evidence for this position.[22] Nonetheless, Japanese investors were major purchasers at the auction, buying 30 per cent of the ten-year issues and 20 per cent of the thirty-year bonds. This may have been connected with the fact that two large Japanese securities firms, Nomura and Daiwa, had a strong interest in a successful performance, having just become primary dealers in US government securities.[23]

Finally, the return of Japanese investors to the US financial markets in 1988 is sometimes offered as a third case in point by those who see a high degree of Japanese government involvement behind Japanese investment behaviour. Because they can see few market-driven reasons to invest in the US in this period, the realists suggest that the Japanese government might have been pushing investment into the US with the objective of helping the presidential campaign of the less protectionist candidate, George Bush, through the provision of a stable dollar.[24] Some even point to the fact that the very moment the election had ended and they had 'their' man in office, the Japanese resumed their more assertive stance of late 1987. As Ian Rodger notes: 'Within hours of the conclusion of the U.S. Presidential election, the Bank of Japan published a study analyzing the Reagan Administration's budget policy and urging the new administration to cut its spending "to avoid the situation where the deficit breeds more debt". The study ... was remarkable not only for the timing of its release but also for the bluntness of its message'.[25]

These realist accounts of three recent trends in the flow of Japanese finance portray the Japanese state as able to use its creditor position to achieve certain political objectives. Creditor status is seen, then, as a definitive source of power for the Japanese state. The fear of a future deliberate 'investment strike' by the Japanese is often invoked by those following this line of reasoning. For example, Eric Lincoln argues, 'As a major creditor to the US, Japan could easily apply conditionality to its lending, refusing to lend unless the US promises to alter its economic policies. More ominously, it could threaten to withdraw capital in retaliation against American trade practices it dislikes. These are real possibilities and some in Japan have begun to speak openly about them'.[26]

At the opposite side of the debate stand those who believe that Japanese financial investment in the US in the 1980s has been entirely a market phenomenon. While acknowledging that in the past the Japanese state has played an important role in controlling financial institutions, this view stresses that recent developments in Japan – including the growth of government deficits, increased competition between financial institutions, and the trend towards deregulation and internationalisation within the Japanese financial system – have reduced the degree of control that the Japanese state can exert over private financial operators.[27] The consequence, in this view, is that Japanese financial investments in the US in the 1980s are more likely to have been directed by the invisible hand than a political one.

To substantiate this case, it is worth going through each of the three examples cited above to show how they are reinterpreted by market-based explanations. To begin with, it can be shown that there were a number of reasons why the falling dollar from 1985 to 1987 did not in fact remove the market incentives for investing in the US. First, many Japanese investors are said to have been unconcerned by exchange rate changes either because they had 'hedged' the currency element in their investment through swaps or futures transactions, or because they had funded their investments from existing holdings of dollars.[28] Second, even for those affected by the dollar fall, the currency loss was more than offset by rising prices on US bonds through 1986, as well as by the continuing substantial yield differential between US and Japanese government bonds. Furthermore, many Japanese investors are said to have a long-run investment horizon and are thus less concerned by short-term losses deriving from changes in exchange rate values.

Similarly, the sudden pullout by Japanese investors after mid-1987, rather than being seen as a deliberately organised investment strike, can be reinterpreted from a market viewpoint. It can be explained as the economic response of private Japanese investors who found that, with continued uncertainty about the value of the dollar and the end of the US bond rally, their money could be better invested at home. Moreover, the fact that the Bank of Japan stepped in to buy dollars and reinvest them in US government securities as private investors pulled out suggests that there was no government-organised investment strike.

Finally, market factors can also account for the return of Japanese investors in 1988. Not only did the interest rate differential between Japan and the US rise to approximately 4 per cent on long-term bonds for most of the year, but also the dollar appeared to stabilise after heavy central bank defence of its value in January.[29]

The market-based account explains the developments since 1985 quite effectively. Does this mean that we should side with those who say that the Japanese state has little control over Japanese financial institutions investing abroad? The difficulty with taking this position is the problem of latent power: the Japanese state may have power that it chooses not to exercise, or has not needed to exercise. It might not have demonstrated its capacity for control because developments have taken the preferred direction without intervention. In early 1985, for example, a proposal to limit capital exports to the US with the objective of forcing a dollar fall – which 'immediately alarmed US monetary authorities' – was turned down by the Prime Minister's Office only after the dollar began to fall of its own accord.[30]

It would be premature, then, to suggest that the Japanese government can exert little control over Japanese financial investments in the US. If nothing else, the fact that Japanese financial institutions are involved in handling the surplus funds, rather than foreign-based institutions (as was true in the case of Saudi Arabia), gives the Japanese government a greater degree of potential control than it might otherwise have. Not only does this give it latitude for a disputed amount of direct control via 'discretionary power', but also the Japanese government can control their behaviour indirectly by changes in tax policies and legal regulations. In March, 1986, for example, the Japanese government helped Japanese insurance companies deal with the currency losses on their US investments by offering them a tax break whereby they were given the option of revaluing their foreign bonds for tax accounting purposes, to reflect the decrease in the yen value of US bonds.

Before concluding this discussion of the degree of state control over Japanese capital exports, it is worth remembering that a growing volume of Japanese capital is flowing abroad as aid. From a value of $3.8 billion in 1985, Japanese official development assistance has grown considerably to a budgeted $12 billion for the fiscal year ending March 1989. Japan is now the world's largest aid donor. This form of capital exports *is* to a certain extent under Japanese state control and thus can be said to be contributing to Japanese power. About two-thirds of Japanese aid is bilateral and much of this, traditionally, has been closely tied to serving Japanese interests, particularly in Asia (which receives roughly 70 per cent of Japan's aid).[31] Japan has less control over the distribution of its aid given through multilateral channels, however, since its influence within the multilateral organisations has often been limited. The United States has fought hard to get the Japanese to contribute more to multilateral institutions without giving them more voting power within the institutions. In the Asian Development Bank, for example, Japan now contributes one-third of the capital but still has only one-eighth of the votes – no more than are commanded by the United States.[32]

Without a doubt, Japan's rapid rise in the 1980s to its current status as a major creditor has dramatically altered its relationship to the world. But how much power has it given Japan? In some circumstances – such as when Japanese money is flowing abroad in forms such as bilateral aid – it is clear that its creditor position has translated into considerable power. In the case of the massive investments in the US, however, the picture is less clear cut. It is likely, on the one hand, that it has acquired more power than some past creditors, such as Saudi Arabia. This is both because of the size and expected duration of its creditor status, and because of the fact that its own financial institutions are very much involved in exporting the funds. On the other hand, the degree of power derived from its creditor status has been less than some other past creditors, such as the US after the Second World War, both because of Japan's overall vulnerability to its major debtor and because of the uncertain amount of control which it exerts over its capital exports.

IMPORTANCE OF THE INTERNATIONALISATION PROCESS

A major argument of this chapter is that Japan's acquisition of power within the international monetary and financial system in the 1980s should not be seen only in terms of its emergence as a major creditor. The other development of importance in the 1980s has been the internationalisation of Japanese finance. While these two trends are interconnected in many ways, they need to be separated for analytical purposes. It is argued here that while Japan's status as a creditor has allowed it to exert a certain degree of 'relational power' in the world – *directly* influencing others by lending or not lending them money – the internationalisation of Japanese finance has increased its 'structural power' within the system – that is, its ability *indirectly* to influence the environment in which others operate.

What is meant by 'the internationalisation of Japanese finance'? This refers to the increasing interaction between the Japanese financial system and the outside world. While in the 1950s and 1960s the Japanese financial system existed to a large extent in isolation from the rest of the world, the two have today become increasingly interconnected. The involvement by Japanese in financial operations abroad has grown, as has the participation by foreigners in the Japanese financial system.

The establishment of a system of controls separating the Japanese financial system from the outside world began in 1931 with Japan's move off the gold standard. It became more rigid in the later years of that decade under the pressures associated with militarisation.[33] After the war, although the US exerted early pressure on European countries to remove exchange controls, the US Occupation authorities in Japan maintained the system of wartime controls and made few moves towards liberalisation.[34] This approach was continued through the 1950s by the Japanese government.

It was not until Japan's balance of payments situation began to appear less precarious in the early 1960s that limited liberalisation moves began. To begin with, Japanese banks were allowed to operate abroad, although on a highly controlled basis. International use of the yen also began in a very restricted way, following the introduction by the Japanese government of free-yen accounts for non-residents in 1960. Finally, foreign purchases of Japanese equities began to increase, slowly, as restrictions were relaxed in the early 1960s.

Symbolically, this liberalisation trend, albeit limited, was confirmed in 1964 when Japan both signed the OECD Code of Liberalisation of

Capital Movements and accepted its IMF obligation to maintain convertibility on current account transactions.[35] In the late 1960s, with Japan's emergence as a creditor for the first time since the war, further moves in the direction of internationalisation took place: banks were allowed to expand abroad in large numbers; foreign exchange regulations were loosened; and outflows of finance began to be encouraged to offset the upward pressure on the yen.

With the first oil price rise and the subsequent balance of payments fluctuations, the Japanese authorities suddenly adopted a more cautious attitude towards the internationalisation process. They turned to manipulating financial movements in order to offset changes in the balance of payments. From November 1973 until 1976, for example, the authorities dealt with the growing deficit by reimposing controls on capital outflows and liberalising inflows. As a surplus re-emerged in 1977–8, these policies were reversed: controls on inflows were tightened while those on outflows were relaxed.

In the 1980s, the internationalisation process accelerated dramatically.[36] In this decade, as restrictions have been lowered, foreigners have markedly increased their financial activity in Japan, while Japanese financial institutions have become increasingly prominent abroad. Tokyo has come to be the third leg of a globally integrated financial system, alongside London and New York.[37]

Why did the internationalisation process proceed so quickly in the 1980s? Some analysts give a central role to US political pressure for liberalisation.[38] Two policy decisions, in particular, are often cited as having resulted from US pressure: the 1980 revision of the Foreign Exchange and Foreign Trade Control Law (which made international transactions 'free in principle' instead of the previous 'restricted in principle') and the 1984 Yen–Dollar Agreement (which set out a detailed timetable of liberalisation moves). While it is true that US pressure played an important role in these decisions, many of those who have studied the internationalisation process as a whole have concluded that the role of the US was not decisive. Rather, domestic factors are said to have been of greater importance.[39]

Several domestic pressures have been at work promoting liberalisation. Of these, the diminution of the feeling of external vulnerability is perhaps the most important. This came about, first, with the successful handling of the second oil price rise and, second, with the emergence of Japan as a creditor in the early 1980s. A second influential domestic change was the growing importance of more 'internationalist' attitudes in the Japanese political system which saw liberalisation in a more favourable light.[40] This change manifested itself most clearly in the response to the second oil shock when the yen bond market was not fully closed to foreigners – as it had been during the first oil shock.[41] It was demonstrated again in 1982, when few restrictions on capital movements were imposed in the face of the balance of payments deficit.

It is worth noting that the new internationalism among policy makers was encouraged by a further development: the growing international interests of Japanese financial institutions. As Japanese financial institutions became more prominent internationally, they began to push for more liberal, outward-looking policies from their government. For example, in the wake of the second oil shock in 1979, Japanese banks successfully lobbied against a repeat of the 1973 suspension of offshore foreign currency loans, arguing that their newly-built international reputations would be hurt by such a restriction. Bankers were also prominent during Nakasone's term in office in promoting liberalisation.[42] It is worth noting that in their lobbying efforts, private financial institutions – especially the banks – were probably aided by their new domestic position as major holders of the expanding government debt.[43]

Liberalisation moves by the government alone cannot account for the greater internationalisation of the Japanese financial system in the 1980s. Strong market pressures have also played a role. Of greatest importance are the effects of the increasing spiral of innovation, competition and deregulation which began to grip the domestic financial system from the mid-1970s onwards. This has promoted internationalisation in several ways. First, the state authorities have less and less control over financial operators, who thus are able to circumvent restrictions on movements in and out of the Japanese financial system. Second, the Japanese authorities' loss of control over the domestic financial scene has made them more resigned to the loss of control which comes with internationalisation. To give one example, the Bank of Japan opposed the creation of International Banking Facilities in Japan in the early 1980s, because it believed that they were incompatible with the maintenance of domestic financial regulation. In 1983, however, it was willing to reconsider its position if domestic deregulation were allowed to take place.[44] International Banking Facilities were introduced in Japan in 1986. Third, the increased competition within the domestic scene has encouraged Japanese financial institutions to move abroad in search of higher profits.[45] Finally, domestic liberalisation has made Japanese financial markets more attractive to foreigners.

IMPLICATIONS FOR JAPANESE POWER: STRUCTURAL POWER

The importance of the internationalisation of Japanese finance lies in the fact that it has given the Japanese state a degree of power to influence the structure of the international monetary and financial system within which others must operate. There are three sources of Japan's 'structural power' in the international monetary and financial system which have emerged with the internationalisation of Japanese finance.

To begin with, it is important to recognise the sheer size and importance of Japanese financial markets within the international financial system. The incorporation of these markets into the global financial system in the 1980s, as well as their growth in both size and complexity (as a result of the aforementioned changes in the domestic financial system), has made it imperative for those involved in financial affairs around the world to pay close attention to their movements. This change has been most dramatic within equities markets, where the Japanese markets now account for 44 per cent of world capitalisation against only 30 per cent accounted for by the United States.[46] In other sectors, however, Japanese markets have also achieved great prominence: annual bond market turnover in Tokyo ($37,400 billion in 1987) has surpassed that of the New York market ($27,700 billion in 1987)[47] and the Tokyo foreign exchange market has grown from relatively unimportant status in the 1970s to come close to equalling New York in terms of daily turnover (although both lag well behind London).[48] These developments have given the Japanese state, through its position as the chief authority over these markets, a great deal of indirect influence over trends and developments in the international monetary and financial system. Regulatory changes and other policy moves that affect Japanese markets have increasingly important indirect impacts on the international monetary and financial system.

The Japanese state, as pointed out earlier, has also gained a certain degree of structural power in the international monetary and financial system through its regulatory authority over Japanese financial institutions. From their limited contacts in the 1960s, Japanese financial institutions began to expand into the international sphere in considerable numbers in the early 1970s, only to receive several setbacks during the rest of the decade. In the 1980s, and particularly since 1985, they have come to play a key role internationally. Japanese banks now dominate the international banking business. They controlled 35 per cent of total international bank assets in September 1987 (compared to 23 per cent only three years before) in comparison to the US banks' 17.6 per cent share.[49] Similarly, Japanese securities firms have been among the top Eurobond lead managers in recent years. It is, however, the total size of Japanese financial institutions that causes the greatest fear in boardrooms abroad. Measured in terms of market capitalisation, the top twenty-one financial institutions in the world in 1987 were Japanese;[50] similarly, nine of the ten world's largest banks are Japanese.[51] Because these institutions listen first and foremost to the Japanese government, and because the rest of the world must listen to them, structural power in the international monetary and financial system has devolved upon the Japanese government from the institutions' new international prominence.

Finally, the position of the yen within the international monetary and financial system affects Japanese power. Just as the international use of the dollar contributes greatly to the 'structural power' of the United States in the international monetary and financial system, a greater international use of the yen could contribute substantially to Japan's structural power. Although the internationalisation of Japanese finance could have led to increased use of the yen internationally, it has not yet done so to any considerable extent. Only approximately 7 per cent of the world's official reserves were denominated in yen in 1988, in contrast to 15 per cent denominated in German marks and 67 per cent in US dollars. In international capital markets, the yen's use has increased somewhat more, but still remains subordinate to the position of the dollar, with only 15 per cent of international bond issues denominated in yen in 1987. Looking at the use of the yen as a unit of account in trade, we find an unusually low use. Only 34 per cent even of Japan's exports (1988) and only 14 per cent of its imports (1985) were denominated in yen.[52]

Why hasn't increased international use of the yen gone along with the internationalisation of Japanese finance? One major inhibition has been the absence of a fully-fledged short-term yen money market, and in particular a short-term market in Japanese government securities. Without an efficient, liquid money market offering high returns in which to hold yen-denominated assets, foreigners have been less willing to use the yen. At present, the most important market to fit this role – the Japanese Treasury bill market – is not sufficiently liquid and deep, and it offers yields that are artificially low. Moreover, foreign investors must pay a withholding tax on their Treasury bill holdings.

Resistance to changing this situation has come primarily from the

MoF. It has preferred to keep the market in its current, regulated state in order that government borrowing costs remain low. There are, however, signs of change. Of particular note was the announcement by Mr Satoshi Sumita, Governor of the Bank of Japan, at the 1988 IMF annual meeting in Berlin that the yen would become a major reserve currency. Moreover, the MoF has recently promoted the deepening of Japan's money markets in two ways: the quantity of Treasury Bills issued in the 1989 financial year was doubled, and three-month Treasury Bills were issued in October 1989 to complement the already existing six-month bills.[53] If such a trend continues, it will add an extra element to Japan's growing influence in the international monetary and financial system.

If Strange concludes that 'Japanese power in finance is relational only', it is because she has concentrated on Japan's 'position as the world's major creditor country and aid donor'.[54] If we look at the internationalisation of Japanese finance, we can see that it has brought the Japan considerable power in the 1980s to shape and influence the environment within which others must operate. It is interesting to compare this 'structural power' in the international monetary and financial system to that held by the United States. With respect to the importance of Japanese financial institutions and the size of some its financial markets, the Japanese have clearly come to challenge the structural power of the United States. The United States, however, has retained much of its predominance through the unequalled position of the dollar, as well as through the depth and range of its financial markets. This remaining US influence should make us wary of dramatic statements such as: 'Clearly, Japan has replaced the US as the world financial leader'.[55]

CONCLUSION

Reflections on the subject of Japan's newfound power within the international monetary and financial system would benefit greatly from some analytical discussion of precisely which factors have changed the nature of Japan's position in the system in the 1980s. Above all, I would like to insist on the need to distinguish between Japan's rise as a creditor and the internationalisation of Japanese finance. As has been argued above, each confers a different form of power on the Japanese state. While creditor status has brought Japan relational power in the international monetary and financial system, internationalisation has bolstered Japanese structural power.

The importance of making this distinction is perhaps best brought out if we turn to make predictions about the future of Japanese power in the international monetary and financial system. Because more attention has been focused on Japan's creditor status, it is often assumed that Japan's newfound power will disappear when its status as a major creditor ends. This, however, ignores the fact that much of Japan's growing influence in the 1980s has been connected to the internationalisation of Japanese finance. If and when Japan ceases to be a major creditor, it is likely that the internationalisation process will be so firmly established that it will not be reversed. In consequence, the disappearance of Japan's position as a major creditor will not mean the end of Japan's influence in the international monetary and financial system. Its 'structural power' will remain.

A conclusion to be drawn from such speculation is that the internationalisation of Japanese finance, rather than the much-discussed growth of Japan's external assets, will probably have the longer-lasting, more profound effect on Japanese power in the international monetary and financial system. The 'structural power' which it has brought to the Japanese state will probably continue to exist, largely independent of Japan's status as a debtor or creditor.

The discussion in this chapter of Japan's power in the international monetary and financial system is by no means complete. Two areas in particular have been neglected. First, the discussion has been limited to a concern about power in the sense of capability. This perspective needs to be complemented by a discussion about Japan's willingness to use its growing power capability. It is perhaps in this respect that the discrepancy between US and Japanese power in the international monetary and financial system will remain for some time to come.

The second area largely neglected in this chapter is the relationship between power in the international monetary and financial system and other types of power. In particular, it is important to ask to what extent Japan can acquire power in the financial and monetary structure without the ideological leadership and military power to reinforce it.[56] While it is easiest to draw on the experiences of British and American financial dominance and reach a sceptical conclusion, it would be interesting also to investigate the experience of Dutch financial preeminence in the second half of the seventeeth century.

This latter example suggests that financial power need not always coincide with leadership in other areas. Indeed, drawing the parallels between a potential Pax Nipponica in the future and the era of Dutch leadership of the world economy is an exercise that may provide an enlightening complement to the more common comparisons with the ages of British and American hegemony.[57]

Notes and References

1. 'In the 1980s, Japan supplanted the United States as the dominant creditor nation and financial power. Never before in the history of international finance has such a dramatic shift taken place in such a relatively short time'.R. Gilpin, *The Political Economy of International Relations* (Princeton, NJ: Princeton University Press, 1987) p. 328.
2. See S. Strange, 'Finance, Information and Power' (mimeo) presented at ISA/BISA conference (March 1989).
3. See S. Strange, *States and Markets: An Introduction to International Political Economy* (London: Pinter Publishers, 1988).
4. S. Wagstyl, 'External Assets at Record Levels', *Financial Times* (27 May 1989).
5. Before 1987, foreign direct investment rarely rose above 15 per cent of total long-term capital outflows, averaging approximately $6 billion per year. Since 1987, however, foreign direct investment is beginning to take a larger proportion of overall capital exports. See *AMEX Bank Review*, 15(3) (24 March 1988) p. 6.
6. See, for example, C. Kindleberger, *International Capital Movements* (Cambridge: Cambridge University Press, 1987) pp. 33–6.
7. D. North, 'International Capital Movements in Historical Perspective', in R. Mikesell (ed.), *United States Private and Government Investment Abroad* (Eugene, OR: University of Oregon Books, 1962) p. 32.
8. E. Lincoln, *Japan: Facing Economic Maturity* (Washington, DC: Brookings, 1988) pp. 99–122. Lincoln stresses that this opposition was largely political. The economic case for reduced government spending was not strong in his opinion.
9. Lincoln, *Japan*, pp. 76–7.
10. Gilpin, *The Political Economy*, p. 330.
11. William Emmott, *The Limits to Japanese Power*, AMEX Bank Review Special Papers. 16 (October 1988) p. 10.
12. Mattione notes that about $141 billion of Saudi Arabia's total $160 billion assets abroad in 1982 were controlled by Saudi Arabian Monetary Authority. Richard Mattione, *OPEC's Investments and the International Financial System* (Washington, DC: Brookings, 1985) p. 60.
13. Gilpin, *The Political Economy*, p. 329.
14. A. Spindler, *The Politics of International Credit* (Washington DC: Brookings, 1984) p. 175.
15. 'Japan's financial authorities have derived another measure of influence over the banking system from their recognized elite status. Finance

Ministry officials, often top graduates of the country's best universities, are perceived as a group to be among the most able of Japan's professional talent', Spindler, *The Politics of International Credit*, p. 106.

16. 'Tokyo asks its banks to stop currency speculation', *Financial Times* (14 May 1987); 'Hedging Helps the Boom', *Financial Times* (3 June 1987).
17. R. T. Murphy, 'Power without Purpose: The Crisis of Japan's Global Financial Dominance', *Harvard Business Review* (March–April 1989) pp. 71–83.
18. *AMEX Bank Review*, 15(3) (24 March 1988) p. 3.
19. R. Gilpin, 'American Policy in the Post-Reagan Era', *Daedalus*, 116(3), (Summer 1987) pp. 48–9. Another 'political' account of continued Japanese investment in this period is provided by Danielian and Thomsen: 'Japan is eager to minimize the political friction with the US by investing much of its $43.5 bilateral trade surplus in US stocks and bonds', in R. L. Danielian and S. E. Thomsen, *The Forgotten Deficit: America's Addiction to Foreign Capital* (London: Westview, 1987) p. 44.
20. Akira Ariyoshi, 'Japanese Capital Flows', *Finance and Development* (September 1988) pp. 28–30.
21. Nicholas Brady, now US Treasury Secretary, cited the Japanese pullout as the principal cause: 'The real trigger [of the stock crash] was that the Japanese came in for their own reasons and sold an enormous amount of US Government bonds and drove the 30-year Government [bond] up through 10 percent ', quoted in 'Japanese selling blamed for crash', *Globe and Mail* (23 April 1988).
22. See Rich Miller, 'Japan seems set to end U.S. domination of world monetary system', *Financial Times* (2 November 1988).
23. C. Rapoport, 'Home is best in unstable times', *Financial Times* (16 November 1987).
24. John Plender makes this case. The Japanese authorities, he writes, 'show every sign of understanding the wider politics of the situation and the advantages to Mr. Bush of exchange rate stability. They have gone out of their way to publicize an addition of nearly $60 billion to their budget for foreign exchange intervention, while warning Japanese insurance companies not to depress the dollar by dumping stock at the start of the new financial year in April. A Republican victory could no doubt be expected to deliver a more accommodating stance on trade policy after the election, though Japanese officials, predictably enough, deny any such quid pro quo for dollar support', John Plender, 'No Foreign Capital Please', *Financial Times* (16 May 1988).
25. Ian Rodger, 'Bank of Japan presses US to reduce spending', *Financial Times* (10 November 1988).
26. E. Lincoln, 'Reassessing US–Japan Relations', *Fletcher Forum*, 12(1) (Winter 1988) p. 68. Even *The Economist* has taken up this possibility: 'But what about a deliberate investment strike? ... Organized by the government, a collective refusal to finance America's twin deficits might be feasible', 'Hooked on T-Bonds' (7 February 1988).
27. L. Pauly, *Regulatory Politics in Japan: The Case of Foreign Banking* (Ithaca, NY: Cornell University Press, 1987) pp. 6–7.
28. 'Hooked on T-Bonds'.

29. *The Economist* concluded: 'Japanese investors should be willing – on strictly commercial grounds – to carry on lending dollars to America', 'Hooked on T-Bonds'.

30. Y. Funabashi, *Managing the Dollar: From the Plaza to the Louvre* (Washington, DC: Institute for International Economics, 1988) p. 87.

31. There are, however, also cases in which Japanese state control over the distribution and administration of their bilateral aid money has been very small. In Africa, for example, which now receives 11 per cent of Japanese ODA, the Japanese have often had to funnel their money through institutions dominated by governments who have greater expertise in the area, such as British Crown Agents who are administering part of Japan's $500 million aid programme to Africa. I. Rodger, 'Crown Agents to administer part of Japanese aid', *Financial Times* (31 January 1988).

32. 'The Young Pretenders', *The Economist* (15 October 1988).

33. See M. Barnhart, *Japan Prepares For Total War: The Search for Economic Security 1919–45* (Ithaca, NY: Cornell University Press, 1987).

34. See. L. Hollerman, 'International Economic Controls in Occupied Japan', *Journal of Asian Studies*, 38(4) (August 1979) pp. 707–19.

35. Although these two moves signified a liberalising trend, it is important to see how limited they were. With respect to the OECD code, Japan diluted its effect by taking out a large number of exemptions. See T. Adams and I. Hoshii, *A Financial History of the New Japan* (Tokyo: Kodansha, 1972) p. 463. In terms of convertability, although it had accepted the IMF's Article 8 obligations only three years later than most European countries, the manner in which it did so was more restrictive than most European countries. All current and capital account transactions still went through special, authorised Foreign Exchange banks, and private citizens were not allowed to retain foreign exchange until 1971. This centralised control gave the government enormous discretionary power.

36. See, for example, R. Feldman, *Japanese Financial Markets: Deficits, Dilemmas, Deregulation* (Cambridge, MA; MIT Press, 1986); Y. Shinkai, 'The Internationalization of Finance in Japan', in T. Inoguchi and D. Okimoto, *The Political Economy of Japan: Vol. 2, The Changing International Context* (Stanford, CA: Stanford University Press, 1988).

37. Judging by price indicators, Feldman concludes that 'the Japanese capital market has been fully internationalized since mid-1981', Feldman, *Japanese Financial Markets*, P. 186.

38. See, for example, Calder's discussion of 'the reactive character of the Japanese state in foreign economic policy', in K. Calder, 'Japanese Foreign Economic Policy Formation: Explaining the Reactive State', *World Politics*, 40(4) (July 1988) p. 537.

39. See J. Horne, *Japan's Financial Markets: Conflict and Consensus in Policymaking* (London: Allen & Unwin, 1985) p. 192. The 1980 and 1984 decisions are seen by some authors as no more than a formal declaration of decisions which the Japanese government had already decided, largely independent of US pressure, to pursue for its own reasons. See, for

example, E. Lincoln, 'Infrastructural Deficiencies, Budget Policy, and Capital Flows', in M. Schmiegelow (ed.), *Japan's Response to Crisis and Change in the World Economy* (London: M. E. Sharpe, 1986) pp. 250–2.

40. For the growing 'internationalism' in the Japanese political scene, see J. Pempel, 'The Unbundling of "Japan Inc."': Changing Dynamics of Japanese Policy Formation', *Journal of Japanese Studies*, 13(2) (Summer 1987); K. Pyle, 'In Pursuit of a Grand Design: Nakasone Betwixt Past and Future', *Journal of Japanese Studies*, 13(2) (Summer 1987).

41. See J. Horne, Japan's Financial Markets, p. 181; and E. Hayden, 'Internationalizing Japan's Financial System', in D. Okimoto (ed.), *Japan's Economy: Coping with Economic Change in the International Environment* (Boulder, CO: Westview Press, 1982) p. 104.

42. 'The Advisory Friends Group, an informal circle of Nakasone's long-time friends, including bankers, businessmen, and former officials, strongly recommended that he pursue the high-yen strategy. Prominent among them was Goro Koyama, senior banker at Mitsui, who provided consistent support for appreciation of the yen and the liberalization of Japanese capital markets', Y. Funabashi, *Managing the Dollar*, p. 89.

43. 'As the government deficit surged, the bargaining power of government and banks reversed', M. Crum and D. Meerschwam, 'From Relationship to Price Banking: The Loss of Regulatory Control', in T. McCraw (ed.), *America vs. Japan* (Boston, MA: Harvard Business School Press, 1986) p. 289.

44. R. Dale, *The Regulation of International Banking* (Cambridge, MA: Woodhead–Faulkner, 1984) p. 44.

45. J. Horne, 'Politics and the Japanese Financial System', in J. Stockwin *et al.* (eds), *Dynamic and Immobilist Politics in Japan* (London: Macmillan, 1988) pp. 176–7.

46. Alison Maitland, 'Economic News Gives US a Starring Role', *Financial Times* (25 April 1989) p. 45. Clive Wolman, 'Investing in the Power of Zen', *Financial Times* (9 June 1989), however, points out that Japan's weighting drops to about 30 per cent while that of the US increases to about 35 per cent if one accounts for the fact that extensive cross-holdings in the Japanese stock market exaggerate the overall size of the market.

47. *Far Eastern Economic Review* (15 December 1988) p. 79.

48. The latest figures, measured in April 1989, show daily turnover in foreign exchange trading in Tokyo worth $115 billion, compared with $129 billion in New York and $187 billion in London. 'London Still Top Exchange Centre', *Financial Times* (14 September 1989).

49. Bank for International Settlements, *Annual Reports*.

50. *Euromoney* (February 1978) p. 6.

51. Murphy, 'Power without Purpose', p. 72.

52. I. Rodger, 'Still a Long way to Go', *Financial Times* (13 March 1989).

53. 'Opening the door to Japan's short-term money markets', *The Economist* (1 April 1989).

54. S. Strange, 'Finance, Information and Power', pp. 16 and 1.

55. Murphy, 'Power without Purpose', p. 74.

56. With respect to ideological leadership, it is interesting to remember

Woodrow Wilson's comment in 1916 as the age of US financial dominance was beginning: 'those who finance the world must understand it and rule it with their spirits and with their minds', quoted in J. Frieden, 'Sectoral Conflict and U.S. Foreign Economic Policy: 1914–40', *International Organization*, 42(1) (Winter 1988) p. 71.

57. If nothing else, it is interesting to note, as Ruggie has, that in common with today Dutch hegemony 'co-existed with mercantilist behavior', J. Ruggie, 'International Regimes, Transactions and Change: Embedded Liberalism in the Postwar Economic Order', *International Organization*, 36(2) (Spring 1982) p. 382.

4 The Japanese Industrial Presence in America: Same Bed, Different Dreams

Michael Hodges

The United States welcomes foreign direct investment that flows according to market forces ... We believe there are only winners, no losers, and all participants gain from it.

(President Ronald Reagan, 9 September, 1983)

This is one of the real national mistakes that's going to haunt us for years to come. There is a strong sentiment on the part of the Western governors that there is something really wrong here. I do not want the Japanese coming in and buying up American technology. I do not want them in our state. I don't want the Arabs owning our banks or the Japanese owning our means of production.

(Governor Richard Lamm [Colorado] 25 February, 1985)

In the winter of 1986 ... a group of congressmen from Kentucky asked me to brief them before they travelled to Japan ... At one point I asked whether they realized that for every Japanese plant that opened in Kentucky, an American one in Michigan was likely to close. Their response was, 'We're not the congressmen from Michigan'.

(Clyde V. Prestowitz, former Counsellor for Japan Affairs to the Secretary of Commerce)[1]

JAPANESE INVESTMENT IN THE UNITED STATES:
EMOLLIENT OR IRRITANT?

The Japanese epigram in the title of this chapter originally described mismatched marriage partners, but could equally be applied to the divergent and unrealistic expectations of both the US and Japan regarding the role of Japanese direct investment in America. The rapid increase in Japanese direct investment in the United States – by March 1988 the location for 38 per cent of total Japanese foreign direct investment and over half of Japanese outward FDI flows during the first half of the 1988 financial year – has provided further ammunition for one of America's remaining growth industries: writing books about the declining US hegemony as a result of 'imperial overstretch'.[2]

This chapter, however, does not seek to join the debate on 'declinism', as Samuel Huntington has termed it,[3] or even to analyse the likelihood of a Pax Nipponica emerging in its place.[4] Its rather more limited purpose is to examine the evolution and profile of Japanese direct investment in industrial plants in the US, outline American public policy responses at federal and state levels, and suggest the likely outcome of present trends. In doing so, it ignores the role of Japanese portfolio investment in the US – investment in stocks, bonds and bank deposits not involving control over management of the assets involved – which in 1986 was seven times higher than direct investment coming from Japan.

The essential thesis of this chapter is that the Japanese industrial presence in the US, although growing very rapidly, is still too small to constitute a credible threat to American economic security, but that the lack of a coherent US policy toward foreign direct investment in general – and Japanese investment in particular – is likely to add a further source of friction in American foreign economic relations. This friction is likely to be increased by unrealistic expectations about the benefits of foreign investment, nurtured by individual congressmen running for re-election and state economic development authorities justifying the rental of expensive office suites in Tokyo. In the long term, the benefits of Japanese foreign direct investment are unlikely to materialise to the extent expected. An uncritical emphasis on them will be as damaging to US–Japan relations, and as ill-founded, as the current worries about the 'Selling of America' to foreign investors.

Economists who stress the benefits of liberal trade and investment policies have one advantage over politicians: they do not have to run for office. In all political systems in which legislators are elected from a geographic constituency, and particularly in the US where members of the House of Representatives have to run for election every two years, the political salience of foreign trade and investment increases where the economic effects are geographically concentrated and when they are quick to materialise. In the case of trade competition through imports, the costs (and hence the political repercussions) are concentrated within particular localities and industries, while the benefits, in terms of cheaper goods or a wider choice, are diffused among the population as a whole. The result is political unhappiness and calls for restriction or retaliation. In the case of foreign direct investment, the opposite is true: the benefits are localised and fairly immediate (creation of new jobs, increased tax revenues) and the costs – in terms of loss of indigenous capabilities through increased competition – are diffused and may take some time to work through. Here the result is political happiness and the urge to encourage more such ventures.

As the Japanese presence grows, the drawbacks of the American policy of 'neutrality with encouragement' are becoming more apparent. From the US perspective, the gains from Japanese industrial investment have been less than anticipated, and there is an increasing tendency to view Japanese investment as another lever in the attempt to change Japan's domestic and foreign economic policy. At the same time, fears of American decline stimulate support for restrictions on Japanese trade and investment. In one 1989 opinion poll, 68 per cent of respondents agreed that Japan's economic threat is a greater danger to the US than the military threat from the Soviet Union and, in 1988, 40 per cent favoured a ban on further foreign investment in the US.[5]

From the Japanese point of view, direct investment has done little to reduce trade friction and has impeded Japanese efforts to prevent economic and military security issues from becoming linked in US policy initiatives. Unless something is done to modify the contradiction between the official American policy of an undiscriminating welcome for foreign investment and the increasing use of ad hoc (and hence unpredictable) policy decisions obstructing specific Japanese investment projects, we must add 'investment friction' to the catalogue of ailments afflicting US–Japan relations.

There is a real danger that domestic political reaction in Japan will no longer permit its government to adopt a low-key public response to practices that seemingly single out Japan as more dangerous or untrustworthy than Britain or the Netherlands, both of whom have larger direct investments in the US. The recent travails of the governing Liberal Democratic Party in Japan increase the likelihood that a vigorous Japanese response may be utilised in order to solidify support behind the government; xenophobia is not monopolised by American congressmen from the Midwest.

Japanese foreign direct investment has since 1983 been seen by Japan's Ministry of International Trade and Industry (MITI) as part of a strategy of 'industrial collaboration', a concept that also includes joint ventures and transfer of technology, as a means of alleviating trade friction with its major export markets. The strategy of replacing exports by local production in the US is an obvious way of surmounting trade barriers and protecting against unforeseen shifts in exchange rates, and replicates the pattern established by European and American multinational corporations in earlier years.

Nevertheless, the rapid growth of Japanese investment in the US – 'Bring salt to your enemy', as the Japanese proverb goes – has tended to exacerbate American fears that Japan is 'Buying into America', to quote the title of a best-selling book of 1988, and that this investment is (in the title of another book) a 'Trojan Horse'.[6] Serving the largest and most consumption-oriented market in the world through local production is a logical development in the internationalisation of Japanese business, and the relative decline of the dollar has made asset acquisition in the US by Japanese firms all the more attractive.

The fears of some Americans, that the Japanese industrial presence in the United States is a mixed blessing, are not irrational. Japanese firms are not simply responding to trade friction by building an industrial presence in the US, but are pursuing a long-term strategy of creating an infrastructure which will enable them to sustain their market share above present levels, insulated from currency fluctuations and the vagaries of protectionist sentiment. The consequences of this process for the US government and US corporations alike (whose strategic plans have for the most part ignored the long-term implications of the collective Japanese presence in the US) will be profound.

The decision by many Japanese manufacturers to establish plants in the US (notably in the automobile and consumer electronics sectors) has also stimulated investment by Japanese firms associated with them in the home country: component suppliers, construction firms and providers of financial services. At the same time, the previous preference for 'greenfield' investments (i.e. establishing a brand new plant) has been modified by an increase in Japanese take-overs of American firms (as well as the continuing formation of joint ventures with indigenous companies). In addition, the years 1985–90 have witnessed a significant flow of technology licensing agreements from Japan to the

US, reducing but not eradicating the technology surplus the US has long enjoyed with Japan.

MITI has described this process as 'Industrial Cooperation', and since 1984 has energetically promoted it, with approving noises from the US State Department, Treasury and (usually) Department of Commerce as well as enthusiastic competition among state economic development offices to attract Japanese investors. While the official attitude toward foreign direct investment in the United States has been overwhelmingly (and often indiscriminately) positive, there have been significant differences of opinion between the Department of Defense and the federal economic agencies on the costs and benefits of foreign penetration of defence-related industries.

Although the Federal Government has long conducted a regular statistical review of FDI, there has been little attempt by the US federal authorities to formulate a coherent national policy toward FDI in general or Japanese investment in particular; nor has there been any movement toward co-ordination of the investment policies and incentives of the individual states, which continue to compete with each other to attract investment and employment creation by Japanese and other foreign firms.

JAPAN'S FDI IN PERSPECTIVE

Although Japanese manufacturing investment in the United States has attracted a great deal of attention, in fact Japan lags well behind the UK and the Netherlands as an investor. The foreign-controlled share of US industry as a whole is below 10 per cent in terms of assets, sales and employment – compared to approximately twice that level in the UK, France and Germany.[7] The official US policy toward inward investment is 'neutrality with encouragement' and, with the exception of a few alarums in 1974–5 (occasioned by fears of petrodollars buying up the land from sea to shining sea), there has been a general belief in the Federal Government that more rigorous reporting requirements would have the undesirable effect of deterring foreign investors. Despite the attempts made in Congress since 1987 to pass Representative John Bryant's Foreign Ownership Disclosure Bill, which would require foreign investors (including privately-owned firms) to disclose more information about their owners and activities than their American competitors, vigorous lobbying by foreign investors and opposition from the Bush Administration will probably prevent it from being enacted during the 101st Congress.[8]

According to US Department of Commerce figures, the cumulative book value of Japanese direct investment in the United States at the end of 1987 was $33.4 billion (third in the ranking after $47.9 billion from the UK and $47.0 billion from the Netherlands) out of a total foreign direct investment of $261.9 billion. This compares with total US direct investment abroad of $308.8 billion.

The US Department of Commerce figures on FDI have to be treated with some caution, however. On the one hand they include minority stakes of 10 per cent and over, thus making Du Pont a 'Canadian' company because the Bronfman family owns 23 per cent of the stock, and ignore the locus of effective control of the firm concerned. On the other hand, they exclude the element of any foreign investment financed by dollar loans from US banks or grants from state economic development agencies – deemed irrelevant for balance of payments purposes. In addition, the American FDI statistics are based on 'book value' (i.e. the amount the assets are declared to be worth in the firm's accounts), which tends to understate the value of older investments that have not been revalued.

These factors mean that US official statistics on FDI are somewhat out of date and tend to underestimate the level of foreign participation in US industry. A Congressional investigation in 1980 indicated that Department of Commerce figures on FDI may represent only 15 per cent of the actual value of foreign-controlled assets in the US, and criticised the Bureau of Economic Analysis for not using industrial census data to make its surveys of foreign investment more accurate and comprehensive. Thus far this recommendation has not been followed, although Senator Frank Murkowski introduced a bill (S 856) in July 1989, to remove legal barriers preventing the use of Census Bureau data by the Bureau of Economic Affairs.[9] Martin and Susan Tolchin state that at least 50 per cent of all foreign investment goes unreported, although their estimate does not distinguish between direct and portfolio investment and one would guess that the ultimate owner of direct investment is inherently easier to trace.[10]

Within the $33.4 billion total for Japanese FDI in the US, only $5.2 billion was in manufacturing – just under 16 per cent of the total – with the bulk of remaining Japanese FDI in wholesaling (44 per cent), banking and finance (18 per cent) and real estate (13 per cent). This compares with 1987 figures for American FDI in Japan of $14.3 billion, of which $7.1 billion (50 per cent) is in manufacturing.

As far as manufacturing is concerned, therefore, the US remains ahead in bilateral FDI, but Japanese manufacturing investment in the US is growing at a faster rate than US manufacturing FDI in Japan (Japan's registered 46 per cent growth in 1986–7 as against 30 per cent for the US). Total Japanese FDI in the US has also been growing rapidly: up from $7.7 billion in 1981 to $33.4 billion in 1987. According to 1985 estimates from MITI – almost certainly conservative in view of the subsequent appreciation of the yen – it is projected to increase by 15 per cent annually until the end of the century, when Japanese firms may be responsible for over 800,000 jobs in the United States.[11] Once most of the internationally-oriented Japanese firms have established a presence in the US, further expansion will probably be by expansion of existing plant or take-overs of American firms rather than the more visible (and politically desirable) greenfield ventures.

Another important asymmetry lies in the relative importance of each country as an investment location for the other. Less than 5 per cent of America's $308.8 billion FDI is in Japan (although this still makes the US the largest investor in Japan, with about half of the total)[12] while over a third of Japan's $139.3 billion world-wide FDI is located in the US (on Japanese Ministry of Finance (MoF) figures, which are defined differently from US FDI statistics). This clearly shows that the United States is far and away the most important location for Japanese investment – more than Japan's investment in Asia ($26.7 billion) and Europe ($21 billion) combined.

Given that 36 per cent of Japan's exports in 1987 went to the US, while only 11 per cent of US exports went to Japan, this imbalance in bilateral direct investment is not surprising. The trade figures do, however, underline the extent to which US FDI in Japan is disproportionately low; it is not clear whether that is due to a lack of investment opportunities in Japan (and the 'invisible barriers' non-Japanese complain about) or the disinclination of American firms to exploit those that do exist. Certainly there are few legal barriers to foreign direct investment in the US (aside from restrictions in limited sectors such as broadcasting and aviation, and regulations governing eligibility of alien-controlled firms for defence contracts) and there is no formal notification and approval procedure for FDI in the US, although since the 1988 Trade Act there has been a requirement for all foreign take-overs of American firms to be screened if they are likely to affect national security (see the discussion of the Committee on Foreign Investment in the US, below).[13]

While these FDI figures and their underlying growth rates are impressive, it is important to view them from a wider perspective; the $14.7 billion of direct investment made by Japan in the US in 1987 was less than 25 per cent of its average bilateral trade surplus for that year. The total value of Japanese investment in automobile manufacturing in the US was $4.1 billion by 1986 – or about equivalent to five weeks' worth of Japanese transport equipment exports during that year. By comparison, General Motors invested $20 billion between 1980 and 1986 on updating its facilities, and in Ohio alone employs 70,000 workers (Honda's plants in Ohio currently employ 7,000).[14]

Nevertheless, Japan Economic Institute (JEI) surveys of Japanese-affiliated manufacturers in the US indicate that increasing numbers of Japanese firms are entering the US – 160 in 1987 alone – for a cumulative total of 628 companies operating 815 plants and employing 145,000 people.[15] Most are small to medium-size firms, with two-thirds

Table 4.1   Location of Japanese manufacturing plants in the US

	Number of plants			
	1980	*1983*	*1986*	*1987*
Total plants (Continental US) Of which in (1987 rank):	314	479	620	815
1. California	80	128	153	179
2. Illinois	14	20	40	55
3. Ohio	6	15	30	51
4. Georgia	18	25	32	41
5. New Jersey	18	26	32	40
6. Michigan	10	16	28	38
7. Texas	11	26	29	34
8. Tennessee	9	12	21	29
9. New York	12	15	26	28
10. Kentucky	2	6	15	26
North Carolina	8	16	21	26
Washington	9	19	20	26
11. Indiana	5	10	16	24
12. Pennsylvania	10	14	16	20
Total no. of states with Japanese plants	42	44	45	46*

Sources: Japan Economic Institute Surveys; *Wall Street Journal*; Kyodo News Service.
*Idaho, Montana, North Dakota and Wyoming had no Japanese manufacturing plants by the end of 1987.

of them being greenfield investments rather than joint ventures or takeovers involving American companies. (There were only 16 publicly recorded take-overs by Japanese purchasers in the US in 1986, none of them hostile, compared to 89 by UK purchasers and 64 by Canadian buyers.)[16] Nevertheless, the advantages of joint ventures or acquisitions of American firms (a local management team, quicker returns, and plant well-placed for distribution) are likely to prove more attractive in future, especially if US–Japanese relations deteriorate and local colouration is a necessary defence.

Most of this investment in manufacturing is comparatively recent; the first JEI survey in 1980 found 213 companies (operating 314 plants), only 12 of which had been established in the US prior to 1970.[17] During the period 1980–7 the number of Japanese firms with manufacturing plants almost tripled, spurred from 1983 onward by the rise in the yen's value and the US economic rebound (see Table 4.1). Japanese firms have far to go before they internationalise their production to a significant extent; only 3 per cent of the production of Japanese companies is outside Japan (rising to 10 per cent by 2000 on MITI estimates), compared with 15–20 per cent for American companies.[18]

THE CHANGING NATURE OF JAPANESE FDI IN THE UNITED STATES

Japanese manufacturing investment in the United States has proceeded in three distinct phases. The first Japanese manufacturing investment in the US was to gain access to raw materials or cheaper production costs – such as the integrated aluminium maker Alumax, established in 1974 as a joint venture between Mitsui/Nippon Steel and AMAX Inc. The second phase, beginning in the late 1970s, was prompted by orderly marketing agreements or other results of trade friction (consumer electronics and automobiles were most prominent). Although trade friction continues to be a frequently-cited motive for Japanese firms establishing themselves in US manufacturing, a September 1986 survey by the Long-Term Credit Bank of Japan indicated that of companies intending to invest overseas (a quarter of them in the US), the aim was more often to increase market share (42 per cent) or reduce costs (17 per cent) than avoid trade barriers (14 per cent). Moreover, a JETRO survey published in August 1987 indicated that 43 per cent of Japanese FDI is now being undertaken by small and medium-sized companies, with the main motivation for investing in the US being market access and improved market intelligence.[19]

This suggests that we are now witnessing a third stage in Japanese overseas investment, especially with the rapid appreciation of the yen in the last four years (the US dollar fell from ¥258 in March 1985 to ¥132 in March 1989) and the resultant squeeze on direct exports from Japan. This third wave can be seen as a turning-point in the internationalisation of Japanese manufacturing, as overseas production increasingly replaces exports from Japan – not only in the US, but in third markets as well. An example of this is Honda's plan to export American-assembled cars to Europe rather than increase exports from Japan (at current exchange rates and productivity levels its unit costs for US-made cars are comparable to or lower than Japanese-made models) or Canon's attempt to export American-assembled copiers to Europe; over 20 Japanese companies now export from North America back to Japan, with about as many again exporting American production to third markets.[20]

Certainly the move overseas by the major Japanese manufacturers has caused their suppliers of goods and services to follow suit. The establishment of US vehicle production by the major Japanese car-makers resulted in 104 Japanese automobile component suppliers investing in US facilities by mid-1987, while most of the vehicle factory construction contracts have gone to Japanese firms and much of the financing has been effected through local branches of Japanese banks.[21] This has provoked protests from American firms that they are being excluded, and this source of tension may intensify if the Japanese camp-followers begin to supply indigenous manufacturers as well.

Indeed, the third wave of Japanese manufacturing investment in the US could be described as a dollar-zone clone of the domestic Japanese industrial complex, aimed at increase in market share rather than substitution for imports from Japan (although fears of 'hollowing out' of firms in the home country have prompted Japanese unions to lobby their American counterparts, without conspicuous success). Some American analysts have argued that the Japanese determination to retain high value-added and technologically advanced component production in Japan will perpetuate the bilateral trade deficit and aggravate American technological dependency on Japan.[22]

US POLICY TOWARD INWARD INVESTMENT: A CASE OF BENIGN NEGLECT

The longstanding US policy of 'neutrality with encouragement' toward inward FDI is undoubtedly a reflection of the relatively small scale of foreign investment in the United States and the pragmatic view that American investors overseas might suffer retaliation if FDI in the US were restricted. Although FDI in the US has grown rapidly (up 215 per cent between 1980 and 1987), it is still smaller than US direct investment abroad – in 1987, $262 billion compared to $309 billion.

It is notable that, among the OECD countries, only the US and West Germany have never had a formal review process for inward investment. Since 1979, FDI matters have been the responsibility of the US Trade Representative (perhaps as a result of a tendency to see FDI as import-substituting in effect). Although the Treasury-chaired interagency Committee on Foreign Investment in the US (CFIUS) was established in 1975 in response to fears of massive petrodollar acquisitions of US assets by foreigners, it met rarely (twice a year on average in the period 1975–88), to review foreign acquisitions where defence or national security considerations were involved.

Apart from some partial prohibitions on foreign investment (in broadcasting, aviation and uranium enrichment), prior to the Exon–Florio provisions of the 1988 Trade Act (see below), only two statutory methods were available to the Federal government to prevent or roll back an unwanted investment. One was to invoke the anti-trust laws, which usually were of little use unless the investor already had a substantial share of the US market. The alternative to this was to use the International Emergency Economic Powers Act, invoked at the time of the US freeze on Iranian assets in 1979 and derived from the earlier Trading with the Enemy Act. Since this required a declaration of national emergency, it was not a useful vehicle for controlling or screening foreign investment. Even now, there is no screening or approval process for foreign investments not involving national security or one of the proscribed sectors, although informal pressures have been exerted to dissuade unwelcome foreign investments on an ad hoc basis.

Well before the Exon–Florio provisions of the 1988 Trade Act, the Federal Government had successfully blocked or discouraged Japanese acquisitions in industries with dual-use, defence-related technology. In 1983, the Department of Defense pressured Kyocera to reverse its acquisition of Dexcel Inc., a manufacturer of semiconductor devices used in the avionics of F-15 and F-16 fighter aircraft, and also prevented Nippon Steel from acquiring Special Metals, an Allegheny Corporation subsidiary producing superalloys used in airframes and engines.[23] While Department of Defense officials denied direct involvement in either case, the Japanese Government trade body JETRO in New York commissioned a confidential report on the impact of the two cases on Japanese FDI in the US. It is somewhat ironic that these attempts to deny access to dual-use technology came at the same time as the US was seeking to persuade the Japanese government to permit the transfer of Japanese technology with potential military applications. Indeed, criticism from high-level American government officials of links between US and Japanese companies in the information technology field has emerged on several occasions in recent years. In 1984, the late CIA Director William Casey, speaking before the Commonwealth Club (a Silicon Valley business study group) criticised Japanese incursions into the computer industry – specifically the Hitachi–National Semiconductor and Amdahl–Fujitsu links – on the ground that it compromised future national security.[24] No such criticism has been directed toward acquisitions by British, French or German companies in dual-use technology sectors.

An example of apparent double standards where Japanese acquisitions are concerned occurred at the end of 1986, when Fujitsu proposed to buy 80 per cent of Fairchild Semiconductor from Schlumberger Ltd of France. Fairchild supplies radiation-resistant semiconductors to the Pentagon. The Pentagon's advisory panel, the Defense Science Board, issued a report in January 1987, warning of the dire consequences of dependence on foreign semiconductors. This prompted then Commerce Secretary Baldridge to oppose Fujitsu's bid, and after un-named Department of Defense sources said that French ownership of Fairchild was preferable (perhaps because France, unlike Japan, does not threaten American output of high-technology products), Fujitsu withdrew its offer.[25]

The absence of an effective interdepartmental co-ordinating body (although CFIUS may assume that role in future with its new powers under the 1988 Trade Act), and a distaste for anything which smacks of *dirigisme*, has meant that Federal policy toward Japanese FDI in the US has been incoherent and inconsistent. The Exon–Florio provisions in the 1988 Trade Act, which gave the President power to block foreign take-overs on national security grounds (though not on the ground that they would affect 'essential commerce', as the sponsors of the amendment originally wanted), seem likely to give a higher profile to CFIUS.

Of 646 US companies acquired by foreigners in 1988–9, the CFIUS reviewed approximately 125, most of them small companies with less than $100 million a year in sales.[26] The Committee represents nine agencies and offices (including Treasury and Defense), but has only six part-time staff to serve it and is obliged to complete its review of foreign acquisitions within 90 days of referral: 30 days to decide whether to investigate the case, then 45 days to complete the investigation, with a final 15 days for the President to act on the Committee's recommendations.

By early 1990, the CFIUS had undertaken only six formal 45-day investigations under Section 5021 (the Exon–Florio provisions) of the 1988 Trade Act. In formulating its recommendations, the CFIUS reviews a number of factors including:

- The domestic production needed for projected national defence requirements.
- The capability and capacity of domestic industries to meet these requirements, including availability of human resources, technology and materials.
- The control of domestic industries and commercial activity by foreign citizens as it affects US ability to meet the requirements of national security.
- The past record of the participants in fulfilling export control regulations.

The CFIUS has been catholic in its investigations. Acquiring companies investigated have come from West Germany, Japan, Sweden/Switzerland, India, France and the PRC. In only one case so far – the acquisition of Mamco (a supplier of metal aircraft components) by the China National Aero-Technology Import and Export Company – has CFIUS recommended a Presidential order requiring divestiture.[27] Of the cases investigated, only one involved a Japanese company: Tokuyama Soda, which deferred its bid for General Ceramics, a producer of components for nuclear weapons, until CFIUS-imposed restrictions requiring divestiture of the division concerned were met.[28] It seems that the CFIUS has made a great effort to avoid 'Japan-bashing' in its investigations, although its operating principles are still far from clear. In other cases the Committee has declined to review takeovers without giving reasons, or has informally persuaded the parties to modify their terms without proceeding to a formal decision.

On the available evidence, it seems that the Treasury Department's Office of International Investment is trying to devise a system that appears to screen foreign take-overs of American firms, but does not deter foreign investors by onerous mandatory notification requirements. The Exon–Florio regulations, which do not define 'national security', therefore call for *voluntary* notification of foreign acquisitions except in the case of products and services that clearly have no relation to national security, such as toys, food, hotels and restaurants, and legal services.[29]

A former Commerce Department representative on CFIUS has remarked, 'The policies and practices that control [the CFIUS] . . . have been passed down largely by word of mouth, like some ancient tribal wisdom.'[30] In the absence of more detailed regulations, Japanese and other foreign acquirers of American companies have every incentive to notify CFIUS – and thus start the 90-day Exon–Florio clock ticking – even if national security issues do not seem to be involved, rather than risk later forced divestiture as a result of non-notification. This, of course, would add to the work-load of CFIUS and probably undermine its effectiveness as a screening and evaluating body.

Although it is somewhat early to evaluate the impact of these regulations, their vagueness, and the power of the CFIUS to review consummated acquisitions in the event of non-disclosure of material facts, seems likely to discourage foreign acquisitions. The obstacles to US acquisitions, however, are still less significant than they are in some other OECD countries.

At least sixteen Federal agencies collect data on some aspect of inward FDI, but there is no apparent co-ordination between them. The House of Representatives Committee on Government Operations commented that 'federal efforts to monitor foreign direct investment in the U.S. and its impact on American national interests are so inadequate, disjointed and poorly implemented that Federal estimates of the total amount of FDI constitute little more than guesswork'. This unco-ordinated approach is mirrored by increasing independence of Federal agencies when it comes to US foreign economic policy toward Japan. Although in the past the State Department has taken the lead on policy toward Japan in general, the trade deficit and Japan's growing economic importance (coupled with the suspicion in the Department of Commerce and the office of the US Trade Representative that State is more concerned with good diplomatic relations than changing Japanese policies) has encouraged the US economic agencies to make independent initiatives toward Tokyo, leading to a decline in co-ordination and policy coherence.

This lack of co-ordination and coherence was exemplified by the controversy in 1989 over the FSX jet fighter co-production agreement, when an arrangement initiated and approved by the Departments of Defense and State (as a means of forestalling an independent Japanese fighter project, and to encourage the transfer of defence-related technology from Japan to the US) had to be amended after signature as a result of pressure by the Department of Commerce and Congress. Even then, a presidential veto was necessary to prevent Congress imposing further restrictions on the renegotiated agreement.[31] It is perhaps significant that no one on the staff of the US National Security Council (NSC) has full-time responsibility for Japan; the *New York Times* quoted an NSC aide's explanation: 'The Japanese don't have nuclear missiles pointed at us.' The FSX affair prompted a California congressman to introduce a bill in March 1989, making the Commerce Secretary a statutory member of the NSC.[32]

Despite the lack of support for a US industrial policy, many US leaders in government and business are reluctantly prepared to admit that the US does indeed have industrial *policies* – i.e. policies that affect various aspects of industrial development – even though there seems to be negligible support for the idea of a coherent and concerted American industrial *strategy* administered by a US version of MITI. In the Reagan Administration, it might have been possible to argue that the emphasis on substantial increases in the defence budget constituted an industrial policy, but the prospect of diminishing defence expenditure as a result of warmer relations with the Soviet Union and the pressing need to reduce the US budget deficit are likely to reduce the influence of the Department of Defense. Secretary of Commerce Robert Mosbacher has resisted calls for a civilian equivalent of DARPA (Defense Advanced Research Projects Agency) to provide federal funds for commercially-critical technology development such as high-definition television.[33] On the other hand, Secretary Mosbacher favours modification of US anti-trust law to permit US firms in all sectors, not only high-technology ones, to collaborate in meeting foreign competition.[34]

Prospects for more formal co-ordination of US industrial policies seem rather remote at present. In March 1985, President Reagan decided not to ask Congress to create a Department of International Trade and Industry, combining portions of the Commerce Department with the Office of the US Trade Representative – a move which the then Secretary of Commerce Malcolm Baldrige had strongly advocated – because of near-unanimous opposition from the rest of the Cabinet (in particular Secretary of State Shultz) who believed it would be an advocate for more protectionist policies.[35] As yet there is no evidence that the Bush Administration is likely to take a different view on this matter, although its willingness to revise US anti-trust law to permit greater collaboration among firms indicates that it is willing to engage in policies explicitly intended to promote the international competitiveness of US industries.

If Japan's industrial policy is consensual, it must be said that America's is vectorial – an unco-ordinated and often conflicting set of policies, practices and programmes affecting industry arising from varied political pressures and often having unintended results. The Export Administration Regulations, for example, have the effect of discouraging research in the US by foreign firms – although the US encourages such activities by Japanese firms as a move beyond low-tech assembly plants – since Part 379 dealing with export and re-export of technical data effectively impedes the transfer of data to affiliates abroad, even where militarily critical technologies and communist countries are not involved.[36]

Policy incoherence, and often outright incompatibility, is compounded by the division of power between federal and state authorities. The Keidanren (trade federation) and other groups in the mid-1980s protested the imposition by certain states of a unitary tax on worldwide profits of multinational firms, much to the embarrassment of Washington, which for some time had been pressing the states to stop taxation at the water's edge. By 1987, the protests had forced California, Florida and virtually all the other states with unitary taxes to abandon them.

COMPETITION BETWEEN THE STATES FOR JAPANESE INVESTMENT

The geographic distribution of Japanese-owned plants has shifted significantly as investment flows have increased. Japanese factories are now located in all but four states (see Table 4.1), and almost 40 states maintain representative offices in Tokyo to attract Japanese investment. Not all are equally successful. Table 4.1 indicates that attention is turning to the Southeastern and Midwestern states after an initial emphasis on California, which remains the location for almost a quarter of all Japanese plants in the US.

It is notable that the sun-belt states with non-union 'right to work' laws have not monopolised Japanese inward investment, and that states such as Michigan, Ohio and Illinois (with a fairly strong union tradition) have benefitted from the camp-followers of the automobile manufacturers. It should be noted, however, that only the auto plants involving a US partner or participant are unionised – Diamond–Star Motors (Chrysler–Mitsubishi), Mazda Motor (Ford owns 25 per cent of Mazda) and New United Motor (GM–Toyota joint venture). In many cases Japanese managers (such as in Honda's Ohio plant or Nissan's Tennessee factory) have been able to avoid union recognition in the plant or (as in Mazda's Michigan factory) negotiate pay scales substantially below those prevailing in American-owned unionised plants. For both production reasons ('just-in-time' inventory methods require reliable deliveries of components) and social requirements (availability of Japanese schooling, food, etc.), there has tended to be some 'clustering' in location of Japanese-owned firms – as in the 'auto alley' surrounding Interstate highways 75 and 65 as they traverse Kentucky, Tennessee and Ohio, or in the Norcross industrial area just north of Atlanta which contains a quarter of the Japanese plants in Georgia within a few square miles.

The quotation from Clyde Prestowitz introducing this chapter indicates the degree of competitiveness existing among the states as they seek to attract foreign investment. Despite recent concerns that uncontrolled foreign investment – particularly where trade and investment reciprocity is absent – is not an unmitigated benefit for the United States, there has been no movement to limit the spiralling investment incentives offered by the states to prospective investors.

Unfortunately, there has been little attempt to quantify the local or regional costs and benefits of any foreign investment, especially Japanese investments. What might be termed the Ichiban Complex – the prestige attached to attracting a Japanese plant as affirmation of a locality's economic dynamism – is sufficient to cause state economic development offices to suspend scepticism and loosen purse-strings. The directory of state investment incentives (the 'Goodies Book' as it is known) runs to over 300 pages, listing the tax-breaks, subsidised loans, road and sewer improvements, and outright grants offered to attract industrialists.[37]

The competition between the states to attract investment has produced an escalating spiral of incentives. In the case of Diamond–Star Motors, four states (Illinois, Indiana, Michigan and Ohio) competed for the plant in 1985, with Bloomington–Normal, Illinois eventually selected. To succeed, Illinois offered Diamond–Star a ten-year package of direct aid and incentives worth $276 million – or about $25,000 for each of the planned 11,000 direct and supplier jobs created (2,500 direct employees and 9,500 employees of suppliers).[38] In fact, Michigan withdrew from the contest a week before the decision as a result of Mitsubishi's 'excessive' demands for incentives, as Governor James Blanchard characterised them.

In order to counter such criticism, Illinois published estimates which indicated that the cost of the incentives would be recouped by the end of 1989 (the Diamond–Star plant's first full year of operation), through lower unemployment benefit payments and increased tax revenue. It did not give as much publicity to such ploys as the $100,000 non-refundable option it paid for four possible plant sites included in the package it had prepared[37] – an example of the increasingly comprehensive and expensive packages used in the investment war between the states. Honda had been given a $22 million package in 1977 to build its plant in Ohio; in 1986 Kentucky gave Toyota a package valued at $100 million to create the same number of jobs (3,000), including payment for screening, training and employing the workers for the first six months.[40]

These dowry contests between states, although aimed at foreign investors generally and not targeted toward the Japanese in particular, are in some measure a reaction to the ineffectual attempts at the Federal level to attract desirable forms of foreign direct investment. In essence, the official Federal policy of 'neutrality with encouragement' has had to be modified cosmetically in order to deflect Congressional attempts to deter or restrict FDI (thus leading to ambiguity, uncertainty and, in the case of CFIUS deliberations, more than a hint of ad-hocery). At the same time, there are no Federal performance criteria or incentives for 'good' foreign investors that might supplant the promotional packages being offered by state economic development agencies.

The Treasury Department has sought to discourage incentive wars between the states, but without success – even though a General Accounting Office survey in 1980 showed that half of the states complained that foreign investors used a state's aid package as leverage in bargaining with another state: 'From the standpoint of the national economy, interstate tax competition is a zero-sum game'. One possible solution might be a Federal ceiling on investment incentives (such as exists in the European Community), but such a limitation would confront the longstanding tensions between Washington and the state capitals on control of commerce.[41]

The states themselves have not been any more successful in devising an armistice in these foreign investment incentive wars. Efforts to promote regional co-ordination of economic development have yet to produce any meaningful results; for example, the meetings of the Southeast United States–Japan Association (composed of elected officials and business executives from six states and Japanese Keidanren members), are used as vehicles for promoting each individual state rather than the region as a whole.[42] This state-level competition is intensified by the competition between local chambers of commerce, port authorities and regional development groups, often poorly co-ordinated by state authorities. This is especially unfortunate in the case of Japanese investors, since at least one survey indicates that for Japanese location decisions factors such as tax and other state and local incentives were much less influential than the quality (and non-militancy) of labour and proximity to markets.[43]

There are reasonable grounds to believe that a ceiling on state aid would not deter Japanese investors, who are probably more impressed by long-term consistency and effort in developing the overall invest-ment climate. Georgia, for example, began its efforts to attract Japa-nese investment in the early 1970s, deciding that it would first be necessary to attract Japanese banks to Atlanta, together with a Japanese consulate, and that this would help to promote Georgia's desirability as an investment location. Its success in doing so, and the creation of an informal intelligence network through the 'Georgia Nihonjin Shokokai' (Georgia Japanese Businessmen's Association) in Atlanta has served to make Georgia fourth among the states in terms of the number of Japanese plants located within its borders, and by far the most successful in the southeastern US (see Table 4.1).

The awareness of the states that these long-term relationships are of the utmost importance can lead to some intriguing cross-pressures in American politics. When Toshiba Machine was threatened with trade sanctions in 1987 over the sale of sensitive high technology to the Soviet Union, the Governor of Tennessee urged the state's Congressional delegation to vote against trade sanctions being applied to Toshiba because 'retaliatory measures directed at Toshiba Corp. can have a direct impact on over 600 employees in Tennessee and approximately 4,000 nationwide'.[44] In this context it is also worth noting that a number of American firms also lobbied Congress to prevent trade sanctions against Toshiba from being included in the 1988 Trade Act, since they were dependent upon uninterrupted supplies of components manufactured by Toshiba. Senator Jake Garn of Utah later said that 'In all the 21 years I have been in public office, I've never seen such a lobbying campaign orchestrated at so many levels'.[45] In the end, Congress did impose sanctions, though only on its machine-tool subsidiary and not on the Toshiba Group as a whole. Although some analysts have taken this as an example of the increasing lobbying power of Japanese firms and their allies, it was not perceived as such in Japan, where news-film of congressmen smashing a Toshiba radio on the Capitol steps has been repeatedly shown as a symbol of American hostility toward Japanese business.

ANTI-TRUST AS INDUSTRIAL POLICY

Both the Reagan and Bush Administrations have pursued a pro-Japanese policy in all but trade-related matters, only deviating from it in defence-related cases or in response to congressional pressure (and even then, as the implementation of Exon–Florio has shown, only in a half-hearted and superficial way). The official US position remains one of welcoming all foreign investment, based on a belief that it reduces imports and boosts employment and tax revenues. While a more restrictive policy toward foreign (and in particular Japanese) direct investment has not been favoured, both President Bush and his predecessor have supported moves to modify US anti-trust regulations in order to promote the international competitiveness of American firms and preserve an indigenous capability in key industrial sectors. Paul McGrath, a former Assistant Attorney-General in charge of the anti-trust division, remarked that 'in a technology war against Japan, even a consortium involving virtually every American player in an industry could well pass antitrust scrutiny'.[46]

The years since 1985 have witnessed some significant amendments to US anti-trust policy, permitting American firms to co-operate in pre-competitive research consortia (under the provisions of the 1984 National Cooperative Research Act), notably the Microelectronics and Computer Technology Corporation, a 20-company consortium initially headed by Admiral Bobby Inman, former Deputy Director of the CIA. The Semiconductor Research Corporation, composed of 40 electronics firms, also received similar anti-trust clearance to support university research; in late 1987 Sematech, a 14-firm collaborative venture (including IBM, AT&T, Intel, Texas Instruments and Motorola) set up to develop semiconductor manufacturing technology, received a $100 million annual matching grant from the US Department of Defense. By March 1989, there were 110 such consortia registered, with further consortia proposed for high-definition television (HDTV) and superconductivity applications.[47] Currently several bills are before the US Congress to permit collaborative consortia in manufacturing, as well as in research; the major US computer and semiconductor manufacturers have proposed a large-scale memory chip manufacturing collective (US Memories Inc.) which is supported by the Departments of Defense and Commerce and a substantial section of Congress.[48]

Recent decisions and official pronouncements indicate that the Justice Department's definition of the appropriate competitive arena is becoming increasingly global, and that restriction of competition domestically in order to compete internationally is now an acceptable goal of anti-trust policy. This is a long way from the position in 1977, when the Justice Department blocked a GE–Hitachi joint colour television venture, even though GE was only sixth in the US market and Hitachi twelfth (and had at that time no US manufacturing base), on the ground that it would restrict competition.[49]

TROJAN HORSE OR SCAPEGOAT? THE FUTURE OF JAPANESE FDI IN THE UNITED STATES

It is evident that the Bush Administration is beginning to undertake a much more critical, focused examination of Japan's strategy of 'industrial co-operation', although the overall attitude remains a positive one. In the short term, Japanese direct investment is indeed an antidote to trade friction, and the immediate benefits of foreign investment are more politically salient than the longer-term costs. In the long term, however, the accumulation of Japanese investment and its failure to live up to some of the more extravagant expectations of its host communities will tend to increase fears of lost autonomy and diminished indigenous capabilities.

Opposition to Japanese investment is still fragmented and subject to cross-pressures. Although some US labour unions, concerned about the alleged anti-union attitudes of Japanese firms, are continuing to press for domestic-content legislation in Congress and were successful in having Japanese cars excluded from the recent US–Canada Free Trade Agreement (they are now pressing to have automobile component kits included in the Japanese 'voluntary' car export quotas), they face considerable domestic opposition. Many of the larger American firms are now already linked to, or in some way dependent upon, Japanese companies (all the major automobile companies now use Japanese components or technology to some degree, and most major electronics firms second-source components from Japan) and consequently would probably oppose restrictions on Japanese inward investment or trade restrictions that might threaten their own offshore assembly and component procurement. Indeed, it might be argued that it is archaic to attribute national identity to any firm whose business takes it abroad. Robert Reich has pointed out that when US Trade Representative Carla Hills accuses Japan of excluding Motorola from the lucrative Tokyo cellular telephone market, she is promoting products designed and manufactured in Malaysia.[50] The announcement in 1989 that Sony (a leading exporter of US-made televisions) was considering an application to join the proposed US HDTV consortium is a further example of this globalisation process.

It is not clear that even the largest American companies, such as General Motors, have done very much hard thinking about the long-term consequences of Japan's industrial presence in the United States; by 1990, for example, Japanese firms will be making 1.3 million cars in America, a third of them in joint ventures with US car-makers, and will collectively pass Chrysler to take their place as the third biggest car manufacturers. Anthony Harris has noted that the Japanese auto firms in the US are called transplants, 'suggesting a vital organ that the host might reject', but that in future they may make an important contribution to US car exports, an arena in which the indigenous firms have not excelled.[51]

Although the US-based multinationals are likely to support a laissez-faire policy toward Japanese investment, this is less likely to be true of smaller and medium-sized American companies (in automobile components, for example). Such firms are finding that Japanese manufacturers bring in their traditional suppliers – who then start selling to US firms as well. This is likely to be a growing source of friction as US component suppliers find that their hopes of selling to Japanese firms are not fulfilled because of stringent design, quality and delivery requirements.

A certain level of domestic discontent is useful for the US administration as a means of putting pressure on Japan to open up its markets and perhaps even accept minimum import quotas for US goods exported to Japan. Recent bilateral trade figures indicate that, despite the rise of the dollar in mid-1989, the Japanese bilateral trade surplus with the US is most unlikely to be substantially reduced in the near future, leaving the 'Japan problem' as a live political issue. It is also unlikely that Japanese manufacturing investment will continue to be seen as a solution to the trade gap, or even as affecting it in any material way. A debate in the US reminiscent of Europe's preoccupation with '*le défi americain*' twenty years ago is now in progress, with unpredictable consequences. The results of the rapid increase in Japanese FDI in the

1980s will soon start to show up in the US current account in the form of service and royalty payments and profit remissions, with the probability of sustained imports of components and high value-added items from Japan.

Protectionist and anti-Japanese sentiment in Congress has receded slightly from its peak four years ago, but remains a potent factor which the Democratic majority may seek to exploit in the 1990 mid-term elections. Certainly the Japanese have cause to be concerned by the trends indicated by recent opinion polls, such as the *Washington Post–ABC News* poll in which 54 per cent of the US sample said that Japan was now the world's strongest economic power and eight out of ten favoured limits on Japanese investments in American companies.[52] The FSX affair has indicated that Japan may be less willing to avoid a public confrontation with the US on technology and investment matters, and it might be that any American attempt to use the Japanese industrial presence in the US as a hostage would be counter-productive.

The Japanese government and many firms and industry associations from Japan have spent large sums on engaging well-connected Washington lobbyists (as the Toshiba affair showed) and employees of Japanese subsidiaries in the US have created well-funded political action committees to support the election expenses of sympathetic legislators at state and federal level. While this does not distinguish them from most indigenous American firms, it does indicate that Japan is rapidly learning the arcane arts of influence-wielding in the polycentric American political system.

Given the fragmented and incoherent nature of US public policy at state and federal levels, it is very difficult to predict the outcome of the problems arising from the growing Japanese industrial presence in America. Just as two decades ago European concern over the potential dominance of its industry by US-owned multinationals aroused alarm and apocalyptic visions of Europe's industrial helotry, so current American sensitivity over their relative loss of power may be causing them to draw too close a link between the internationalisation of Japanese firms and the rise of Japan as a new hegemon. This use of Japan as scapegoat for the US loss of competitiveness is clearly exaggerated and ill-founded. The Trojan Horse analogy may be as false as it is tempting, or perhaps history tells us no more than that Trojan horses are dangerous when they have armed Greeks inside them. Japan may be the new Phoenicia rather than a reincarnated Greece, especially if it sells its horses rather than employing them as machines of war.

Notes and References

1. Clyde V. Prestowitz, *Trading Places: How We Allowed Japan to Take the Lead* (New York: Basic Books, 1988) p. 214.
2. Two recent and influential examples of this genre are: David P. Calleo, *Beyond American Hegemony* (New York: Basic Books, 1987); Paul Kennedy, *The Rise and Fall of the Great Powers* (New York: Random House, 1987).
3. Samuel P. Huntington: 'The U.S. – Decline or Renewal?', *Foreign Affairs*, 67(2) (Winter 1988/89) pp. 76–96.
4. Theodore H. White: 'The Danger from Japan', *New York Times Sunday Magazine* (28 July 1985); Daniel Burstein, *YEN!: Japan's New Financial Empire and its Threat to America* (New York: Simon & Schuster, 1988); Clyde M. Prestowitz, *Trading Places*; Larry Martz *et al.*, 'Hour of Power?', *Newsweek* (27 February 1989) pp. 26–31.
5. *Business Week* (7 August 1989); *The Economist* (19 March 1988). To put this in perspective, it should be noted that another poll (*Newsweek*, 3 April 1989) found that 77 per cent of the Americans responding believe there is a heaven, and 76 per cent that they have a good or excellent chance of getting there.
6. Martin and Susan Tolchin, *Buying Into America* (New York: Times Books, 1988); Barrie G. James, *Trojan Horse: The Ultimate Japanese Challenge to Western Industry* (London: Mercury Books, 1989).
7. DeAnne Julius and Stephen E. Thomsen, *Inward Investment and Foreign-Owned Firms in the G-5*, RIIA Discussion Paper, 12 (London: Royal Institute of International Affairs, 1989) pp. 3–9.
8. *International Herald Tribune* (21 February 1989) p. 6; *JEI Report*, 2B (13 January 1989) p. 10.
9. House Committee on Government Operations, *The Adequacy of the Federal Response to Foreign Investment in the United States*, 96th Congress, 2nd session: House Report 96-1216 (Washington, DC: Government Printing Office, August 1980) pp. 66–7; *Japan Economic Institute Report*, 30 (4 August 1989) pp. 6–8.
10. Tolchin and Tolchin, *Buying Into America*, pp. 264–5.
11. *The Economist* (2 May 1987) pp. 67–70.
12. American Chamber of Commerce in Japan and Council of the European Business Community, *Direct Foreign Investment in Japan: The Challenge for Foreign Firms* (Tokyo: ACCJ/EBC, 1987).
13. Elliott Zupnick, *Foreign Investment in the U.S.: Costs and Benefits*, Headline Series, 249 (New York: Foreign Policy Association, 1980) pp. 20–2.
14. *Financial Times* (7 December 1987, Supplement on Japanese Industry) p. iv; Japan Economic Institute, *Japan's Expanding U.S. Manufacturing Presence: 1987 Update* (Washington, DC: JEI, 1988) p. 18; *Business Week* (24 July 1989) p. 54.
15. Japan Economic Institute, *Japan's Expanding U.S. Manufacturing Presence*, pp. 2–3.
16. W. T. Grimm survey, quoted in *Financial Times* (8 August 1987).

17. Susan MacKnight, *Japan's Expanding Manufacturing Presence in the United States: A Profile* (Washington, DC: JEI, 1981) pp. 2, 6–16.
18. *The Economist* (2 May 1987) p. 68.
19. Tomoichiro Aoki, 'Increasing Japan's Direct Overseas Investment', *LTCB Monthly Economic Review*, 88 (September–October 1986) pp. 3–4; *Financial Times* (22 Sept 1987).
20. *Financial Times* (18 Sept 1987 and 7 Dec 1987).
21. US General Accounting Office, *Foreign Investment: Growing Japanese Presence in the U.S. Auto Industry* (GAO/NSIAD-88-111) (March 1988) pp. 41, 53–6.
22. Lester C. Thurow, 'Paradise Lost', *New York Times* (24 February 1988).
23. *Yearbook of U.S.–Japan Economic Relations in 1983* (Washington, DC: JEI, 1984) p. 63.
24. *Japan Economic Journal* (30 October 1984); *Allentown Call-Chronicle* (18 November 1984).
25. *New York Times* (9 November 1986); *Wall Street Journal* (17 November 1986); *Financial Times* (27 Jan 1987); *JEI Report* 30A (7 August 1987).
26. *Business Week* (12 June 1989) pp. 40–1.
27. *Financial Times* (3 February 1990).
28. *Financial Times* (10 May 1989)
29. *Financial Times*, 19 July 1989; *The Sunday Times* (London), 23 July 1989; *Federal Register*, vol. 54 no. 134 (14 July 1989) pp. 29744–55.
30. Joseph F. Dennin, 'Getting a Transaction Past CFIUS', *International Trade Reporter*, vol. 6 (22 March 1989), p. 377.
31. *Financial Times*, 31 May and 1 August 1989.
32. House Committee on Government Operations' *The Adequacy of the Federal Response*, pp. 19–20; *New York Times* (20 March 1989); *JEI Report*, 12B (24 March 1989).
33. *Financial Times* (18 May 1989).
34. *Financial Times* (27 July 1989).
35. *Wall Street Journal* (18 March 1985).
36. US Department of Defense, *Department of Defense Directive, 2040.2 (International Transfers of Technology, Goods, Services, and Munitions)* (17 January 1984).
37. *Morning Call* (Allentown, PA) (14 October 1985); for an overview of the range of state aids, see *The Economist* Intelligence Unit, *US State Investment Incentives* (Special Report, 187) (January 1985).
38. *Chicago Tribune* (13 October 1985).
39. *New York Times* (17 September 1985).
40. *New York Times* (10 September 1986); *Wall Street Journal* (24 September 1986).
41. US General Accounting Office, *Foreign Direct Investment in the United States – The Federal Role* (June 1980) p. 33.
42. *National Journal* (16 January 1988) p. 130.
43. Mamoru Yoshida, *Japanese Direct Manufacturing Investment in the United States* (New York: Praeger, 1987) pp. 66–8.
44. *New York Times* (19 August 1987).

45. Quoted in Robert J. Samuelson, 'America for Sale?', *The New Republic* (12 June 1989) p. 33.
46. *New York Times* (23 April 1985).
47. Louise Kehoe, 'Japanese electronics threatens the American Way', *Financial Times* (9 March 1989).
48. *Financial Times* (22 June 1989).
49. Sanford M. Litvack, 'The Urge to Rewrite the Antitrust Laws', *Across the Board* (January 1984), p. 15.
50. Robert B. Reich, 'Members Only', *The New Republic* (26 June 1989) p. 14.
51. *The Economist* (12 December 1987) p. 79.; Anthony Harris: 'When Detroit catches a cold. . .', *Financial Times* (31 July 1989).
52. *The Economist* (25 February 1989) p. 42.

5 The Third World in Japanese Foreign Policy

William Nester

The continued and growing access of Japanese firms to the markets and resources of the Third World has been a vital aspect of Japan's rise to economic prominence. In 1986, 38 per cent of Japan's total trade and 46 per cent of its accumulated foreign investments (1958–86) was with the Third World.[1] For the most part this access has had minimal costs and maximum benefits. Japan's immensely successful foreign policy was geared toward maintaining a low political profile while concentrating on maximising its overseas economic penetration. Tokyo managed to avoid getting entangled in any significant political issues, and even when it was forced to take a stand, as in the Middle East in 1973, succeeded in minimising its difficulties. By tying most foreign aid to the purchase of Japanese goods and services, Tokyo gave its producers a tremendous export subsidy which enabled them to capture markets from their foreign competitors while 'fulfilling' Japan's obligations as an OECD member. The chief purpose of its intermediary role in various regional conflicts was to solidify and justify its continued economic links with both sides, rather than conflict resolution.

Japan's foreign policy toward the Third World will be explored in three parts. The first part will put Tokyo's Third World policy in the context of its overall foreign policy and development goals. It will then identify a number of key diplomatic strategies Tokyo has used to secure its interests in the Third World. The second part will analyse Japan's economic interests in trade, investments and aid in different regions of the Third World. The third section will look at how skilful Japanese diplomacy in several regional or bilateral conflicts effectively secured Japan's economic and political interests in those respective areas.

JAPAN'S FOREIGN POLICY AND THE THIRD WORLD

Although the means have changed, Tokyo has continually pursued four interrelated foreign policy goals since the country was forced into the world economy by Commodore Perry's gunboats in 1853: (1) economic and military security; (2) rapid modernisation; (3) great

71

power status; and (4) world recognition of its accomplishments. Before 1945, Japan used state-led industrialisation and imperialism to achieve these goals, and these means were initially very successful. By 1919, Japan had become an industrial and military Great Power, was recognised as one of the 'Big Five' at the Versailles Conference and enjoyed an alliance with Britain. Unfortunately, these accomplishments were tossed away during Japan's imperialist drive after 1931. The trauma of Japan's devastating defeat during the Second World War convinced its leaders that militarism was a bankrupt means of achieving the nation's foreign policy goals. Instead, Tokyo has single-mindedly used neomercantilism – a combination of industrial targeting at home, export of the resulting products into a rapidly expanding world economy and import barriers against competitive foreign products. Japan made use of the shelter of America's nuclear umbrella, largely open market and sales of advanced technology at bargain prices to achieve its four longstanding foreign policy goals.

Japan's post-war foreign policy can be divided into two phases. From 1952 to 1973, Tokyo followed its 'separation of economics and politics' (*seikei bunri*) strategy whereby it avoided involvement in almost all international issues, while concentrating on trading with virtually everyone (although during this time much of its trade with the Third World was concentrated in East Asia). This phase came to an abrupt end in late 1973, with OPEC's quadrupling of oil prices and the oil embargo by the Arab states. It became clear to Tokyo that it was no longer possible to separate economics from politics – at least in the Middle East. Japan responded with its 'comprehensive security' (*sogo anzen hosho*) strategy which involved active diplomatic involvement in relatively non-controversial issues while diversifying its sources of foreign markets, cheap labour, energy and raw materials. While reducing Japan's dependence on any single source, Tokyo in turn attempted to make its sources dependent on Japanese goods, services, capital and technology.

As Japan's foreign economic presence throughout the Third World expanded rapidly, Tokyo has had to confront a range of problems in its quest for diversified sources of markets, raw materials, cheap labour and energy. The 'laser beam' character of Japan's export offensives, which target and deluge certain market niches with underpriced goods, have continually caused resentment and protest among Japan's trade rivals. At the same time, its trade surpluses with all its Third World partners except for the oil and raw material producers are the source of continual complaints by those countries. Third World nations are joining the chorus of the industrial states in demanding that Japan halt its neomercantilist policies and open its markets to competitive imports. Japan is also criticised for the composition of its trade, as Japan predominantly exports manufactured goods and restricts its imports to raw materials or semi-finished goods, even when Third World manufactured goods with a comparative advantage are available.

Japanese direct foreign investment has been heavily criticised as well. Japan's manufacturing investments in simple technologies like textiles tend to squeeze out local entrepreneurs. When Japanese firms form a joint venture with local entrepreneurs, they tend to prefer minority groups like the overseas Chinese in Southeast Asia or the Indians in Africa rather than indigenous businessmen, a practice which causes considerable resentment among the latter. There are also widespread complaints that Japanese firms refuse to transfer technology to their partners, staff the venture with as many as four times the number of expatriate managers as American and European foreign investors and thus completely control decision making. Japanese expatriates tend to remain isolated from the local culture and few are seen to mingle with the local people. Riots in Thailand and Indonesia in the early 1970s, and protests in China in 1985 reveal the depth of these resentments. Another complaint involves Tokyo's foreign aid programme, which is criticised for being used essentially as an export subsidy for Japanese firms since most aid remains tied to the purchase of Japanese goods and services. Japan's grant component of its ODA is the lowest of the 18 OECD countries, while the interest rate on its loans is the highest.[2]

Tokyo has used extremely sophisticated diplomacy to finesse these problems. Its most common response to foreign demands that it halt its neomercantilism has been continual Japanese promises of fewer export offensives, more open markets and more beneficial foreign investments and aid terms. Many of these promises are conveyed as 'gifts' (*omiyage*) by Japanese prime ministers and other cabinet officials when they travel abroad. This '*omiyage* diplomacy' hides continued neomercantilist practices. Japan's diversification policy has supported the practice. The wider Japan spreads its sources of markets and resources and the more firmly it makes its partners dependent on Japanese goods, services, capital and technology, the stronger its negotiating position against any one country or even region will be should an attempt be made to extract trade, investment or aid concessions from Japan's government or firms.

By acting as a go-between in regional conflicts, Japan has maximised both its trading position and its diplomatic prestige. Japan first began playing both sides of regional fences in the early 1950s, when Washington forced Tokyo to sever its diplomatic ties with Beijing and recognise Taipei. Instead, Japan continued to trade and conduct diplomacy with both countries and by the mid-1960s was China's largest trade partner. Chalmers Johnson describes this as 'one of the most skilfully executed foreign policies pursued by Japan in the postwar era – a clever, covert adaptation by Japan to the Cold War and a good example of Japan's essentially neomercantilist foreign policy'.[3] To varying degrees, Tokyo has played the same intermediary role in conflicts between North and South Korea, ASEAN and Vietnam, the Arab states and Israel, Iran and Iraq, and Black African states and South Africa.

Another interesting variation of its go-between role has been Tokyo's attempts to mediate North–South issues in the United Nations and elsewhere. Japan has been elected to the Security Council more often than any other country, in part because of its effective go-between policy which generates widespread support. In UN votes, Tokyo tries to avoid taking any stand on controversial issues, and will even vote for a proposal it actually opposes if it knows the United States will veto it, all in an attempt to gain as much favour in the Third World as possible.[4] Japan has played the same role in the annual 'Big Seven' industrial nation summits. Since 1975, it has acted as the spokesman for East Asia at each summit, a role every country in the region accepts, barring China. In particular, Japan has raised the issue of bringing the Newly Industrialising Countries (NICs) and eventually the New Exporting Countries (NECs) into the OECD. At the Toronto Summit in June 1988, Prime Minister Takeshita warned against the rise of European Community and North American trade blocs, and hinted that Japan could convert its strong position in East Asia into a similar trade bloc if necessary.[5]

This neomercantilist foreign policy has been supremely successful. In the sincerest form of flattery, most NICs have used Japan's strategy as a model for their own development. Tokyo has overwhelmingly achieved the national goals of economic and military security, rapid modernisation, economic superpower status, and foreign recognition of these tremendous accomplishments.

JAPAN'S POLITICAL AND ECONOMIC TIES WITH THE THIRD WORLD

Although Japan's comprehensive security policy makes virtually any region or country a potentially important economic partner, some regions of the Third World are obviously far more important to Japan than others. East Asia and the Middle East are Japan's most important economic partners for both economic and political reasons. Latin America is important primarily for economic reasons, and Africa trails last in importance. Between 1958 and 1987, the value of Japan's trade with the developing world grew an astonishing 24-fold, from $6 billion to $145 billion.[6] Yet, during this time, trade with the Third World as a proportion of Japan's total trade remained virtually constant at about 40 per cent. In 1958, Japan's largest trade flow with the Third World was with Asia and the Pacific, worth $1.6 billion (amounting to 27 per cent of total Japanese trade), followed by the Middle East with $479 million (7 per cent), Latin America and the Caribbean with $464 million (7 per cent) and Africa with $78 million (1 per cent). In 1987, Asia was still the focus of Japan's Third World trade, with $9 billion, although its proportion of Japan's total trade had dropped to 23 per cent. This again was followed by the Middle East with 10 per cent, Latin America with 4 per cent, and Africa with 2 per cent.

Japanese foreign investments have inevitably followed trade. Until the late 1960s, MITI used its powers under the 1949 Foreign Exchange and Foreign Trade Control Law to regulate carefully all foreign investments in Japan or Japanese overseas investments. Competitive foreign firms were prevented from investing in Japan so that they would instead sell their technology to their Japanese rivals. Japanese firms were prevented from investing overseas to prevent the balance of payments deficit from eroding further. Between 1956 and 1967, the accumulated total of Japanese foreign direct investment (FDI) in developing countries was $686 million, starting at $10 million in 1956 and rising in a roller coaster pattern to $84.6 million, with peaks of $98.4 million in 1961 and $97.1 million in 1966.[7]

Harry Chernotsky identifies several key reasons why MITI began to allow a growing amount of Japanese foreign investment after 1968:

... as a defensive measure to relieve pressure on the domestic economy and to assist in the realization of key economy policy goals. It is also an integral part of Japan's enduring 'export or die' philosophy ... It seems predicated largely on the need to acquire direct access to raw material supplies to support industrial activity, to secure established and additional markets for the sale of Japanese products and to enhance further the country's worldwide competitiveness.[8]

To these reasons can be added the desire for access to cheap labour and land, and the wish to export heavily polluting firms to relieve a growing pollution problem within Japan.

Since then, Japanese FDI has passed through two distinct phases, and seems to be entering a third. From the late 1960s to the early 1970s, 64 per cent of all Japanese FDI was in Third World countries, of which 63 per cent was in mining and labour intensive manufacturing sectors. The majority of investments were by small or medium-sized firms which formed joint ventures with local partners; in 1972 only 41 per cent of the Japanese ventures in Asia were majority owned.[9]

Throughout the 1970s, larger firms began to invest overseas and an increasing percentage of FDI went to other industrial countries, particularly the United States. Although trading companies continued to help small and medium-sized firms invest overseas, the larger firms largely financed themselves and generally preferred majority ownership in joint ventures.[10] From the mid-1980s, the steady stream of Japanese FDI became a flood. Between 1980 and 1985 alone, accumulative Japanese FDI doubled from $36 billion to $70 billion, of which 32 per cent went to North America, 23 per cent to Latin America, 23 per cent to Asia, 12 per cent to Europe, 5 per cent to Africa, 2 per cent to Australia, and 2 per cent to the Middle East. This flow generally followed the historical pattern of Japanese FDI.[11]

The largest recipient of Japanese FDI through 1986 was the United States; the second ranking country was Indonesia (although FDI in the US was three times greater). Eight of the next 12 largest recipients were developing countries, among them Panama and Liberia, where the investment was mostly in flags of convenience rather than manufacturing. In other recipients such as Hong Kong, Singapore, Saudi Arabia and Mexico investments were largely in manufacturing or manufacturing and resource extraction.[12] This pattern began to shift in 1986, as much of that year's investments flowed toward North America (47 per cent of the total), Latin America (21 per cent), and Europe (16 per cent), while the flow to Asia dropped to 10 per cent, as did that to Africa (1 per cent) and the Middle East (0.2 per cent).[13] Japanese firms have been tapping into Latin America's rich resources and growing domestic markets for several decades, and the flow will continue. Most Japanese investments are either manufacturing ventures in Mexico whose products are targeted for North America's markets or both resource and manufacturing ventures in Brazil.

Japan's aid policy has always been geared toward promoting Japanese trade with and investments in the recipient country.[14] Aid tied to the purchase of Japanese goods and services had always been the most important goal of Japan's aid policy. Although Japan's official development assistance (ODA) has risen gradually since the 1950s, it still remains low by OECD standards.[15] As a proportion of world ODA, Japan's share has risen little over the past 15 years, from 9 per cent in 1970 to 13 per cent in FY 1986–87. As a proportion of GNP, Japanese aid has risen steadily from 0.2 per cent in 1976 to 0.3 in 1987. During these years, Japan's ratio of ODA to GNP was well behind the OECD average of 0.35 per cent of GNP. Japan's grant element of total ODA continues to lag at the bottom of the OECD countries, and has actually dropped recently. In 1987, Japan's grant element to the poorest countries was 86 per cent compared to the OECD average of 96 per cent, while statistically Japan and Italy shared the ignominy of having their private grants as a proportion of GNP recorded as zero compared to an OECD mean of 0.03 per cent.

After 1973, as part of Japan's comprehensive security policy, Tokyo began significantly to expand its aid programme both in volume and geographical spread. Increasing amounts of aid were given to strategic countries bordering conflicts (*funso shuhen koku*) which did not necessarily have large markets or resources. In the 1980s, Japan has increasingly co-ordinated its strategic aid with the United States, and has picked up the slack of Washington's declining aid in countries like Sudan, Egypt, Pakistan, El Salvador, the Philippines, Jamaica, Honduras and Costa Rica. Despite these changes, the geographical distribution of Japanese aid has remained fairly constant over time. About 50 per cent of Japanese aid continues to go to East Asia and Oceania. The proportion of Japan's total aid going to the Middle East and North Africa also stayed about the same at between 7–8 per cent. However, Japan's aid to Subsaharan Africa and Latin America and the Caribbean increased as proportions of total Japanese aid during this decade.

At the Paris summit of the Group of Seven industrial countries in July 1989, Prime Minister Sosuke Uno announced a five-year, $35 billion aid programme. Whether aid will remain a carefully formulated set of export subsidies for Japanese industries remains to be seen. But it is extremely unlikely that Japan will reverse a tied aid policy that has been so beneficial to Japanese firms. If Japan's aid levels reach the

OECD average, that aid may still be wholly or partially tied. Where competition is restricted to companies from Japan and firms of the recipient nations (in 'LDC-tied' aid), Japanese companies land the contracts most of the time, as they are easily the more competitive.[16] In 1988, only 47 per cent of Japan's ODA was estimated to be wholly untied compared to 78 per cent for France, 90 per cent for the United States, and 99 per cent for Britain.[17]

BILATERAL AND MULTILATERAL RELATIONS

Two Chinas Policy

Japan's leaders never shared Washington's fears of a communist China. As early as 1948, Prime Minister Yoshida succinctly summed up Japan's neomercantilist policy when he said: 'I don't care whether China is red or green. China is a national market and it has become necessary for Japan to think about markets'.[18] Yoshida went on to say that 'Japan viewed without any anxiety, the possibility of a total seizure of China by the communists . . . [because] the CCP would soon turn as nationalistic and anti-foreign as previous Chinese regimes. The CCP would actually help to mitigate Soviet power in Asia. Sino–Japanese contacts could be built to mutual advantage'.[19] It took Washington another quarter century before it reached the same sensible conclusion. Meanwhile, although Japan had dutifully complied with Washington's demands in 1951 that Japan sever its relations with the mainland and recognise Taiwan, it continued to trade with both Chinas. In 1964, surpassing the Soviet Union and United States respectively, Japan became the leading trade partner of both China and Taiwan. Since then it has had continually growing trade surpluses with both.

Prime Minister Yoshida signed not only the September 1951 security treaty forming an American–Japanese alliance, but also the December 1951 'Yoshida letter', drafted by John Foster Dulles, in which Japan committed itself to Taipei and condemned communist China, although future relations were hinted at if Beijing 'changes its present ways'.[20] Yoshida's 'commitment' to Taipei was followed up by the April 1952 Japan–Taiwan peace treaty. Although Tokyo seemed to knuckle under to Washington's pressures, both the security and Taiwan treaties proved to be outstanding Japanese foreign policy coups. Japan's military security was guaranteed at minimum cost while diplomatic recognition of Taipei and continued trade ties with both countries maximised the economic benefits for Japan while making Tokyo appear a faithful US ally in the Cold War. In 1972, Tokyo followed Washington's lead and simultaneously restored relations with Beijing while breaking them with Taipei. Its economic ties with both have accelerated since.

Sino–Japanese relations before 1972 were a roller coaster that reared and plunged according to shifts in the continual power struggle within Beijing between pragmatists and radicals. Throughout this time, Japan skilfully rode out each crisis so that the trade volume expanded despite temporary setbacks. Chalmers Johnson describes Japanese strategy throughout this period as *'fumie* diplomacy',[21] whereby a 'private' political or business group would sign lucrative trade agreements with China with the requirement that they then harshly criticise Western 'imperialism' and sometimes the Japanese government itself, before they could reap the benefits of greater wealth for their corporations and Japan.

Since 1972, diplomatic recognition has shifted from Taipei to Beijing while trade continued to flourish with both Taiwan and China. Six years later, on 12 August 1978, Tokyo signed the Sino–Japanese Treaty of Peace and Friendship in which both sides agreed to expand trade to $20 billion over the next eight years. The standard *fumie* 'anti-hegemony clause' was offset by another clause stating that 'the present treaty shall not affect the position of either contracting party regarding its relations with third parties'.[22]

Southeast Asia

From the late 1940s through the 1960s, Washington and Tokyo worked carefully to reassert Japan's economic presence in Southeast Asia. In this dynamic triangular economic relationship, a division of labour was agreed upon whereby the United States would provide capital and high technology, Japan intermediate goods, and Southeast Asia raw materials. During this period, American embassies helped Japanese business get a foot in local markets while both American aid and Japanese reparations were tied to purchases of Japanese goods and services.[23] By the mid-1970s, as its economic development continued to advance, Japan replaced the United States as the region's most important source of trade, investment and aid. Tokyo's economic hegemony over Southeast Asia has steadily strengthened since.

Although Japan's economic and geopolitical interests and power are now world-wide, Southeast Asia remains an especially important pillar of Japan's comprehensive security for several reasons. Economically, South-east Asia provides a tremendous source of markets and natural resources, and a potential ally to counter a possible protectionist North American or European trade bloc. Southeast Asia is almost as important geopolitically since 70 per cent of Japan's oil flows through the Straits of Malacca. In 1987, Prime Minister Takeshita made his first overseas visit to the ASEAN summit, rather than to Washington – one illustration of Southeast Asia's importance to Japan.

As in other regions, Tokyo's policy toward Southeast Asia has focused on maintaining access to benefits flowing from the region's continued economic growth and political stability. But, with one notable exception, Tokyo did not take any significant political initiatives in the region until the mid-1970s. Instead, it simply pursued a subtle, behind the scenes diplomacy geared to enhance Japan's economic interests. After the American withdrawal from Indochina and the fall of South Vietnam in 1975, it became clear that the United States would no longer underwrite Japan's regional economic hegemony. Instead, Tokyo embarked on a series of diplomatic initiatives to fill the political vacuum left by America's reduced regional presence.

Before 1977, Tokyo successfully followed its policy of attempting to separate economic from political issues. Although it joined several important regional organisations – the Colombo Plan (1954), Economic Commission for Asia and the Far East (1955), Asia and Pacific Council (1966), and Asian Parliamentarian Union (1966) – Tokyo always used these organisations to fuel its economic penetration of the region while remaining aloof from political controversies. Although at first it hoped to become a member when the Association of Southeast Asian Nations (ASEAN) was formed on 8 August 1967, Tokyo snubbed the organisation after it was refused membership. Prime Minister Sato visited Southeast Asia in September and October 1967, but refused to discuss, let alone recognise, ASEAN. Tokyo feared ASEAN would become a powerful pressure group on economic issues and thus felt the less encouragement given the better.[24] Tokyo's only significant diplomatic initiative during this time was to create and lead the Asian Development Bank (ADB), an action which simultaneously enhanced both Japan's economic security and prestige goals, as well as offsetting foreign criticism about Tokyo's inattention to regional responsibilities.[25] Japanese have served as presidents of the ADB since its formation in 1967.

Japan's deepening economic penetration of Southeast Asia has encountered some difficulties. The rapid influx of Japanese goods and investments in the early 1970s caused economic disruptions and subsequent backlash in several countries. In 1972, there was a widespread boycott of Japanese goods in Thailand in protest against what Thais described as Japanese businessmen acting like 'economic animals'.[26] Prime Minister Tanaka's visit to Thailand and Indonesia was greeted with mass protests in both countries. The protests forced Tokyo to take its first step in recognising ASEAN, when Tanaka agreed to establish the Japan–ASEAN Forum on Rubber in March 1974 to allay some of the criticism.

But it was only after 1975, with Indochina under communist rule and Southeast Asia's future uncertain that Japan embarked on several significant diplomatic initiatives. The Japan–ASEAN Forum was created in March 1977, and Prime Minister Fukuda attended the ASEAN prime ministers' summit in August of that year. At the summit, Fukuda announced that Japan was firmly committed to a 'special relationship' based on equality and a 'heart-to-heart understanding' with ASEAN that did not include a military dimension. In the months leading up to the summit, ASEAN negotiated a pledge from Tokyo of $1 billion for five ASEAN regional projects. Although the entry price seemed high, Tokyo was able to divert criticism of its policies in Southeast Asia and elsewhere by using the regional stage to act like a responsible power.[27] As it turns out, Tokyo had to fund only two of the five projects (the other three failed to materialise), while it successfully rejected ASEAN demands that Japan cut its trade surplus, open its markets, buy more manufactured goods, improve the quality of its aid, transfer technology and agree to a stable price system for commodity imports (STABEX).

In Southeast Asia, Tokyo perfected the policy of *'omiyage* (gift) diplomacy' that it now pursues so successfully everywhere in the world. Every prime minister after Fukuda visited either ASEAN or its individual countries, bearing a 'gift' of promises that were, more often than not, simply a reworking of his predecessor's promises. These promises generally dampen regional criticism temporarily. Meanwhile, although forced to deal with Southeast Asia multilaterally rather than through its divide-and-conquer bilateral policy before 1977, Tokyo has consistently attempted to dilute its own dependence on ASEAN resources while reinforcing ASEAN dependence on Japanese goods, services and capital. It has also sought to draw ASEAN into more diversified settings in which its force as a regional grouping might be swamped: for example, since 1978 Tokyo has tried to include the

United States, Canada, Australia, New Zealand and even the European Community in the Japan–ASEAN Forum to divert attention from bilateral economic problems towards regional political issues. Between 1978 and 1980, the Ohira government promoted its Pacific Community Concept designed to push economic problems under the carpet of widespread political concerns. Both ASEAN and the Pacific Forum countries successfully opposed this plan which would have undercut their respective regional organisations.

Cultural diplomacy was yet another device to divert attention from the worsening economic relationship. Sueo Sudo describes Tokyo's rationale for this strategy: 'Since growing economic interdependence and a more complex political relationship will inevitably increase the chances for a collision of interests, the most effective way to building a strong foundation for mutually beneficial relations between Japan and ASEAN is to foster more extensive cultural exchanges'.[28] Though largely successful in forestalling any significant Japanese concessions, '*omiyage* diplomacy' has not escaped criticism. ASEAN continually complains that it benefitted little from Japan's seven 'market opening steps' of the 1980s, since most concessions went to the West. Also, Japan faces an image problem in the region. In 1982, Malaysian Prime Minister Mahathir told his people to 'look East' to Japan as a development model. But a mere two years later he complained openly that relations with Tokyo still 'conform . . . to the classic pattern of economic colonialism'; the 'Look East Policy' was not an invitation to Japanese 'arrogance and insensitive behaviour'. Mahathir questioned Japanese motives in assisting Malaysian development.[29] In 1985, the Malaysian Trade and Industry Minister publicly wondered 'whether the ugly past has returned in a different guise', protested Japanese 'trade selfishness and parochial protectionism' and feared that the Look East Policy may have actually hindered Malaysian development while enhancing Japanese economic hegemony over his country.[30]

A key element of Japan's policy toward the region is ostensibly to act as the go-between for ASEAN in international conflicts. Takeshita claimed to speak for Southeast Asian interests at the Toronto summit, but Japan's go-between diplomacy goes back at least a decade earlier. Since the late 1970s, Japan attempted to mediate tensions between ASEAN and Vietnam. Tokyo's motives for acting as go-between were mixed. On one level, it shared with ASEAN the fear of a powerful, expansionist Vietnam. Yet, more importantly, Tokyo had its eye on a potential 60-million person market in Indochina, led by huge orders for reconstruction.

Between 1977 and 1981, Japanese diplomats conducted shuttle diplomacy between ASEAN and Vietnam and aired several peace plans for the region. Tokyo justifies its continued diplomatic links by claiming they would moderate Hanoi and wean it from dependence on Moscow.[31] But Japan's diplomacy did not prevent Vietnam from invading Cambodia in 1979, while ASEAN protested that Tokyo's aid and investments merely strengthened Hanoi and Japanese industry.[32] In 1980, after tremendous pressure, Japan finally agreed to freeze its aid programme and condemn Vietnamese aggression. The following year, Tokyo announced a regional peace plan which included provisions for a UN supervised phased withdrawal, free elections, and repatriation of refugees. In July 1984, Foreign Minister Abe upped the ante when he announced at the Japan–ASEAN foreign ministers' meeting that Japan would bear the costs of the UN peacekeeping forces, provide personnel and facilities for the election and give economic aid to all concerned countries. Tokyo reiterated the same points in June 1987.

These statements were cost-free and temporarily diverted ASEAN attention from more pressing bilateral trade issue. They also help justify rapidly expanding Japanese economic ties with Vietnam. Tokyo has resumed its aid to Vietnam, particularly targeting infrastructure projects like roads, water supply, power, communications and docks, tied to purchases of Japanese capital equipment. As a result of these efforts, after a dip in the early 1980s, Japanese exports to Vietnam more than doubled, from $92 million to $189 million, while its imports went from $36 million to $83 million between 1982 and 1986. Fearing criticism from the United States and ASEAN, which impose economic sanctions on Vietnam, only the trading company Nissho Iwai has a permanent official office in Hanoi, but such huge corporations as Mitsubishi, Mitsui, C. Itoh and Marubeni maintain a permanent presence through dummy firms.[33]

Tokyo has played both sides of the diplomatic fence to its economic benefit with Burma as well. Japan has enjoyed a trade suplus with Burma, which in 1986 imported $213 million of goods from Japan while exporting only $49 million to Japan. Although trade has hovered at the same level for over a decade after rising rapidly in the mid-1970s, Japan remains Burma's largest trade partner. Tokyo is also Burma's largest aid donor – by 1988, Japan had given Burma $3.8 billion, or four-fifths of all foreign assistance received. After the 18 September 1988 coup in which General Saw Maung took power, killing hundreds of protestors in the process, Japan suspended all development aid and supplied only $450,000-worth of emergency food aid, mainly through

UNICEF. Japan is the only country with leverage over the regime, and is thus in a prime position to benefit economically should Burma rejoin the world economy.[34]

Japan's hegemony over East Asia will only intensify in the decades ahead; while Japan's importance to ASEAN in trade, investments and aid will steadily increase, ASEAN's importance to Japan will just as steadily decline, further enhancing Tokyo's clout in the region. Regional criticism of Japan will increase with its power. Tokyo is at some times condemned both for not playing a big enough role in the region and at other times accused of trying to turn it into another 'East Asian Co-prosperity Sphere'. But the complaints will have little effect. Japan has achieved all of its political economic goals in Southeast Asia at minimal cost.

The Korean Peninsula

South Korea is the only country in the world whose geopolitical importance for Japan exceeds its economic importance. Often described as a 'dagger pointed at the heart of Japan', the Korean peninsula is the most obvious jumping off point for any ambitious invader from the continent. The 1945 division of the Korean peninsula between North and South was the perfect solution to this security problem. South Korea serves as a vital buffer zone against possible aggression from the Soviet Union or China. Prime Minister Sato succinctly articulated the peninsula's importance when on November 1969 he said the security of South Korea 'is essential to Japan's security'.[35]

But the creation of an American-protected buffer in the South also prevented the emergence of a powerful Korea that could rival Tokyo. Divided against each other, the two Koreas focus much of their foreign policy energy across the 38th parallel rather than against their traditional enemy, Japan. A peninsula united under the Communist North would pose a serious security threat to Japan, forcing Tokyo to undertake a significant rearmament, including possibly the employment of nuclear weapons. A peninsula united under the dynamic South would pose a great economic challenge to Japan. With a huge domestic market of 60 million consumers, a united capitalist Korea would be far less dependent on export-led growth and could achieve economies of scale for its products even more quickly than it does now.

Tokyo's policy for the peninsula is thus focused on enhancing stability and peaceful coexistence between South and North, while checking both the economic threat from the South and the security threat from the North. Mutual antagonisms resulting from Japan's brutal colonisation of Korea (1910–45) and refusal to pay reparations delayed the restoration of relations for twenty years after the Second World War. Finally, in 1965, after years of bitter negotiations, the two countries signed a treaty normalising relations in which Tokyo promised to accept Seoul as the 'sole legal' government of the entire peninsula as defined in the 1948 UN General Assembly Resolution 195 (III) and to extend an aid package worth $800 million over the following ten years. In return, Japan was allowed to maintain unofficial economic, social and humanitarian relations with North Korea.

Economic relations between Japan and South Korea boomed following the agreement, as Tokyo's aid package facilitated the rapid re-emergence of Japanese business in South Korea. In 1965, 60 per cent of South Korea's trade and 75 per cent of its foreign investment was with the United States. Only four years later, Japan had become South Korea's largest trading partner with 41 per cent of the total compared to America's 30 per cent share. Japan not only remains South Korea's largest trading partner today, but continues to enjoy a huge surplus whose cumulative total between 1965 and 1985 was $30 billion. In 1971, Japanese foreign investments in South Korea surpassed those of the United States, a gap which has steadily widened. By 1981, Japan had invested $3.1 billion in South Korea, supplying 57 per cent of the total value and 76 per cent of the total number of foreign ventures.[36]

Tokyo's two-Korea policy, whereby it limited official diplomacy to the South but carried on economic relations with both North and South, has been almost as successful as its policy toward China before 1972. In place of official diplomatic contacts, Tokyo has used such intermediaries as the Japanese Red Cross, Japan–North Korean Diet leagues, business associations, Liberal Democratic Party study groups and the Japan Socialist Party to negotiate a range of economic and humanitarian agreements.

Despite squabbles with both sides, Japan's two-Korea policy has been immensely successful. Japan is not only South Korea's largest trade and investment partner, but continues to enjoy an immense trade surplus, which in 1986 exceeded $5 billion. Meanwhile, Japan accounts for two-thirds of North Korea's non-communist trade. Although Japan's trade with North Korea is a small fraction of its trade with South Korea, its continued relations with Pyongyang remain very important. As in Vietnam, Japan is in the perfect position rapidly to expand its economic ties should North Korea ever launch the sort of sweeping economic reforms that China and the Soviet Union are undergoing.

Seoul long ago gave up demands that Tokyo recognise it as Korea's sole legitimate government, and tolerates Japan's extensive unofficial diplomacy with the North. Even after North Korea sponsored terrorist acts such as the Rangoon bombing that killed most of President Chun's cabinet in 1983 and the Korean Airlines explosion in 1985, Seoul did not press Tokyo to embargo its trade with North Korea. In addition, Seoul's continual demands that Tokyo cut its trade surplus, open its markets, transfer significant technology and stop discrimination against people of Korean descent living in Japan have been met with many promises but no significant action.

The Middle East

In less than a quarter century, Japan's economy has been transformed from near self-sufficiency in energy to almost total dependence on foreign energy sources.[37] In 1950, domestic coal satisfied most of Japan's energy needs; foreign oil accounted for only 7 per cent. By 1973, 95 per cent of the energy used in Japan was imported, three-quarters in the form of oil of which 80 per cent came from the Middle East. In those halcyon days before OPEC's quadrupling of oil prices in December 1973, Tokyo's energy policy consisted mostly of trying to get the cheapest oil possible to fuel Japan's average annual growth rate of 10 per cent.

More dependent on foreign energy sources than any other industrial nation, Japan's economy came to a screeching halt after the embargo. Hoarding and panic buying stimulated price rises of 20 per cent or more for a wide range of goods. In 1974, GNP actually declined by more than 1 per cent. But the government responded creatively and effectively to the energy crisis. The embargo was soon lifted in January 1974, after Tokyo agreed to give up its 'neutrality' and become 'pro-Arab' by denouncing Israel and extending considerable aid to the Middle East. Behind the schemes, government and business embarked on a vast, interrelated, comprehensive security policy designed to reduce Japan's energy dependence. This included diversifying energy and particularly oil sources as widely as possible, conserving energy at home, stockpiling, developing alternative energies and upgrading the economy into low energy-consuming, information-based industries.

This policy has been an enormous success. Between 1973 and 1987, the share of oil in total energy consumption sank from 78 per cent to 55 per cent, oil consumption dropped by over one-third, the share of Middle East oil in total oil imports fell from 78 per cent to 68 per cent; Persian Gulf oil was then only 48 per cent of oil imports, while oil from Iran and Iraq was only about 12 per cent of the total.[38] Between 1981 and 1987, Japan's imports from the Middle East were cut in half, to 13 per cent of total imports. While reducing its own dependence on the Middle East, Tokyo has also in turn increased the dependence of Middle Eastern countries on Japanese goods, services, and capital. For example, in 1983 Japan surpassed the United States as the leading exporter to Saudi Arabia.[39] In part, Tokyo has accomplished this through an extensive tied aid programme – untied direct loans are under 3 per cent of Japan's total aid to the Middle East.[49]

Japanese diplomacy in the Middle East has centred on promoting the image of a significant shift from a 'neutral' to a 'pro-Arab' stance. Between 17 October 1973, when OPEC first announced its production cutbacks and embargo, and 25 December, when it restored 'friendly' status and oil shipments to Japan, Tokyo followed the EC lead in breaking with Washington and called on Israel to withdraw from the occupied territories. It also recognised the Palestinian people's right to self-determination and sent them $5 million in aid, and for the first time sent several high-ranking delegations to the Middle East promising extensive aid. Japan was the first OECD nation to recognise the PLO as a legitimate (though not sole) representative of the Palestinian people. In December 1976, it allowed them to open an office in Tokyo in return for agreeing to renounce terrorism and stop aiding the Red Army. On 21 October 1981, Yasser Arafat was hosted in Tokyo by the Japan–Palestinian Parliamentarian League (JPPL). Arafat met with Prime Minister Suzuki, and was accorded full diplomatic honours.

There has been a significant shift in UN votes on Palestinian issues. From 1966 to 1970, in a classic attempt to 'separate economics and politics', Japan abstained on 80 per cent of resolutions concerning the Palestinians, and voted in favour of 20 per cent involving non-controversial humanitarian questions. But Japan's support for the Palestinians shifted to steady support in the 1970s and 1980s. Generally, Japan would abstain if a resolution appeared to be too anti-Israel and voted against the five resolutions that, if realised, would have radically changed the balance of power in the Middle East.[41]

During events such as the American hostage crisis, the doubling of oil prices, the Soviet invasion of Afghanistan and the Libyan terrorist bombings in 1985 and 1986, Japan either openly defied Washington's requests for sanctions or went along only after the EC fell in line. Tokyo would counter Washington's requests by reminding it of Japan's energy vulnerability. Ronald Morse writes that

> Japan never fully appreciated the emotional nature or the 'human rights' aspect of the hostage issue in the U.S. It was primarily concerned with obtaining adequate oil supplies and protecting its billion dollar Mitsui petrochemical project at Bandar-Khomeini on the Persian Gulf ... From the beginning Japanese officials spoke of Japan being caught in a dispute between 'two friends', presumably of equal value, and not wishing to take sides.[42]

This strategy is nothing new. In 1953, Japan continued to buy Iranian oil secretly despite a Western boycott after President Mossadegh nationalised the oil industry.[43] Tokyo has a record of putting Japan's immediate economic needs ahead of any less profitable notions such as alliance solidarity or humanitarianism.

Japan tried to maintain neutrality during the Iran–Iraq War, since it had extensive trade and investment interests in both countries. Between 1984 and 1987, it made a number of attempts to mediate an end to the war, and repeatedly called on both sides to use restraint and respect international shipping rights. Although Japan's role has been described as more a message carrier than a mediator, its diplomatic activities were an excellent cover for continued economic ties. Although half of all the oil flowing through the Straits of Hormuz goes to Japan (and only 5 per cent to the United States) and seven Japanese oil tankers were attacked there in 1987 alone, Washington and its NATO allies continue to provide the immensely expensive fleet in the Persian Gulf to protect shipping. In 1987, Prime Minister Nakasone did ask his Cabinet to consider sending Japanese mine sweepers to the Persian Gulf, but the idea was quickly rejected. Japan did, however, contribute a $10 million navigational device. Japan enjoyed all the benefits of the alliance while contributing only a fraction of the costs.

Despite recognising the PLO, voting in favour of most UN resolutions concerning the Palestinians, and refusing to support the United States in problems like the hostage crisis or Libyan terrorist bombings, Japan's policy toward the Middle East has not changed fundamentally since 1973. Most of Japan's shift to a 'pro-Arab' position in the Middle East consists of costless rhetoric and gestures of no real substance. Essentially, Japan's policy toward the Middle East remains unchanged from the September 1957 Foreign Ministry Blue Book which states 'it is desirable that peace be maintained in this area in order for commercial relations between Japan and the Middle East to make smooth progress'.[44]

Although in 1952 Israel became the first Middle East state with which Japan established relations, Tokyo reduced relations to a minimum after 1973. However, as the comprehensive security policy has steadily lessened Japan's dependence on the Middle East, Tokyo is beginning to re-establish better relations between the two countries. Israel's 4.2 million population is a large, affluent market by Middle East standards, and Japanese firms are eager to take advantage of it as the Arab blacklist of companies trading with Israel continues to lose effectiveness. Bilateral trade doubled from $600 million in 1985 to $1.2 billion in 1988, and diplomacy swiftly followed to accelerate it. In June 1988, Foreign Minister Uno paid the first visit of a high-ranking Japanese official to Israel. However, he followed this with visits to Syria, Jordan and Egypt, during which time he met with the PLO and assured his hosts that Japan's policy to the Middle East had not changed. The trip was classic Japanese strategy, maintaining good diplomatic relations with both sides in order to maximise economic ties with both. Some analysts, however, believe the reason for Uno's visit to Israel may have been as much to dampen the negative impression of Japan among American Jews during a time of continued trade conflict as to increase trade with Israel.[45]

Subsaharan Africa

South Africa's trading partners seem to be engaged in a game of musical chairs in which each tries desperately to become 'number two'. In 1987, Japan was left 'standing up' like the proverbial nail about to be hammered, as Japanese firms took advantage of foreign rivals that had cut back their South African ties. That year, while American trade with South Africa dropped 20 per cent to $3 billion, Japanese trade rose just as rapidly from $3.6 billion the previous year to $4.3 billion. Japanese exports were up 37 per cent while imports rose by 8 per cent, for a total increase in trade of 19 per cent. These figures are, however, artificially inflated by the appreciation of the Japanese currency: if denominated in yen, the trade increase was only 2 per cent.[46] Japan was also criticised for selling computers and vehicles to South Africa's police and military forces while importing uranium and gold.

The embarrassment and criticism Japan experienced when news of its number-one trade position with South Africa emerged disrupted a very careful strategy whereby Tokyo has been cultivating ties on both sides of the diplomatic fence in Subsaharan Africa. Since 1961, when Japanese were granted 'honorary white' status by Pretoria, Tokyo has followed a classic 'separation of economics and politics'. Tokyo would echo the various condemnations by the other industrial countries or the United Nations while continually increasing its trade and investments.

Japan's strategy in Subsaharan Africa mirrors its policy in the Middle East. Thus it was no surprise that in 1974 Tokyo publicly denounced apartheid and became the first major industrialised state to prohibit its citizens from directly investing in South Africa. It downgraded its diplomatic relations to a consular level; suspended all sports, cultural, and educational exchange between the two countries; and refused to issue visas to South Africans. Tokyo followed up this action by dispatching Foreign Minister Kimura on a 10-day tour of Black Africa which took him to Ghana, Zaire, Nigeria and Tanzania. A decade later, after Pretoria's declaration of martial law, Japan followed the lead of the United States and EC in refusing to buy Krugerrands or sell computer equipment to South Africa. The following year, after the US Congress passed the Comprehensive Anti-Apartheid Act, Japan banned imports of South African iron and steel. In April 1987, ANC President Oliver Tambo met with Prime Minister Nakasone and Foreign Minister Kuranari in Tokyo.

These actions seem impressive until it is realised that Japanese trade with South Africa rose about eight-fold between 1961 and 1973, and then quadrupled again by 1987, to reach $4.3 billion. This represents a steadily rising proportion of its trade with the other Subsaharan countries. In 1961, Japan's $131 million trade with South Africa was one-third the size of its trade with the other Subsaharan African states. By 1987, its bilateral trade had soared to over 80 per cent the size of its $5 billion multilateral trade.

Meanwhile Tokyo's refusal to issue visas to South Africa did not prevent Japanese citizens from travelling to South Africa to conduct business. Although Tokyo's 1985 sanctions, bolstered by a public condemnation of apartheid – 'the most serious and systematic denial of freedom and equality anywhere in the world' – and a call for the release of Nelson Mandela seemed to put Japan squarely alongside its allies, Japan continued to buy Krugerrands and gold through third countries and dummy companies.[47] Likewise, the following year, after placing sanctions on South African steel and iron – thus providing some relief to Japan's own hard pressed steel and iron industries – Tokyo continued to buy South African coal on national security grounds despite persistent American attempts to sell its own coal to Japan.[48] In fact, in 1986 Japan secretly sold a $50 million steel plant to the South African-owned Iron and Steel Corporation. Once the plant is operating it will annually save South Africa $25 million in foreign exchange, making the country self-sufficient in certain types of coated steel.[49]

Although Tokyo theoretically forbade Japanese firms from doing so, they actually have invested hundreds of millions of dollars in scores of manufacturing, mining and service industries. Japanese firms use a variety of ingenious means to get around the official ban on investments. There are at present 30 Japanese firms with offices in South Africa, and 150 with marketing representatives.[50] One method is to set up subsidiaries and dummy companies (*yurei kaisha*), which build their factories with South African capital. Payne points out that the Japanese investors have 'no equivalent of the Sullivan Principles or EEC code for black employees may of whom are employed in low-level jobs and receive substandard wages at Toyota. The same applies to other Japanese companies'.[51]

Another means of getting around the ban is through licensing and franchising agreements which allow South African firms to assemble Japanese products. For example, as its rivals from other industrial countries cut back their investments, Toyota tripled its operating revenues by selling 87,000 kits in 1987 and enjoyed a 10 per cent sales rise in 1988. Toyota's South African plant is its largest outside Japan and the biggest in South Africa. Japanese cars now account for over 60 per cent of all cars sold in South Africa.[52] Japanese firms have taken over American markets in mainframe computers, automated office equipment, photocopiers, facsimile machines, chemicals and automobiles.

The announcement that Japan has become South Africa's largest trade partner set off what became a bitter policy debate within Tokyo's foreign policy establishment. At first both MITI and the Foreign Ministry took a hands-off stance. MITI argued that there was no reason to impose stronger sanctions. It further claimed that the dollar value of bilateral trade had grown because of 'natural causes' (chiefly the appreciation of the yen, although over time the fact that the yen had almost doubled in value over the previous two years could be expected to reduce trade).[53] MITI also proclaimed a belief in free trade which made it 'ideologically' opposed to sanctions.[54] In a similar vein, the Foreign Ministry claimed it was very difficult to do anything about

Japan's trade surplus since the responsibility lay with private sector initiatives, and the government had no control over trade.[55]

The Foreign Ministry, however, began to shift its position as criticism of Japan's trade practices mounted from all sides. In January 1988, the Foreign Ministry's Middle East and African Affairs Bureau Chief Takashi Onda asked two of Japan's most important business federations – Keidanren and Doyukai – to 'exercise restraint' in trade with South Africa. Then in early February, the Foreign Ministry met with South African anti-apartheid leaders visiting Japan to assuage feelings in the international community, and allowed the ANC to open an office in Tokyo. At this time Allan Boesak eloquently expressed his bewilderment that Japanese would accept 'honorary white' status, considering Tokyo's claim to be against racism. Boesak called on Japanese to put 'pressure on your government and the business community to stop collaborating with the South African regime'.[56]

Under this pressure, on 9 February 1988, MITI finally reversed its previous indifference when MITI Minister Hajime Tamura said: 'Japan should take some action against South Africa from a humanitarian point of view, and MITI will talk to Keidanren on the need to do something over growing Japan–South African trade'.[57] These words were later echoed by Foreign Minister Uno who asked Keidanren and Doyukai to cut back their trade with South Africa.

Contrary to their claims that the government has little influence over business, the 'administrative guidance' soon had the desired effect. Both NEC and Pioneer Electronic promised to suspend exports by 1989; the Mitsubishi group dropped out of bidding on an industrial plant; while Nissan, which sells 40,000 vehicles to South Africa a year, will stop exports of its Safari model which is used by both the police and defence forces.[58] Japan gets 43 per cent of its uranium from either South Africa or Namibia, which is sold to Japan through several dummy companies. When the imports were revealed, the Foreign Ministry first denied that Japanese firms were violating the ban, but with new revelations the four Japanese electricity firms agreed to import uranium from Australia and Canada instead – after their current contracts run out. MITI said the four were acting in compliance with government guidelines set two years earlier.[59] A Japanese trading company executive, who obviously did not want to be quoted, summed up the Japanese attitude to its South Africa trade very succinctly when he said: 'We have to trade with South Africa more inconspicuously to avoid being criticized'.[60] In this, the Japanese have clearly been successful: in January 1989, it was reported West Germany had inherited Japan's crown as South Africa's largest trading partner. Some African states have talked about blocking Japan's coveted seat on the UN Security Council, but to date no action has been taken. In a pattern similar to its votes on Middle East issues, Japan votes in favour of resolutions condemning racial discrimination and apartheid, but abstains on calls for economic sanctions. Voting aside, Tokyo has in the past not hesitated to violate UN resolutions and sanctions when they threaten Japanese interests. For example, Japan continued to import high grade Rhodesian chromium through South Africa even though it claimed to support the UN sanctions.[61] More recently Mitsubishi, in co-operation with the Japanese government, delivered nuclear power technology to South Africa in partial payment for 8,200 tons of uranium from the Rossing Mining Group's Namibian mine, despite UN resolutions prohibiting trade with Namibia.[62]

Tokyo has been just as successful in maintaining profitable relations with other Black African countries. The 1961 Ministry of Foreign Affairs Yearbook summed up Japan's previous 75-year relationship with Africa as being 'nothing but an export market for consumer goods which centred mainly on textile products'.[63] Although Africa's share in Japan's trade has never exceeded 3 per cent of Japan's total trade, it is important in several key products. Africa has become an important market for such Japanese products as telecommunications, heavy electrical equipment, vehicles and consumer electronics, and a vital source of such raw materials as chromium, vanadium, manganese, uranium and platinum.

Japanese investments have been split between manufacturing ventures in countries with sizeable domestic markets such as Kenya, South Africa and Nigeria or mining ventures in countries with rich natural resources such as Niger, Zambia and Zaire. About 80 per cent of all Japanese investments, however, are concentrated in Liberia, which has liberal flag of conveyance, tax and disclosure laws. Although Japan's investments in Africa account for little more than 2 per cent of its total foreign investment, they include 24 per cent of its foreign investments in oil, 15 per cent in iron ore, and 24 per cent in copper.[64]

Under the guidelines of comprehensive security, the government has taken an active role in promoting Japanese interests in Black Africa. For example, the Metal Mining Agency is supporting chromium exploration in Sudan; iron ore deposits in Liberia, Senegal and Mauritania; and manganese in Gabon. As elsewhere, Tokyo has solidified its economic interests with aid. Before 1973, Japanese aid to Africa was never as much as 3 per cent of its total foreign aid. Then, with OPEC's quadrupling of oil prices and the fears that similar cartels would emerge among other mineral-producing countries, Tokyo doubled its African aid to over 5 per cent of its total, from which it rose steadily to 19 per cent of its total aid in 1980. Since then it has dropped to the current level of 10 per cent.

The quality of the aid has varied greatly over the years. Before 1980, 62 per cent of the loans were tied while only 29 per cent were LDC-untied and 10 per cent totally untied. Since then Japan's aid policy has become increasingly liberal. Between 1980 and 1985, only 5 per cent of the total loans were tied, while 80 per cent were LDC-untied and 15 per cent were generally untied. This liberal aid policy was capped in 1987, when Tokyo handed out $500 million to 11 African countries disbursed through the London-based Crown Agents. Japanese aid is targeted on countries in which it has extensive economic interests. The main recipients of aid have either large markets or natural resources, although considerable aid has flowed to Tanzania because of ex-President Nyerere's powerful diplomatic prestige.[65]

Latin America and South Asia

Japan has avoided significant political conflicts in either Latin America or South Asia. Of the two regions, Japan's trade ties with Latin America are much more important. Japanese trade with Latin America and the Caribbean in 1987 totalled $14 billion, of which $8 billion was exports and $6 billion imports. In comparison, Japan's trade with South Asia was only $8.5 billion: $4.9 billion of exports and $3.3 billion of imports.

There are several reasons why Latin America is more important. First, Latin American countries are on average more affluent and industrialised than South Asian countries, thus presenting Japanese firms with more potential buyers of consumer and capital goods. Latin American countries are generally more open to foreign investment than the South Asian countries, and most of them particularly welcome Japanese investments to offset the dominance of American investments. The Amazon Basin is rich in natural resources which Japanese mining, logging and oil firms are busily trying to develop. South Asia, on the other hand, is relatively resource poor. Finally, Latin America contains several million people of Japanese descent, some of whom still speak Japanese and can serve as business intermediaries.

Most Japanese investment in Latin America has been split between Mexico and Brazil – Mexico largely as an export platform for the United States and Brazil to serve its vast mass market and adjacent ones in Uruguay, Argentina, and Chile. Japan's ties with Mexico have grown increasingly close in the 1980s; it is now Mexico's second largest source of trade, investments and loans. In 1987, bilateral trade was $3 billion, almost evenly divided between exports and imports. Mexico is Japan's largest Latin American trading partner. In addition, Japan held $16 billion of Mexico's $100 billion debt as of 1987. These loans constitute Japan's biggest stake in any Third World country.[66] Japan's total investment is growing rapidly, although it is still only a fraction of its worldwide total and one-tenth the American share.[67] Cultural and diplomatic relations are reinforcing the growing web of economic ties.

Japan and Mexico have formed a de facto economic alliance to deal with the American giant – both countries share an interest in reducing their dependence on the United States. Mexico offers Japan a protection-proof production platform for the vast American market as well as stable oil imports; while Japan offers Mexico finance, technology and a range of cheap products. Most of Japan's investments are located in Tijuana and other export-processing zones along the border with the United States or on the Pacific coast. To date Japanese firms like Sony, Hitachi, Canon, Casio and Matsushita have built 40 factories in the 'maquiladora' assembly plants geared for American markets. Although the Japanese plants represent only 1 per cent of the total number of foreign plants, they are much bigger and more capital intensive than other plants. A second wave of Japanese subcontractors is arriving to serve the Japanese flagship corporations.[68] Leon Hollerman describes these Japanese investments as a Trojan Horse for the day Mexico becomes part of a North American free trade zone.[69]

Like Mexico, Brazil is following a strategy of diversifying its economic relations away from its traditional dependence on the United States. Japan has become Brazil's third largest trading partner – in 1987 bilateral trade reached $2.9 billion, approximately one-third being Japanese exports and two-thirds imports. Japan's outstanding loans of $6 billion to Brazil are its second highest to any country.[70] In 1987, Japan's $2.5 billion worth of investment put it third behind the US and West Germany.[71]

Japanese investors have had no trouble dealing with Brazil's tough investment terms, such as the 85 per cent domestic content requirement for manufacturers or Brazil's use of state companies to compete against the foreign multinationals. Japanese firms have strong allies in the over one-million strong Japanese–Brazilian community centred in São Paulo. Japanese analysts ranked Brazil very highly as an investment market, second only to Canada with an 'AA' rating for resource industries, and an 'A' rating for mass market industry opportunities.[72]

Japan's trade and investments are growing rapidly elsewhere, although on a lower scale. After Mexico and Brazil, Japan's largest Latin American trade partner is Panama, whose bilateral trade reached $2.5 billion in 1987, consisting almost entirely of Japanese exports. As with Liberia, Japan has taken advantage of Panama's liberal flag of convenience, banking and tax rules to tranship huge quantities of goods there. Japan's other important trade partners include Chile, whose bilateral trade was $978 million in 1987; Venezuela with $869 million; Argentina with $750 million; Colombia with $618 million; and Peru with $537 million.

Japan's relations with South Asia contrast sharply with those with Latin America. Japan runs large trade surpluses with all the South Asian countries, unlike in Latin America where it runs deficits with the resource rich countries. Yet South Asia's poverty, limited industrialisation and inward looking economic policies have limited Japan's economic penetration of the region, illustrated by the fact that Japan's largest trade partner is the small though relatively affluent Sri Lanka. Japan's bilateral trade with Sri Lanka of $4.7 billion is well ahead of its $3.5 billion trade with India or $1.4 billion with Pakistan. As in Latin America, Japan has avoided entanglement in regional political conflicts such as the three Pakistan–India wars or the Soviet invasion of Afghanistan. Japanese trade continued to flow to both India and Pakistan after each war while Japan's bilateral trade with Afghanistan remained constant despite the decade-long war.

CONCLUSION

Since 1945, the Japanese government has focused its policies on achieving the interrelated goals of economic and military security, rapid modernisation, economic superpower status and international recognition of its accomplishments. These goals are linked through the notion of comprehensive security, in which government policies attempt to minimise Japan's dependence on its trade partners while maximising its trade partners dependence on Japan. Specifically, Tokyo actively attempts to spread its sources of foreign markets, resources and energy as widely as possible while tying them to Japanese products, finance, technology and markets.

Japan's policy toward the Third World has been a key pillar toward achieving its comprehensive security policies. Japanese investments and aid have followed and reinforced its trade relations with the Third World. In addition to developing the dependence of Third World nations on Japan, Tokyo has actively played both sides of the diplomatic fence in several regional conflicts across the globe. More often than not, Tokyo's diplomatic initiatives have been means with which to maintain or enhance its economic ties with both sides. Since the mid-1970s, Tokyo has also attempted to act as the go-between in North–South issues at the United Nations and as spokesman for East Asia at the annual economic summits of the Big Seven industrial countries.

Japan has been overwhelmingly successful in achieving its national goals. As an economic superpower, and with its military security guaranteed by America's nuclear and conventional umbrella, Japan is as secure as any nation in the world today. Tokyo's Third World policy will continue to be a vital component of its comprehensive security.

Notes and References

1. Muthiah Alaggappa, 'Japan's Political and Security Role in the Asia-Pacific Region', *Contemporary Southeast Asia*, 10(1) (June 1986) pp. 19–21.
2. *OECD Economic Assistance Report* (1989).
3. Chalmers Johnson, 'The Patterns of Japanese Relations with China, 1952–82', *Pacific Affairs*, 59(3) (Fall 1986) p. 405.
4. See William Nester and Kweku Ampiah, 'Japan's Oil Diplomacy: Tatemae and Honne', *Third World Quarterly*, 11(1) (January 1989).
5. Noboru Takeshita, *Far Eastern Economic Review* (17 July 1988).
6. Unless otherwise noted all trade statistics are compiled from the International Monetary Fund annual *Direction of Trade Statistics Yearbook*.
7. *OECD Development Assistance* (1968 report).
8. Harry Chernotsky, 'Trade Adjustment and Foreign Direct Investment: Japan in the United States', *Pacific Focus*, 1(2) (Fall 1986) p. 69.
9. Chernotsky, 'Trade Adjustment', pp. 69–71.
10. Philip McMichael, 'Foundations of U.S./Japanese World-economic Rivalry in the Pacific Rim', *Journal of Developing Societies*, 3 (1987) p. 74.
11. McMichael, 'Foundations', p. 72.

12.   Chikara Higashi and G. Peter Lauter, *The Internationalization of the Japanese Economy* (Boston, MA: Kluwer, 1987) p. 201.
13.   Alaggappa, 'Japan's Political and Security Role', pp. 19–21.
14.   See Juichi Inada's study (Chapter 6 in this volume); Alan Rix, *Japan's Economic Aid: Policymaking and Policies* (London: Croom Helm, 1980); Sukehiro Hasegawa, *Japanese Foreign Aid: Policy and Practice* (New York: Praeger, 1975).
15.   Unless otherwise noted all aid statistics come from the annual *OECD Economic Assistance* reports.
16.   *International Herald Tribune* (27 June 1988).
17.   *International Herald Tribune* (27 June 1988).
18.   Shigeru Yoshida, *The Yoshida Memoirs: The Story of Japan in Crisis*, trans. Kenichi Yoshida (London: Heinemann, 1961) pp. 127–31.
19.   Yoshida, *The Yoshida Memoirs*.
20.   Johnson, 'The Patterns of Japanese Relations', p. 407.
21.   Johnson, 'The Patterns of Japanese Relations'. *Fumie* were the plates engraved with images of Jesus and the Virgin Mary upon which Japanese Christians were forced to tread in the seventeenth century to prove their loyalty to the Tokugawa regime.
22.   Johnson, 'The Patterns of Japanese Relations', p. 417.
23.   See William R. Nester, *Japan's Growing Power over East Asia and the World Economy: Ends and Means* (London: Macmillan, 1989) for an in-depth study of these and related questions.
24.   Sueo Sudo, 'From Fukuda to Takeshita: A Decade of Japan–ASEAN Relations', *Contemporary Southeast Asia*, 10(2) (September 1988) p. 511.
25.   See Dennis Yasutomo, *Japan and the Asian Development Bank* (New York: Praeger, 1985).
26.   Yasutomo, *Japan*.
27.   Sueo Sudo, 'Japan–Asian Relations', *Asian Survey*, 28(5) (May 1988) p. 512.
28.   Sudo, 'Japan–Asian Relations', p. 513.
29.   Kit Machado, 'Malaysian Cultural Relations with Japan and Korea in the 1980s', *Asian Survey*, 27(6) (June 1987) p. 657.
30.   Machado, 'Malaysian Cultural Relations', p. 657.
31.   Sudo, 'Japan–Asian Relations', p. 515.
32.   Seuo Sudo, 'The Road to Becoming a Regional Leader: Japanese Attempts in Southeast Asia, 1975–80', *Pacific Affairs*, 61(1) p. 37.
33.   *Japan Economic Journal* (1 October 1988).
34.   *The Economist* (8 October 1988).
35.   Kwan Ha Yim, 'The Japanese Role in the Korean Unification Process', *Asian Perspective*, 10(1) (Spring–Summer 1986) p. 165.
36.   Hong Kim, 'Japanese–Korean Relations in the 1980s', *Asian Survey*, 27(5) (May 1987) p. 498.
37.   See Nester, *Japan's Growing Power*.
38.   *Middle East Economic Development Report* (1988) p. 22.
39.   Ronald Morse, 'Japan's Search for an Independent Foreign Policy: An American Perspective', *Journal of Northeast Asian Studies*, 3(2) (Summer 1984) p. 34.
40.   *Middle East Economic Development*, p. 11.

41. Nester, *Japan's Growing Power*.
42. Morse, 'Japan's Search', p. 36.
43. Nester, *Japan's Growing Power*.
44. See *Waga Gaikyo no Kankyo* (1957).
45. Nester, *Japan's Growing Power*.
46. *Japan Economic Journal* (20 February 1988).
47. Jun Morikawa, 'The Myth and Reality of Japan's Relations with Colonial Africa, 1885–1960', *Journal of African Studies*, 12(1) (Spring 1985) p. 133.
48. Richard J. Payne, 'Japan's South Africa Policy: Political Rhetoric and Economic Realities', *African Affairs* (Spring 1986) p. 175.
49. *Los Angeles Times* (3 April 1988).
50. *International Herald Tribune* (7 April 1988).
51. Payne, 'Japan's South African Policy', p. 174.
52. Payne, 'Japan's South African Policy', p. 172.
53. *Japanese Economic Journal* (20 February 1988).
54. *Far Eastern Economic Review* (17 March 1988).
55. *Japan Economic Journal* (20 February 1988).
56. Kweku Ampiah, 'Succour from Japan', *West Africa* (7 December 1987) p. 2385.
57. *Japan Economic Journal* (20 February 1988).
58. *The Economist* (2 April 1988).
59. *Independent* (2 November 1988).
60. *Los Angeles Times* (3 April 1988).
61. Payne, 'Japan's South African Policy', p. 170.
62. Payne, 'Japan's South African Policy', p. 169.
63. *International Herald Tribune* (7 April 1988).
64. Payne, 'Japan's South African Policy', p. 172.
65. Kweku Ampiah, 'A One-sided Partnership: Japanese–African Relations', *West Africa* (28 November 1988) p. 2221.
66. *The Economist* (21 May 1988).
67. *The Economist* (27 October 1988).
68. *The Economist* (27 October 1988).
69. *The Economist* (27 January 1988).
70. David Bruce, 'Brazil Plays the Japan Card', *Third World Quarterly*, 5(4) (October 1983) p. 857.
71. *The Economist* (21 May 1988).
72. Bruce, 'Brazil', p. 851.

6 Japan's Aid Diplomacy: Economic, Political or Strategic?

Juichi Inada

In recent years Japan's foreign aid has often been raised both as a domestic and as an international political issue. Domestically, for example, the propriety of aid to the Philippines became the subject of debate in the National Diet in 1986, and this legislative discussion led to serious questioning of the nation's foreign aid policy. On the international level, meanwhile, the United States has been seeking increases in Japanese aid, mainly as a way to share the cost of promoting international security. For example, the increase in Japan's official development assistance to the countries of the South Pacific in recent years is said to be partly in response to the increasing presence of the Soviet Union in this region.

Observers have often complained that Japan's aid programme is motivated by narrow economic interests. It cannot be denied that in the early stages of the programme, which started with post-war reparations, the economic assistance that Japan provided was linked to the expansion of its own exports, especially in the late 1960s. Similarly, after the first oil shock in 1973, Japan's desire to secure steady supplies of energy and other resources influenced its aid policy as well.

Over time, this self-interested posture became the target of resentment. As the Japanese economy grew in scale, people in other countries came to expect Japan to do what it could to promote global peace and prosperity. Partly in response to this pressure from abroad, in 1977 the government announced a three-year plan to double Japan's official development assistance (ODA). Since then, appropriations for ODA have grown steadily, having been exempted from the fiscal austerity drive of the 1980s. In assistance to Asian countries in particular, Japan surpassed the United States in 1977, and Japan now gives considerably more aid to the region than does the United States (see Figure 6.1). The total ODA appropriation in the draft budget for FY 1989 (April 1989– March 1990) comes to ¥1,369.8 billion, or about $10 billion at the 1989 exchange rate. Meanwhile the US ODA budget in the FY 1989

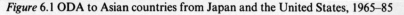

Figure 6.1 ODA to Asian countries from Japan and the United States, 1965–85

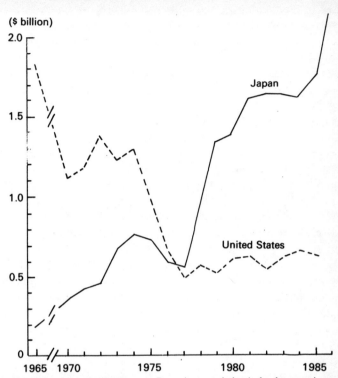

Source: OECD Development Assistance Committee statistics (calendar years)
Note: Figures represent the total of net disbursements to East, Southeast and South Asia.

(October 1988–September 1989) was expected to be at most $9 billion. If the disbursement of these appropriations proceeded smoothly, Japan will have passed the US in 1990 to become the world's largest ODA donor.

Provision of aid as a means of fulfilling the country's responsibilities as a major economic power is itself a significant aspect of Japanese diplomacy. But to date, little serious research has appeared on Japanese aid as an instrument of foreign policy.[1]

Aid is by nature an integral element of foreign policy. The Marshall Plan undertaken by the US after the Second World War, for example, was designed to help the countries of Western Europe recover and become stronger as a means of counteracting the influence of the Soviet bloc. Since then, the US has continued to make security concerns an explicit part of its aid policy. Britain and France, meanwhile, have placed heavy emphasis on the maintenance of ties with their former colonies through their aid programmes.

In the late 1970s, Japan also began to define its aid in terms of its overall foreign policy, taking the provision of aid to be part of the cost of maintaining the country's 'comprehensive security'.[2] And recent years have seen prominent US observers suggesting that Japan should increase the volume of its foreign aid as a way of compensating for the limits on its military spending, which until 1986 was subject to an official ceiling of 1 per cent of gross national product. Former US National Security Advisor Zbigniew Brzezinski, for example, proposed that if Japan was going to hold its military spending far below that of other Western countries, it should increase its aid to the point at which the sum of the two reach 4 per cent of GNP.[3] Even after the decision to lift the 1 per cent ceiling, former Secretary of State Henry Kissinger, among others, has suggested that Japan should still give priority to increasing economic assistance rather than defence expenditures.[4]

Alongside discussion relating Japan's aid to its defence posture, there have been repeated calls from abroad for qualitative improvements in the country's aid programme and criticisms of the economic self-interest that it is seen to reflect. Some of the specific complaints are that too little of Japan's aid is provided in grant form (and too much in the form of loans) and that too little is in the 'general untied' category, unlinked to exports from Japan.

This international attention is partly attributable to Japan's huge trade surplus. It may reflect the onset of what has been dubbed 'aid fatigue' among the other major donors of the industrial world. Like it or not, therefore, Japan finds that its aid programme involves political and diplomatic issues beyond the realm of purely economic concerns.

In the midst of this growing attention, however, some of what is said about Japan's aid is misleading. One reason is that perceptions have tended to lag behind the reality: in fact, Japan's ODA has grown sharply in value in recent years and is gradually improving in quality as well. Aid policy – in particular, the process of deciding how the aid should be distributed by country and what specific projects should be funded – is mainly in the hands of bureaucratic administrators. This has tended to make it hard for observers to determine how the programme is being conducted and to discuss it in an informed manner.

In this chapter it is my intention to shed some light on the actual state of Japan's aid programme as I consider three questions in the Japanese context: (1) Is aid becoming more political, or 'strategic', in nature? (2)

What political and diplomatic considerations go into the formation of aid diplomacy? (3) Is aid still dominated by commercial interests? I hope that this will offer a new perspective on the issues surrounding Japan's aid policy and its political role.

JAPAN'S AID: BECOMING MORE POLITICAL?

What is 'Strategic' Aid?

The term 'comprehensive security' was first used officially in expressing the conceptual framework of Japan's aid policy in 1980. The previous year, Iranians had seized the US embassy in Teheran and taken the Americans working there hostage, and the Soviets had invaded Afghanistan. These events created additional pressure, particularly from the US, for Japan to play not just an economic but also a political role as a member of the Western bloc. This pressure was brought to bear on the formulation of Japan's aid policy.

In the wake of the Soviet invasion of Afghanistan, the Japanese government stepped up its assistance to neighbouring Pakistan. It also started building up its assistance to Thailand and Turkey, which were similarly defined as 'countries bordering on areas of conflict'.[5] And in 1981, it declared its intention to strengthen its assistance to 'those areas which are important to the maintenance of [the] peace and stability of the world'.[6] The media in Japan took these government actions to mean that the country had embarked on a programme of what the media termed 'strategic aid'.

In the years from 1981 to 1983, the Japanese media gave extensive treatment of South Korea's appeal to Japan for 'security-related economic assistance'. Similarly, the press gave a great deal of attention to the issue of Japan's assistance to the Philippines in the years following 1984, as the Marcos administration grew increasingly unstable, and after Corazon Aquino became president in 1986, at which point the volume of Japanese aid was greatly increased. Aid to the Philippines was also a major topic of discussion in the Diet. Since aid was increased partly in response to the wishes of the US, which viewed the Philippines as a strategically important country, the larger issue of defining Japan's political and economic roles as a member of the Western industrialised community was also involved.

The Japanese government – the Ministry of Foreign Affairs in particular – has not officially used the term 'strategic aid', the appearance of which has been limited for the most part to newspapers and other media. The very concept of 'strategic aid' lacks a precise definition. Within the Foreign Ministry, in fact, there are some who deny that the assistance that is so labelled has anything to do with military security or with support for existing local governments; one official has suggested that it should be called 'peace aid'.

In order to discuss whether or not Japan's foreign aid is strategic, we must clarify what this term means. One point that is clear is that even what might be called strategic aid in Japan's case is not military aid, since Japan's assistance to other countries is limited entirely to economic co-operation. Some countries may aim to satisfy overtly military objectives even when they extend economic aid, but in Japan's case the government has been explicitly enjoined, in a resolution adopted by the Foreign Affairs Committee of the House of Representatives on 5 April 1978, to 'take all precautions not to carry out external economic assistance of a sort that will be applied toward military use or that will promote international conflict'. The committee subsequently reconfirmed this resolution on 30 March 1981.

When people suggest that Japanese aid is strategic, what they are apt to mean is that it is being conducted in accord with US strategy. It is true that, ever since 1978, Japan and the US have undertaken repeated policy-planning talks on assistance, supplemented since 1985 by Japan–US consultations between vice-ministers in charge of political affairs. These and other talks that frequently take place on a working level have served as fora for numerous US requests for Japan to increase its economic aid to countries that America perceives as important for military or diplomatic reasons.

It is also a fact that the US has in recent years expected Japanese aid to play a much larger role, partly because the mammoth US federal budget deficit has forced foreign needs to take a back seat to domestic priorities. The US government has feared that its diplomatic strategy will be undermined by congressional budget cuts in aid to areas of conflict, like Central America and the Middle East, and for strategically important countries such as Pakistan and the Philippines. This is the background against which the Americans have sought a greater Japanese contribution in aid, particularly to the regions that are of special strategic significance to the US.

Cases of 'Strategic' Aid

To what extent have these American requests affected the actual conduct of Japan's foreign aid programme? Let us first consider how Japanese ODA is distributed by country. One feature that has remained unchanged is the emphasis on other Asian countries (excluding the Middle East), which have been receiving about two-thirds of Japan's net disbursements (63 per cent as of 1988). In America's case, these countries' share is less than one-tenth of the total (9 per cent in 1987), indicating how much greater an emphasis Japan places on the region in its aid programme.

The amount of Japan's aid to specific countries has changed during recent years (see Table 6.1). The countries in question are those in areas that may be considered 'important to the maintenance of the peace and stability of the world'. They can be divided into two broad categories (see Table 6.1). The first (Group 1) consists of countries whose aid receipts jumped sharply at some point and subsequently declined or levelled off; examples include Jamaica (to which aid peaked in 1983), Somalia (1982), and Turkey (1981). An intermediate category consists

Table 6.1   Key recipients of Japanese aid (¥ billion)

	1979	1980	1981	1982	1983	1984	1985	1986	1987
Group 1									
Jamaica	0.05	0.03	2.18	0.03	16.24	0.22	0.17	0.30	0.19
Pakistan	14.99	30.76	48.18	37.84	39.57	10.06	42.13	9.44	44.98
Somalia	—	0.92	0.79	6.31	1.16	2.23	2.50	3.24	1.56
Sudan	1.85	1.49	3.86	7.73	5.90	7.05	7.18	7.07	9.74
Turkey	7.58	50.95	60.03	23.77	32.76	0.36	24.92	28.01	10.67
Group 2									
China	—	—	63.39	73.56	79.88	79.67	84.94	92.38	98.22
Indonesia	93.78	81.43	70.49	12.09	145.95	88.09	92.04	95.00	104.31
Malaysia	21.03	23.07	57.54	5.29	66.35	24.54	9.68	17.93	4.74
Philippines	4.40	44.12	52.25	61.23	69.28	56.44	62.43	15.52	136.61
South Korea	19.00	19.44	0.44	0.48	45.54	50.42	55.25	45.72	1.35
Thailand	46.37	65.00	72.89	89.26	87.53	89.58	92.25	18.78	102.29

Note: Figures are for ODA on a notes-exchanged basis. (Aid performance may be measured on any of three bases: net disbursements, exchanges of notes, or pledges. Of these, the measurement based on exchanges of pledges is perhaps the best as an indicator of the workings of political forces on aid policy.)

Source: Ministry of Foreign Affairs.

of countries to which aid went up sharply at a particular point but then remained high, such as Pakistan (since 1980) and Sudan (since 1982).

Aid to the countries of the second category (Group 2) has tended to remain steady or increase gradually, although there has been a certain amount of fluctuation in some cases (particularly that of Malaysia). Typical of this pattern are China, Indonesia, the Philippines, and Thailand. Aid to South Korea shows a sharp increase in the years since 1983, but large quantities of aid had also been provided in the years up to 1978, which are not shown in Table 6.1.

A characteristic of the countries of the first category is that developments in international affairs catapulted them into a position of importance for the security of the Western bloc, with the result that the US strongly urged Japan to increase its aid to them. The jump in aid to Turkey, for example, reflects the deteriorating situation in Iran in 1979–80, that to Pakistan the Soviet invasion of Afghanistan, that to Sudan and Somalia the increasingly close Soviet involvement in Ethiopia dating from about 1980 and that to Jamaica the switch from a socialist to a pro-American administration following the election in October 1980. In each of these cases, the change of circumstances prompted the US to seek an increase of aid from Japan to the country or countries in question. In this sense it is therefore possible to refer to the increased assistance provided in these cases as 'political' in the narrow sense of the term that many would consider to be synonymous with 'strategic'.

We also find cases that are just the opposite of the first group, that is to say, countries to which aid was cut off because of changes in their international circumstances. This might also be considered a type of strategic aid, or rather, strategic non-aid. After the end of the war in Vietnam, for example, that country had become the recipient of around ¥14 billion a year in Japanese aid, but this assistance was suspended following the Vietnamese invasion of Kampuchea in December 1978. It still has not been resumed.

There are some countries in the second category for which the US Government requested an increase in Japanese aid: Thailand in 1980 and the Philippines in 1984, to cite two examples. However, even among 'countries bordering areas of conflict', there is a difference in Japan's aid policy with respect to Group 1 countries like Turkey and Pakistan and Group 2 countries like Thailand. The 1981 declaration by the Japanese government of its intention to strengthen its aid to 'areas important to the maintenance of the peace and stability of the world' did not refer to the increase of only narrowly defined political aid (in other words, 'strategic aid'). It also included the provision of greater assistance to countries that had traditionally been high-priority beneficiaries of Japan's aid programme.

Cases of 'Political' Aid

Even in those cases where it may be suggested that Japan's aid is strategic, the increased assistance is often provided not so much to respond to narrowly defined security considerations as to strengthen assistance to countries that have been important recipients of Japanese aid all along.

In this sense, it might be possible to consider the 1981 declaration that Japan would strengthen its aid to 'areas important to the maintenance of the peace and stability of the world' as mere rhetoric, reflecting no change from its previous policy. The declaration was significant, however, as an explicit statement by Japan of its intention to do its part as a member of the Western bloc.

In practice, Japan's part as a 'member of the Western community' is also a concept subject to varying definitions.[7] It does not refer only to the provision of 'strategic' aid. It is natural, however, to see the desire to do its part as a factor behind Japan's affirmative response to US requests for additional aid to countries like those of Group 1 in Table 6.1, which the US considers strategically important. This sort of positive response has been one way of demonstrating Japan's co-operative stance to the Americans and improving Japan–US relations.

Japan may also be seen to be striving to play its proper role within the Western community when it extends official assistance to countries where the US, for historical or political reasons, finds it hard to be an active donor. Japanese aid to Turkey and Pakistan, for example, has served to fill gaps left by the Americans: US relations with rival Greece preclude a substantial rise in aid to Turkey, while Pakistan's pursuit of nuclear technology resulted in a temporary freeze on US aid to that country.

Another category of Japanese aid that may be seen as fulfilling a role on behalf of the Western bloc is that to communist countries – not only China but also countries like Laos that do not receive any direct US assistance.

When Japan commenced its aid to China in 1979, one body of supporting opinion was that represented by the Ministry of International Trade and Industry (MITI), which saw China as a major potential market for Japanese goods and as a possible source of oil, coal and other resources. But this was accompanied by the thinking of members of the Foreign Ministry and their sympathisers, who felt that Japan should assist China in its modernisation programme as a means of strengthening the hand of the pragmatists within the Chinese government and thereby helping keep China in line with the Western bloc on major foreign policy issues. Japan is also continuing to provide assistance in the form of grants to Laos as part of its own efforts to contribute to stability in the Indochinese peninsula. The aid to these countries, though it has run into some opposition within the Association of Southeast Asian Nations (ASEAN), may be seen as an action on behalf of the Western bloc, in particular the US, which is not in a position to offer aid to such countries itself.

The main beneficiaries of Japan's ODA programme are the ASEAN member countries, which are also in an area 'important to the maintenance of peace and stability in the world'. Japanese aid to ASEAN countries increased sharply starting in 1978, at a time when the US commitment to Southeast Asia had decreased following the end of the Vietnam War. The increase in Japanese aid represented an attempt to increase the 'resilience' of ASEAN by assisting the economic development of its member states. As mentioned above, Japan suspended its aid to Vietnam in the wake of that country's invasion of Kampuchea, after which it sharply increased assistance to Thailand. Following the assassination of Benigno Aquino in August 1983, as the internal stability of the Philippines rapidly deteriorated, Japan provided large commodity loans. Aid was further increased after Corazon Aquino became president in 1986, in order to promote the country's economic and political stability.

The first objective of Japan's aid to these countries is to help them develop their economies and improve the welfare of their people; over the long run this is expected to contribute indirectly to regional political stability. In this sense the assistance extended to the countries of the second group described above, such as China and the ASEAN members, may be seen as 'political aid' in the broad sense of the term.[8]

The concept that assisting the developing countries should indirectly contribute to regional political stability has long been part of Japanese thinking on aid policy. As early as 1959, in the third edition of its Diplomatic Blue Book, the Foreign Ministry wrote that 'the economic development of the less advanced countries is of extremely great significance for the achievement of permanent world peace'.[9]

In the years following 1965, the Japanese government rapidly stepped up its concessional lending of yen funds to developing countries. In particular, the commencement of yen loans to South Korea and Taiwan in 1965 can be seen as a reflection not only of Japan's increasing prosperity, but also of an awareness of the need to make up for the decrease in US economic assistance to these two countries as its deepening involvement in the Vietnam War took up more of its resources. This same period saw a rise in Japanese aid to Indonesia, where in a de facto military coup the anti-American President Sukarno was overthrown by General Suharto, who set up a more pro-Western administration.

It is thus apparent that political considerations, broadly defined, played a role in the formulation of Japan's aid policy even in the 1960s. Japan had already started providing assistance designed to show its co-operation with the US and its awareness of its role as a member of the community of advanced Western nations well before the 1980s. It is not accurate to see Japan's aid policy as having suddenly taken on strong political overtones in that decade.

AID POLICY MAKING: THE FACTS BEHIND POLITICAL INPUT

The Bureaucratic Process of Aid Distribution

If, as suggested above, the provision by Japan of political aid is not as much of a special recent development as is generally thought and cannot be explained simply as a response to US requests, then what are the political and diplomatic considerations that have gone into Japan's aid policy? To answer this question it is necessary first to look briefly at the decision making process behind Japan's official development assistance.

In Japan, the bureaucracy plays the largest role in the formulation of ODA policy. The legislature is not greatly involved in the process. The contrast with the US is sharp, as the US Congress plays a major part in determining the specifics of foreign aid policy. The appropriation for ODA in the draft budget presented by the Japanese Government to the Diet every year is the sum of the individual categories of aid – such as loans, grants and technical assistance – proposed by various ministries and agencies. The extent of the Diet's involvement is to consider the total ODA budget and the amounts sought by each government organ. The decisions on how much aid will go to which countries and what particular projects will be funded are left up to the administration; exchanges of notes with other governments concerning the provision of loans and grants are authorised by administrative decision and do not require individual legislative approval.

On occasion, to be sure, the nature or the amount of aid being provided to a particular country may turn into a political issue and become the subject of questioning in the Diet, as was the case with Japan's assistance to the Philippines in the final years of the Marcos Administration. In almost all cases, however, the legislature is satisfied with an after-the-fact explanation of the aid agreement into which the government has entered.

The political and diplomatic considerations that go into the formulation of Japan's ODA policy are therefore mainly those of the bureaucrats who dominate the decision making process. Let us look a bit more deeply into the mechanics of this process.

The country-by-country distribution of Japan's ODA is handled on an incremental basis, with the previous year's appropriation levels serving as the starting point. The two major categories of Japan's ODA are yen loans and grants. The decisions on the amounts and recipients of the yen loans each year are made primarily through discussions among four government agencies: the Ministry of Foreign Affairs, Ministry of Finance, Ministry of International Trade and Industry, and the Economic Planning Agency. But in practice, the greater part of the loan budget is predetermined. There are a number of countries that receive yen loans on a regular annual basis, and the amount of each year's lending to them is based on the previous year's loans, increased by a proportion matching the rise in the total ODA budget. The decision makers are constrained by the fact that any sudden cut may adversely affect bilateral relations. As a result, the country-by-country shares of the total yen loan budget tend to change relatively little from one year to the next.

The allocation of grants is not handled through four-agency discussions but rather at the Foreign Ministry, which consults as appropriate with other government bodies. There is potentially greater scope for flexibility in deciding how to distribute these funds, but in practice the previous year's appropriations are, as for yen loans, the starting point for determining the general breakdown among regions and countries.[10]

The second-group countries described in the previous section and listed in Table 6.1 are all regular annual recipients of yen loans. Japan considers these East and Southeast Asian nations to be 'key countries' in the distribution of its ODA budget. Their position reflects the totality of their political and economic relations with Japan and has deep historical roots. Many of these same countries, after all, were among the recipients of the postwar reparations out of which the present aid programme grew.

The Politics of Aid Increases

Though the country-by-country distribution of the ODA budget may be relatively stable in general, changes do occur when political and diplomatic considerations intervene. The clearest examples of such considerations at work involve meetings between government heads, as when a foreign leader visiting Japan strongly requests increased aid or a Japanese prime minister takes along plans to increase assistance as a 'present' when visiting a foreign country.[11] Generally a country seeking increased aid will initiate its request through working-level channels, and the Foreign Ministry may well approve it for diplomatic reasons. The approval of the Foreign Ministry, however, is subject to the checks built into the four-agency discussion process, particularly the budgetary review of the Finance Ministry. Prime ministerial decisions can be important in securing an aid increase in the context of this bureaucratic manoeuvring.

The tendency is for Japan to attempt to meet the requests for increased aid made by foreign leaders both as a means of maintaining friendly bilateral relations with the requesting country and as a demonstration of Japan's readiness to fulfil its international responsibilities as an economic superpower.[12]

More specifically, the first-category countries described in the previous section have all been the recipients of aid increases carried out through the sort of political process mentioned above. These increases may be regarded as strategic, but not in the sense of military considerations. They reflect, rather, Japan's desire to maintain healthy bilateral relations with the US and to demonstrate its contribution to global security – diplomatic concerns, in other words.

Even though political and diplomatic considerations affect decisions about how much aid to provide to particular countries, the decisions about how the aid is to be used are a different matter. The determination of how the aid is to be provided and what specific projects are to be funded are handled non-politically by government ministry bureaucrats and officials of the aid-administering agency. The Japanese government has adhered firmly to the principle that the assistance is to be given for economic and social infrastructure, and it has also taken care to keep commodity loans from becoming political issues by limiting the purposes for which they may be used. In this sense, even when assistance is provided for strategic purposes, its actual content is no different from that of the general development assistance that Japan extends to promote economic development and national welfare.

It is also to be noted that Japan does not increase aid simply because other countries lodge strong requests. To see what kinds of considerations have gone into the political decisions to increase aid, we need to look at individual cases.

Two examples of such increases are the 1979–80 increase in aid to Turkey and the 1983 increase in aid to South Korea. In January 1979, when Turkey's external debt problem had reached serious proportions and the turbulence in Iran led to fears of greater Soviet influence in the region, countries like the US and West Germany requested that Japan increase its aid to Turkey. The Japanese prime minister, Masayoshi Ohira, played a large part in making the final decision. The working-level proposal that year was for an increase to only $80 million, but it was decided that Japan would pledge $100 million in accordance with Ohira's wishes. Japan's global role as a member of the Western community was a major consideration behind this decision.[13]

In the years from 1981 to 1983, South Korea pushed for additional aid from Japan under the rubric of 'security-related economic assistance'. The attainment of a final agreement, under which Japan pledged to provide $4 billion over a five-year period, is said to have been greatly influenced by the position taken by Prime Minister Yasuhiro Nakasone, who decided to recognise in principle the importance of South Korea for Japan's own security and to increase the amount of Japan's offer.[14] It seems likely, however, that the desire to improve bilateral relations by demonstrating Japan's readiness to co-operate in South Korea's economic development had more weight as a factor than the security element advanced by the Koreans.[15]

Regardless of the political motivation and possible security ramifications of increased assistance in cases like these, the actual aid provided has been economic, not military. The bulk of the 1979 yen loan to Turkey went for the building of a dam, and the debt-relief measures and substantial commodity loans that have been provided to that country since 1980 have all been for the purpose of bringing about short-term economic benefits. While South Korea raised the issue of security in its aid request, as a donor Japan held to the position that its assistance was given for economic development purposes only. The projects funded by yen loans were mainly for improvements in the country's social infrastructure, including the construction of waterworks and sewage disposal plants, a multipurpose dam, and disposal facilities for urban waste.

More recently, in the summer of 1987, when several Western countries sent minesweepers to the Persian Gulf to make it safe for shipping, Japan was also expected to do its part. The measures that Japan adopted in October were not military: they consisted of paying the cost of high-accuracy radio aids to navigation, promising to contribute financially upon the establishment of an international peace-keeping framework for the region (such as a team of UN cease-fire observers) and providing about $500 million in economic and technical aid to Oman, Jordan, and other countries of the region. This is another case of economic aid increased for political reasons.

Latin America is an area in which the US government and American banks have special interests. Japan's recycling of funds to this region was announced when Prime Minister Nakasone visited the US in September 1987, as one example of how Japan was shouldering its international responsibilities. Untied grants to Africa are intended to counter the criticisms heard in Europe and America that Japan's aid is over-concentrated in Asia and that it aims to further Japan's own economic interests.

Though different political or diplomatic considerations may be at work in each of these individual cases, Japan has maintained a consistent policy of limiting its aid to economic development purposes. It is not strategic aid in the same sense as US aid, with its emphasis on security concerns.

When Japan provides aid, its intentions are, first, to co-operate in countries' economic development as a means of strengthening bilateral relations with them; second, to foster international economic stability and thereby promote Japan's own economic well-being; and third, to fulfil a part of its international responsibilities by indirectly contributing to the political stability of the countries receiving aid. In a 1981 document, the Foreign Ministry expressed Japan's aid philosophy concisely, describing ODA spending as 'the cost of building an international order so as to achieve comprehensive security for Japan'.[16]

COMMERCIAL INTERESTS: MYTH OR REALITY?

In the previous section, I have outlined what political and diplomatic

considerations go into the formation of Japan's aid diplomacy. However, there are many arguments that Japanese aid policy has been
driven solely by economic interests, by a desire to expand exports, to
acquire natural resources and so forth. Such arguments often neglect
the development of Japan's aid programme in the 1980s. Nonetheless,
they are widely accepted. They are based on the idea that the Japanese
are 'economic animals', and that the Japanese government does not
consider the welfare of the recipient countries, but only the prosperity
of its own country in its aid programme. In this section, I will examine
to what extent, if any, this argument is valid.

Analysts differ over who determines the supposed economic objectives in Japan's aid. Most point to Japanese companies which want to
expand their exports: Japanese firms and trading companies find
specific aid projects in recipient countries, submit aid proposals to the
Japanese government, and then lobby in Tokyo for the projects that
would require procurement orders from their companies. These companies are aided by influential politicians, and the aid bureaucrats then
accept and carry out aid allocations to those projects.[17]

To assess the role of companies in making aid policy, we should
examine two issues: (1) the influence of companies on the decision
making process of Japan's aid programme (2) and the role of Japanese
companies in finding aid projects in the recipient countries.

The Influence of Companies on Aid Policy Decision Making

Historically, it is true that Japan's aid policy has been influenced by
economic or commercial interests. Many analysts argue that Japan's
reparations and aid to the Asian countries led directly to an expansion
of Japanese exports to that region. There are, in fact, some cases in
which Japanese firms influenced procurement orders of tied aid (loans
and grants which are tied to Japanese goods and services). However,
Japan's aid programme has changed considerably in recent years.

For instance, it is true that most of Japan's grants and loans were at
one time tied to the purchase of Japanese goods. However, there has
been significant progress in the untying of Japanese government yen
loans since 1978. In January of that year, the Japanese government
announced that it would promote 'general-untied' loans, which permit
procurement of goods from any country. This was a measure to reduce
Japan's huge trade surplus and soften the Japan–US economic conflict.[18]

Almost half of Japan's untied aid is 'LDC-untied', loans which can be used to buy goods from Japan and from less-developed countries. Still, Japan is criticised by other advanced countries for not untying more of its aid. But, in 1987, 72 per cent of Japan's loans were general untied loans. This is high in comparison with other advanced industrial countries; for example, the proportions of untied loans were 57 per cent for West Germany, 45 per cent for the United States, 56 per cent for France and 38 per cent for the United Kingdom.

Moreover, the Japanese ODA component of the $20 billion capital recycling plan announced at the Venice summit in June 1987 consists entirely of general untied loans. Also in 1987, the Japanese government announced that it would provide $500 million in untied grants to African countries for three years. This is the first case in which grant aid was untied.

Is it really true that Japanese firms are involved in the decision making and implementation of the official ODA programme? Firms are not formally involved in determining loan allocations by the Japanese government. However, four ministries including MITI consult on aid policy, so commercial interests may be reflected in the aid programme through MITI.

For example, in the case of aid to China in 1979, it was an important decision whether or not the aid was to be untied. The initiation of Japanese aid to China in 1979 concerned other advanced countries who feared that Japan would monopolise the Chinese market by giving a large amount of aid (47 million yen over seven years). The US and some European countries requested that the Japanese government make its loans to China general untied loans. The Ministry of Foreign Affairs promoted general untying of its loans, but this was strongly resisted by business circles and the MITI. In the end the loans were LDC-untied.[19]

In contrast, the decision to promote general untying of Japanese loans in January 1978 was made in spite of strong opposition from business circles and MITI. The influence of the business community on Japan's aid policy has not been as strong in recent years as is commonly asserted in international criticism.

On the other hand, there are some cases in which companies are aided by influential politicians. Companies often request that politicians intervene in specific decisions on aid projects or procurement, for instance, and it is reported that some *nourin-giin* (Dietmen who have special interests in agricultural issues) pushed government officials to build water systems as aid projects in the Philippines, Bangladesh and Nepal at the request of Japanese companies which had commercial interests in building them in the recipient countries.[20]

Japan's aid projects are in principle based on requests from recipient countries. Procurement orders for projects funded by general untied aid are offered for public tender in the recipient countries, not in Japan. Whether Japanese companies can get orders for aid projects from the recipient government depends on their competitiveness in price and skill, or their effort in finding good projects, not on their special relationship with the Japanese government or politicians. In effect, the process of untying Japan's ODA has reduced the influence of private companies on Japan's aid allocation.

The Role of Companies in the Recipient Countries

The role of Japanese companies in devising and implementing aid projects in the recipient countries should be examined. The effect of untying Japan's loans will encourage Japanese companies to approach the recipient governments to get the procurement orders for aid projects. Japanese companies, in fact, are actively trying to develop aid projects in the recipient countries in order to get procurement orders. For instance, there was strong criticism in the National Diet in 1986 of Japanese companies in the Philippines that offered large bribes to officials in the Marcos regime.

However, one reason for Japanese participation in the aid process is that many recipient governments do not have sufficient ability to formulate aid projects. Japanese companies are helping them in developing projects. Another reason is that the Japanese government has a limited staff responsible for aid policy in the recipient countries, particularly in contrast with the large number of personnel from the US Agency for International Development (USAID). In that sense, the participation of representatives from Japanese companies in the process of developing and implementing aid projects in the recipient countries has a positive and important role in Japan's aid system.

On the other hand, although Japan decided in principle to untie its loans in 1978, 40 to 50 per cent of the procurement for these untied loans has been, in fact, secured by Japanese companies.[21] This figure is not so very high compared with other donor countries. But it cannot be denied that the increase in Japan's ODA will lead to an expansion of Japan's exports to the developing countries. It will also result in closer economic ties between Japan and the recipients.

This will probably give rise to political frictions between Japan and other advanced countries. For instance, the increase of Japan's aid to

Turkey, which is a typical case of strategic aid, may have helped Japanese companies to get procurement orders for the Second Bosporus Bridge in 1985. Furthermore, the competition over the procurement order for that bridge brought about a diplomatic problem between Japan and the UK.[22] 'Aid friction' seems to be increasing between Japan and other countries as Japan increases its aid budget while other advanced countries decrease theirs.

CONCLUSION

Since the late 1970s, the relative growth of Japan's economic power, along with the occurrence of incidents like the Soviet invasion of Afghanistan, has increased the pressure on Japan to play a political role as a member of the Western community. The Japanese response, as we have seen, has been to strengthen its aid to 'countries bordering areas of conflict' and 'areas important to the maintenance of the peace and stability of the world'. The distribution of Japan's ODA has in fact changed to a certain extent, and there are an increasing number of cases in which Japan provides aid to particular countries in line with American requests. The general view is that this means that Japan's aid is becoming more strategic in orientation.

If, however, we look more carefully at the political and diplomatic considerations involved, we find that even in cases where there has been a US request, this is not the only factor behind the provision of aid. Japan's own desire to maintain good relations with the country in question and to demonstrate its readiness to fulfil its political responsibilities also come into play. Furthermore, the main recipients of Japanese assistance continue to be those countries to which Japan has traditionally directed a large portion of its aid, mainly its Asian neighbours. And even when increased ODA is provided in response to diplomatic considerations, Japan continues to maintain its policy of extending it in the form of economic assistance. In this respect, Japan's stance is quite different from that of the US, which stresses military security concerns.

At first glance this might be taken to mean that Japan's aid programme is independent of political considerations. In fact, however, the exclusively economic nature of the aid programme is itself a clear statement of Japan's definition of its own national interests, including its position concerning the nature of international relations and its view of the role it can play in the context of global realities. A world free of military conflicts is to Japan's advantage, and since it does not possess military power of its own as a means of resolving such conflicts, the provision of economic aid is a major pillar of Japan's 'comprehensive national security' policy.

Toward the end of his book *The Manner of Giving: Strategic Aid and Japanese Foreign Policy* (1986), American political scientist Dennis Yasutomo describes Japan's aid policy as a 'hybrid' that reflects both its recognition of the forces of *Realpolitik* and its striving for a world of 'complex interdependence'.[23] This policy, in other words, has two sides: it is a means of coping with the realities of today's power politics, but at the same time it is part of a fundamental strategy that aims to create a different sort of system, one where security will be based not on military might but rather on the shared economic and social interests of the international community.

When he was president of the World Bank, Robert McNamara often said that economic development is the best form of security. It may also be suggested that the best defence for Japan is to contribute to the economic and political stability of the developing countries by aiding their development. In this sense, economic assistance is a necessary part of the 'diplomacy of peace' through which Japan seeks to protect its own interests, and the growing role of Japanese aid may be expected to contribute to the real security both of Japan and of the entire international community.

However, the proposition that the increase of economic assistance to developing countries will always lead to harmony and friendship is not true. An increase of economic aid can be regarded as a use of economic power. It may cause political conflicts not only with the recipients but also with other donor countries, as seen in cases of 'aid friction'. There are difficulties in aid diplomacy as in all other forms of the art, and that is the reason that Japan is now in search of a comprehensive 'strategy' which calculates and balances the economic, political and diplomatic effects of aid.

Notes and References

1.   Works that have examined Japan's aid programme in the context of its foreign policy include Alan Rix, *Japan's Economic Aid: Policy-Making and Politics* (London: Croom Helm, 1980); and Dennis T. Yasumoto, *The Manner of Giving: Strategic Aid and Japanese Foreign Policy* (Lexington, MA: Lexington Books, 1986).

2. The first definition of 'comprehensive security' appeared in a report issued in May 1978 by the National Institute for Research Advancement (NIRA) and the Nomura Research Institute, *Kokusai kankyo no henka to Nihon no taio – 21 seiki e no teigen* (Changes in the International Environment and Japan's Response to Them: Recommendations for the Twenty-first Century) pp. 145–8.
3. *International Herald Tribune* (23 August 1985).
4. *Daily Yomiuri* (27 January 1987).
5. Ministry of Foreign Affairs, *Gaiko Seisho* (Diplomatic Blue Book) 1980, p. 220; 1981, pp. 42–3.
6. This declaration was contained in the Japan–US communiques issued on 8 May 1981, after Prime Minister Zenko Suzuki and President Ronald Reagan met in Washington.
7. 'One member of the West' (*Nishigawa no ichiin*) is the generally used term. In its *1981 Diplomatic Blue Book* (p. 14) the Foreign Ministry used the phrase 'one member of the advanced democratic community' (*senshin minshushugi shakai no ichiin*); in the 1987 edn (p. 3) the official terminology was 'one member of the [community of] free democracies' (*jiyu minshushugi shokoku no ichiin*).
8. Concerning the political aspects of aid to China and the Philippines, refer to Research Institute for Peace and Security (RIPS), *Asian Security 1985*, pp. 171–5.
9. *Gaiko Seisho* (1959) p. 27.
10. Interview with an aid official of the Ministry of Foreign Affairs.
11. Domestic politicians will also occasionally make requests concerning the foreign aid programme, but almost invariably these are either for an increase in the total ODA budget or for funding for some specific project; they do not entail major changes in the country-by-country distribution of aid.
12. Interview with an aid official of the Ministry of Foreign Affairs.
13. *Nihon Keizai Shimbun* (16 April 1980) and an interview with a politician of the Liberal Democratic Party.
14. Hong N. Kim, 'Politics of Japan's Economic Aid to South Korea', *Asia–Pacific Community*, 20 (Spring 1983).
15. RIPS, *Asian Security 1985*, pp. 170–1.
16. Economic Co-operation Bureau, Ministry of Foreign Affairs, *Keizai Kyoryoku no Rinen–Seifu Kaihatsu Enjo wa Naze Okonau no ka* (The Philosophy of Economic Co-operation: Why Give Official Development Assistance?) (Tokyo: Association for Promotion of International Co-operation, 1981) pp. 75–84.
17. Ken Matsui, *Keizai Kyoryoku: Towareru Nihon no Keizai Gaikou* (Economic Co-operation) (Yuhikaku, 1983) pp. 151–7.
18. Juichi Inada, 'Hatten Tojokoku to Nihon: Taigai Enjo Seisaku no Henyou Katei', in Akio Watanabe (ed.), *Sengo Nihon no Taigai Seisaku* (Yuhikaku, 1985) pp. 298–302.
19. *Nihon Keizai Shimbun* (25 October 1979).
20. Interview with an aid official of the Ministry of Foreign Affairs.

21. Interview with and aid official of the Overseas Economic Co-operation Fund (OECF).
22. *Nihon Keizai Shimbun* (2 May (evening), 22 May, 24 May and 29 May 1985).
23. Yasutomo, *The Manner of Giving*, p. 123.

7 Political and Economic Influences in Japan's Relations with China since 1978

Walter Arnold

Political and economic relations are inextricably intertwined. This axiomatic proposition represents a core concern in international political economy[1] and provides a useful basis from which to examine the nature and structure of China's economic relationship with Japan. Since the conclusion of the Long-Term Trade Agreement (LTTA) in 1978, Sino–Japanese economic relations have expanded rapidly, from a value of $5 billion to a high of $18.8 billion in 1985, greatly exceeding expectations on both sides. Sino–Japanese relations are now characterised by an intricate interplay of political and economic considerations. Japan's initial euphoria over the China market has been replaced by more sober attitudes. The Chinese, on the other hand, are increasingly fearful of economic dependence on Japan. China lists trade imbalances, Japanese restrictions on technology transfer and lack of Japanese investment as major problems in Sino–Japanese economic relations. Together with China's perceived economic dependence on Japan, these problems remain as pressing public policy issues for the PRC. The trade between the two countries makes up approximately 20 per cent of China's foreign trade but less than 3 per cent of Japan's. Japanese foreign direct investment (FDI) in China is only US $1.7 billion, or 1.2 per cent of Japan's world-wide aggregate FDI in 1987. Today, two of the most salient tasks of China's foreign economic policy remain contradictory: to diminish trade dependence on Japan and, at the same time, to increase Japanese investment in China.

The important question to be addressed here is why and how politics have influenced Japanese trade and investment in China. More specific concerns are the causes of China's economic dependence on Japan and the impact it has on the structure of their bilateral relations.[2] The attempt will also be made to determine how the interface of political and economic factors has shaped the overall relationship between the

121

two countries, and how bilateral political conflict has been resolved. The underlying assumption is that Sino–Japanese relations are largely defined by close co-operation, periodic conflict and bilateral political accommodation.

This chapter will analyse Sino–Japanese relations largely from a 'dependency' perspective. It will attempt to determine the extent to which political factors have influenced Sino–Japanese economic relations by applying Albert O. Hirschman's theory of the economic 'influence effect' to Sino–Japanese trade, investment and foreign aid.[3]

HIRSCHMAN'S TRADE AND INVESTMENT INFLUENCE EFFECT THEORY

In a systematic theory of the linkage between economics and politics, Hirschman developed a set of propositions asserting that both trade and investment have more than one kind of effect. While economic relations between nations serve to supply the trading partners with desired goods ('supply effect'), they also create an 'influence effect'. This arises from each nation's need for imports, exports and investment. Hirschman begins with the premise that one nation influences another through trade. Every nation has the sovereign right to stop importing, exporting or investing in others; country A can stop trading with countries B, C, and D at any time. Such a stoppage will injure all countries involved. But if it will injure B, C and D more than A, then A can threaten to stop trade in order to influence the actions of the other countries. Hirschman explains why B, C and D may find a trade stoppage with A an effective threat: if they find trading with A better than not trading and if they would have difficulties replacing A's exports or markets (thus making the adjustment process painful), they are likely to acquiesce in certain of A's demands in order to maintain that trade.[4] As will be illustrated below, Hirschman's theory appears to be a useful analytical device to explain the Japanese government's strategic use of foreign economic policy.

The influence effects of investment work in much the same manner as those of trade. Capital is required for industrialisation and development, and many nations seek it in the form of foreign investment. When a country comes to rely on investment as a substitute for indigenous capital, then the threat of stoppage has an effect similar to that in a trading relationship: the country benefits from the investment of its partner, and would have a difficult time in replacing its capital inputs (assuming a lack of other willing investors). Therefore, a country dependent on foreign investment may be willing to accommodate some of the demands of foreign investors in order to attract capital and thus secure continued development of its economy and industry.

Japanese foreign direct investment in FY 1987 reached a record high of $33.3 billion, up 49.5 per cent over FY 1986 and four-fold from 1982. North America received the largest share, but Asia had the greatest proportional increase – up 109 per cent in the one-year period, with $4.8 billion invested in the area. The 1987–8 increase in Japanese FDI was caused primarily by the sharp appreciation of the yen, trade friction and competition with newly industrialising economies. A combination of these factors is forcing a growing number of Japanese firms to invest abroad.[5]

The effect of Japanese Official Development Assistance (ODA) is similar to Hirschman's 'influence effect' for trade and investment. There are, however, fundamental political differences. Unlike the pecuniary interests that underlie private sector foreign investment and international economic activity, the motive for granting and receiving foreign aid is complex. The desire for greater power, prestige, influence and development are among the motives of most donors and recipients.[6] Many in Japan see ODA as an important means to attain 'comprehensive national security', and acknowledge that Japan is quite capable of global influence through the strategic use of its ODA.[7] Politically, ODA is respectable internationally and has popular support in Japan. It also helps to dissolve Japan's pretence that economics is separable from politics. Moreover, ODA tends to be largely an executive or bureaucratic affair. As a result, bureaucrats and politicians often make discretionary use of ODA to serve specific foreign policy goals as well as to promote national influence and prestige more generally. This is not to suggest that recipient countries remain entirely passive or powerless. On the contrary, in many instances recipient countries have influenced the amount and flow of ODA by taking appropriate political positions *vis-à-vis* the donor.

It is precisely the influence effect exerted by trade, investment and ODA that makes the political aspects of Japanese economic relations such important analytical issues. In the first place, Japanese economic relations cannot be perceived as politically 'neutral'. Instead, they must be seen as instruments of influence, power and possibly domination. By focusing Hirschman's analytical approach on Sino–Japanese economic relations, we link economic trends to political causes and outcomes in this important bilateral relationship.

POLITICAL AND ECONOMIC CHARACTERISTICS OF SINO—JAPANESE RELATIONS

Dominant explanations of Sino–Japanese relations focus on such interrelated variables as politics, strategy and presumed economic complementarity. Many studies suggest that China's foreign policy toward Japan combines economic considerations and strategic calculations in a pragmatic framework.[8] Japan is now widely perceived as a country that uses international trade and investment as political instruments to further its national interest and expand its power in the international arena.[9] It has been conceptualised as a 'reactive' state, that, unlike other middle-ranking powers such as France, fails to undertake major independent foreign economic policy initiatives and is largely incapable of responding effectively and efficiently to outside pressures (*gaiatsu*).[10]

In the context of Sino–Japanese relations, the Japanese state does appear reactive and unwilling to take bold initiatives. It puts a high premium on the economic aspects of the bilateral relationship but is quite oblique about the political aspects of its relations with China – although presumably such issues as national and regional security and stability (in which perceptions of the Soviet Union are important) play a significant role. Conversely, the Chinese have long emphasised the political dimensions of relations with Japan and insist that equality and mutual benefit are the basic principles that must govern Sino–Japanese economic relations.[11] The Chinese attach great importance to reciprocal relations, maintaining that foreign trade should always benefit both trading parties and not one party alone; still less should it be harmful to either party.[12] In addition, China currently manifests a growing nationalist sentiment which started in 1985 with outbursts by students against what they perceived as Japan's 'second invasion', or 'economic aggression'. This increasing anti-Japanese sentiment in some segments of China's population represents yet another political factor in Sino–Japanese relations.

Japan today, owing to the sheer magnitude of its domestic economic and industrial base and its international financial and commercial position, can tie trading partners to its economic orbit.[13] Northeast Asia has particular economic and political importance for Japan, which has fostered close commercial ties with South Korea, Taiwan and, since 1978, with China. Exerting its economic influence through trade, investment and aid, Japan not only established itself as the core industrial and financial power in Northeast Asia – among some of the world's most dynamic economies – but also made itself indispensable for the region's economic development.[14] Through these economic linkages, Japan seeks to promote stability in Northeast Asia and to safeguard its own economic security.

As a major recipient of Japanese trade and ODA, China has been linked very closely to the Japanese economic orbit. Measured in terms of trade statistics, Japan's economic role in China has increased dramatically since the formal conclusion of the Long-Term Trade Agreement and Peace and Friendship Treaty (PFT) in 1978. Since then, Japan has established a visible presence in several of China's major cities and successfully applied its comparative economic advantage, productive capabilities and trading ingenuity to its economic dealings with China. Much to the chagrin of its competitors (and some Chinese) Japan established itself as China's most important trading partner and its largest donor of foreign aid. The record shows that over the years, Japan has been most responsive to repeated Chinese demands for both grants and loans.

The political motives for Japan's high economic stakes in China are usually explained in terms of the influential view in Japanese elite circles that China's socio-political and economic stability are prerequisites for stability in Asia. An important related assertion is that China's leadership depends heavily on Japan for the success of its ambitious programme of economic reform and modernisation on which the leadership's legitimacy, credibility and political fortunes hinge.

Because Japan has been China's single most important economic partner, China is, conceivably, susceptible to Japanese political influence, just as Japan is exposed to Chinese political pressures. For example, during the 1950s and well into the early 1970s, China was vehemently opposed to the Japan–United States Mutual Security Treaty. Since 1972 and especially after 1979, China has become more conciliatory toward, if not openly supportive of, the US–Japan security alliance. This development may be ascribed in part to Japan's increasing economic presence and influence in China. On the other hand, since 1952, China has skilfully played upon the theme of Japan's war debt and guilt. Also noteworthy is the fact that China is now perceived by some as an emerging political and strategic power, and a potential economic force in the region – one that could conceivably challenge Japan's position in Asia. This last point is an important political aspect of Sino–Japanese relations and is often overlooked; in spite of rhetoric to the contrary, Japan and China remain regional – and potentially global – rivals. The consequences of Japan's changing status in international politics will almost certainly have an impact on relations with China, especially as the two countries' interests diverge as a result of rapid and fundamental changes in Northeast Asia and the international political economy in general.

The following sections focus on the causes and political consequences of Japan's growing economic influence in China, which Hirschman's theory of the influence effect would predict.

THE INFLUENCE EFFECT IN SINO—JAPANESE RELATIONS

The international environment in Northeast Asia, unlike that of Europe, is not dominated by two powerful military blocs. Neither the US nor the USSR can claim a pervasive political hegemony. However, the political economy of the East Asian region is greatly affected by the global reach of the Japanese trading state. An open – and highly relevant – question is whether economic integration and interdependence in Northeast Asia has been driven primarily by market forces, political grand design or a combination of both. There can be no doubt that Japan's international economic activities have been a major catalyst for stability and peaceful coexistence in a multipolar Northeast Asia, which includes socialist and market-oriented economies that were once diametrically opposed. Japan's political intentions in the region, however, are far less transparent. From the early 1950s to the 1970s, Japan consciously avoided political entanglements in world affairs and followed a policy of export-led growth with little attention to the costs that might be imposed on other countries.

Today, an economically powerful Japan seeks a political role and asserts itself in the international realm. It has many opportunities to harness its economic influence to foreign policy objectives. The signing of the LTTA with China in 1978, which set the stage for a new era of economic and political ties, is a clear example of the uses of economic power for political purposes.[15] Against this backdrop, the analytical focus may turn to the structural features of Sino–Japanese economic relations and assess their respective political relevance and ramifications.

The LTTA specified that Japan would purchase Chinese coal and oil worth $10 billion in the period from 1978 to 1985. China committed itself to buy Japanese capital goods of equal value. Trade between the two nations rose from $5 billion in 1978 to a high of $19.3 billion in

1988.[16] After the LTTA was signed, an optimistic China committed
itself to a larger number of plant and equipment deals with Japan than
it could handle financially – including the notorious Baoshan iron and
steel plant (about which more below), petrochemical plants and several
colour TV production facilities. As a result Sino–Japanese trade
doubled in less than three years. However, the rapid over-extension led
to the first crisis in Sino–Japanese trade when, in 1981, China unilaterally cancelled or suspended numerous Japanese contracts in an effort to
bring its economy under control.[17] Subsequently, China not only
suffered from large and chronic trade deficits with Japan (these reached
a staggering $6 billion in 1985 alone), but also concomitant foreign
exchange shortages and balance of payment difficulties (see Table 7.1).

The vicissitudes of Sino–Japanese trade are structural, and must be
located in the composition of trade. Chinese exports to Japan consist
primarily of petroleum, textiles, clothing, foodstuffs, and low value-
added manufactured items. China imports mainly high value-added
capital and consumer goods. It is thus exposed to the unfavourable
terms of trade that plague most Third World exporters. China's raw
material exports to Japan – about one-third of the total – are exposed
to wide fluctuations of the world market prices, while prices for Japan's
industrial goods are much more stable. For example, the 1986 drop in
petroleum prices from $26 a barrel to $13 per barrel halved Chinese
revenues from one of its major exports to Japan. Thus far, China has

Table 7.1 Sino–Japanese trade (US$ million)

Year	Imports	Exports	Total	Chinese balance
1978	3049	2030	5080	– 120
1979	3699	2955	6650	– 144
1980	5078	4323	9400	– 755
1981	5097	5291	10400	+ 194
1982	3510	5352	8860	+ 1842
1983	4914	5087	10000	+ 173
1984	7200	6000	13200	– 1200
1985	12450	6300	18800	– 6100
1986	9900	5600	15300	– 4200
1987	8249	7401	15651	– 848
1988	9476	9859	19335	383

Sources: Based on *1987 Almanac of China's Foreign Economic Relations and
Trade* (Beijing: China Prospect Publishing House, 1987); 'Nitchu Keizai
Kankei ni tsuite' (Tsusansho, Tokyo: 1988) p. 8 (mimeo); JETRO, *China
Newsletter*, 77 (Nov–Dec, 1988) pp. 23–4.

been unable satisfactorily to diversify either its export products or its trading partners. The result is asymmetrical interdependence – that is to say, a deepening of China's economic dependence on Japan.[18]

According to the Japan–China Association on Economy and Trade, Sino–Japanese trade, which has declined considerably since 1986, is currently very 'sluggish'.[19] The immediate causes are many: foreign exchange shortages in China, the sharp appreciation of the yen, and MITI's tougher export screening as a result of the Toshiba affair. In addition, China, like most other countries, encounters enormous difficulties in gaining access to the Japanese market.

Japanese foreign direct investment, joint ventures and ODA remain a critical resource for China's economic modernisation effort. They enable China to finance industrial projects and various deficits. These infusions of capital, soft loans and aid packages represent a primary source of Japanese economic influence in China. Since bailing out the Baoshan project, the Japanese government has assumed the role of a major provider of aid to China. Moreover, since most of these funds are tied to the importation of Japanese goods, technology and industrial plants, there is also a substantial 'technology dependence' evolving which is tying China's emerging industrial economy closely to Japanese suppliers. As Table 7.2 and Table 7.3 detail, Japan's commitment of public funds in the form of grants and aid to China's development exceeds that of any other country. It is also Japan's largest involvement with a single recipient.

When Japan's global foreign direct investment began to soar in

Table 7.2   Japanese ODA disbursements in China, 1982–8 (US$ million)

Year	Grant aid	Technical cooperation	Loan aid	Total
1982	25.09	13.52	330.18	368.79
1983	30.62	20.46	299.07	350.24
1984	14.26	27.23	347.86	389.55
1985	11.56	31.16	345.17	387.89
1986	25.68	61.19	410.08	496.95
1987	54.30	76.00	422.8	553.1
1988	52.00	102.70	519.0	673.7

Source: Compilation of table based on *1987 Keizai Kyoryoku no Genjo to Mondaiten* (Tsusansho, 1987) p. 154; *1987 ODA Annual Report* (p. 141); 'Nitchu Keizai Kankei ni tsuite' (Tsusansho, 1988) p. 9; *Beijing Review* (10–16 October 1988) p. 29.

Table 7.3   Major donors of total ODA received by China (US$ million)

Donor	1983	1984	1985	1986	1987
Total	669.6	797.6	939.9	1133.9	
Japan	387.89	389.4	387.7	497.0	553.1
FRG	96.7	57.5	97.6	51.2	
Others	185.01	350.7	454.6	585.7	

Source: Compilation of table based on *1987 Keizai Kyorkoku no Genjo to Mondaiten* (Tsusansho, 1987) p. 154; *1987 ODA Annual Report* (p. 141); 'Nitchu Keizai Kankei no tsuite' (Tsusansho, 1988) p. 9; *Beijing Review* (10–16 October 1988) p. 29.

1985–6, China expected to reap a large portion of it (see Table 7.4). The Chinese reasoned that rapidly rising wages in the East Asian NICs coupled with the sharp appreciation of the Japanese yen and Taiwanese dollar would induce Japanese firms to shift production to China.[20] However, this scenario did not materialise in any significant way; instead, many Japanese firms shifted their offshore production to Southeast Asia – Thailand in particular, which offered a more attractive investment environment. China also presumed that Japanese investment would flow primarily to developing areas in search of comparative advantage in labour. As Japan's direct investment abroad rose during the 1985–7 period, the new investment went principally into the banking and insurance, manufacturing and real estate sectors; the share of the primary sector has diminished considerably. Moreover, the bulk

Table 7.4   Selected Japanese foreign direct investment, 1985–8 by receiving country (US$ million)

Recipient	1985	1986	1987	1988 (first half)
China	100	226	1226	170
Taiwan	114	291	367	192
South Korea	134	436	647	305
Thailand	48	124	250	366
USA	5395	10165	14704	11430
W. Europe	1930	3469	6576	4046
World total	12217	22320	33364	22857

Source: Compilation of table based on *1987 Keizai Kyoryoku no Genjo to Mondaiten* (Tsusansho, 1987) p. 154; *1987 ODA Annual Report* (p. 141); 'Nitchu Keizai Kankei ni tsuite' (Tsusansho, 1988) p. 9; *Beijing Review* (10–16 October 1988) p. 29.

of Japan's FDI went to the United States and Western Europe (see Table 7.5).[21]

Many Japanese companies bypassed China as a potential location for FDI, citing its unsettled investment environment as a major cause, and arguing that more profitable and secure investment opportunities were available elsewhere. Dissatisfaction with China's foreign investment environment dates back to the 1970s, when Japanese enterprises first attempted to invest in China. Since then there have been numerous casualties along with well-publicised success stories.[22] Japanese criticisms of China's investment environment focus primarily on China's legal system, foreign exchange problems, export requirements, and inadequate infrastructure.

Hirschman's 'economic influence effect' theory yields important and interesting political insights into Sino–Japanese relations, which go well beyond the endemic structural problems afflicting Sino–Japanese trade. Ostensibly, China benefits from its trade with Japan. Japan supplies consumer durables as well as technology and above all a wide range of capital goods needed for China's development. Both China and Japan understand very well that adjustment for China would be a long and arduous process should Sino–Japanese trade be interrupted. China would have to find other countries capable of furnishing over 20 per cent of its import requirements. Possible substitutes such as Taiwan, South Korea, and the Soviet Union are not only politically constrained in their dealings with China; they may also lack Japan's sophistication in industrial technology and production, while Western Europe or the United States may not at this point be able to fill China's needs as effectively and efficiently as Japan.

Hirschman's notion of 'vested interests' in trade represents yet

Table 7.5 Sources of foreign investment in China, 1979–87 (US$ billion)

Source	Total
Total FDI 1979–87	45.48
Hong Kong/Macao	17.23
Japan	14.39
North America and Europe	12.39
Others	1.47

Source: Compilation of table based on *1987 Keizai Kyoryoku no Genjo to Mondaiten* (Tsusansho, 1987) p. 154; *1987 ODA Annual Report* (p. 141); 'Nitchu Keizai Kankei no tsuite' (Tsusansho, 1988) p. 9; *Beijing Review* (10–16 October 1988) p. 29.

another political factor to be considered in Sino–Japanese relations.[23] In the course of the past several years powerful vested interests have emerged at the national and regional levels in both China and Japan. These groups would almost certainly oppose any type of severance of Sino–Japanese trade. China's top-level political leadership also has a vested interest in sustaining Sino–Japanese trade, particularly in view of its professed goal of making China a developed nation by the turn of the century. Having committed itself so thoroughly to an ambitious modernisation programme, the Chinese leadership will necessarily seek to maintain its ties with such an important financial and economic power as Japan.[24]

As shown above, China's dependence on Japan extends to investment and ODA as well as trade. Hirschman's theory of the 'economic influence effect' therefore can usefully be applied to these aspects of the bilateral relationship as well. The Chinese leadership is receptive to Japanese economic assistance in the form of aid, grants and technological co-operation of any kind. It has long ago relinquished its policy of self-reliance, and China's economic development seems to benefit from Japanese private investment, joint ventures and ODA. Presumably, China will continue to request additional loans, grants, investment and joint ventures from Japan. Other things being equal, it can be reasonably assumed that Japan will respond positively to such Chinese requests. In the past, political stability, commitment to economic modernisation, rapid economic growth and a good credit rating allowed China to raise foreign loans with relative ease. Nevertheless, the test for China as a borrowing nation will come in the mid-1990s when demands for repayment of foreign debts will reach a peak; much will then depend on whether China has been able to build up its export capacity in the meantime.[25]

There can be no doubt that China would find it extremely difficult to find an alternative to Japan as a major donor. At present, there is no other industrialised country that possesses Japan's financial capabilities and is willing to underwrite China's development effort, which in 1987 alone absorbed $1.2 billion in FDI and $497 million in ODA. It is also most unlikely that international organisations such as the IMF, World Bank, or the ADB could fill any such void, given their limited lending capabilities and competing demands for funds. Should the flow of Japanese FDI and ODA to China be cut for any reason, China's adjustment period would be long, costly and very painful – perhaps even more so than in the aftermath of the Sino–Soviet split in the early 1950s. Therefore, the influence effect of its combined trade, aid and investment should give Japan considerable strength in its bilateral relationship with China, even if this is confined only to the threat of interrupting economic relations. Does this suggest that China alone is dependent and vulnerable? The answer is almost certainly no. Japan remains exposed to a variety of Chinese influences, including accusations of harbouring desires for political expansion and economic domination.

POLITICAL DETERMINANTS OF SINO—JAPANESE ECONOMIC RELATIONS

The Chinese analyst Zhang Xiangshan argued in a 1988 article that political considerations determine Sino–Japanese economic relations: he wrote that because politics is the concentrated expression of economics, Japan has the objective qualifications to emerge as a major political power.[26] An appropriate place to begin a discussion of the specific instances in which political factors have played the leading role in the bilateral relationship is with the Sino–Japanese LTTA and the PFT of 1978. The two countries signed the LTTA in February of that year. Only after very difficult political negotiations over the 'anti-hegemony clause' (directed against the Soviet Union) was the PFT signed. There are several important analytical points to be considered here. First, the Japanese clearly recognised the political ramifications of the 'economically based' LTTA; from a Chinese perspective the LTTA was intrinsically linked to the politically motivated PFT. Second, the Japanese felt that they made great political concessions by signing the PFT with its 'anti-hegemony' clause. 'Siding' with China in the PFT did in fact mark a departure from Japan's 'equidistant' foreign policy which had served it so well in the past. Third, those with 'vested interests' in the China trade, in this instance the top echelon of Japan's business leaders, lobbied very hard for Japan's signing of the PFT.[27]

The LTTA and PFT led to an unprecedented expansion of political and economic ties. There was a remarkable increase in the number of top-level state visits, the beginning of student exchange, the inauguration of regular bilateral meetings at the ministerial level to discuss problems of common interest, the dispatching of Japanese advisers and consultants to China, and training of Chinese technical personnel in Japan. The Sino–Japanese Friendship Committee for the Twenty-first Century was founded to bring together the future leaders of the two countries.

While the overall record of Sino–Japanese political relations has been good, both China and Japan occasionally seem to be driven by a combination of nationalistic sentiment, recognition of their interdependence, and their dual status as regional and potential world powers. Since 1978, a discernible pattern has developed in Sino–Japanese political relations: eruption of political and/or economic conflict, a period of heightened mass media campaigns, public apologies and eventual conflict resolution at the highest political level; in many instances, Japan has smoothed things over with additional aid and assistance.

POLITICAL AND ECONOMIC CONFLICT

In 1981, Sino–Japanese economic relations faced the first in a series of severe bilateral political crises and economic challenges. It is argued here that China has used political conflict to gain leverage over Japan in order to maximise economic assistance. Several major issue areas are discussed below.

Political Conflict

A series of largely symbolic issues have been raised by the Chinese in recent years, evoking their concern at the prospect of renewed militarism or aggressive nationalism in Japan. In 1982 and again in 1986, Japanese secondary school history texts were revised, and references to Japan's invasion and ferocious occupation of China in the 1930s were diluted. In 1982, the textbook crisis led to sharply worded political editorials in China, denouncing Japanese militarism and expansionism. China also filed a formal diplomatic complaint, and revoked an invitation for Japan's Minister of Education to visit China. The Japanese government moved quickly to remedy the situation, reaffirmed Japan's responsibilities for past aggression against China and other Asian countries. The controversy was eventually settled when China accepted Japan's offer to replace the revised texts with another revision.

In 1986, there was a similar incident. In this case, Chinese indignation was exacerbated by the controversial Minister of Education, Masayuki Fujio, who stated publicly that those who complain about Japanese history books should first look back to make sure they have not committed such a thing (invasion) in their own history. Prime Minister Nakasone dismissed Fujio after he refused to step down voluntarily. By this time, there was mounting discontent in Japan over China's interference into Japan's domestic affairs. However, the Japanese government again did its best to placate China and apologised for the affair. Again in 1988, China was 'shocked' by a series of statements by National Land Agency Director Seisuke Okuno who claimed that Japan had not intended to invade China in the 1930s. Okuno eventually resigned and China chose not to elevate the incident to a major issue in Sino–Japanese relations.

In 1985, Prime Minister Nakasone together with members of his cabinet made an official visit to the Yasukuni Shrine (Japan's war memorial) which triggered spontaneous student protests in several Chinese cities. The propriety of such visits by members of the Japanese cabinet to the Yasukuni Shrine, where class-A war criminals are enshrined together with millions of Japanese war dead, has been questioned in Japan and abroad. China has indicated that it would not object to official annual commemorations by Japanese cabinet members of Japan's war dead, provided that the physical remains of class-A war criminals were removed from the Yasukuni Shrine. Nakasone did not repeat his controversial visit in an official capacity, nor have his successors.

In 1985, Chinese students also denounced Nakasone's intention to 'settle the account of the Pacific War', which played to Chinese fears of a revival of Japanese militarism. The protests quickly turned to 'Japan's economic invasion'. China's huge trade deficit provided a safe outlet for rising anti-Japanese sentiment. Students, many dissatisfied with conditions on their campuses as well, took to the streets on several occasions in Beijing, Wuhan, Chengdu and Xian to protest Japanese economic aggression and militarism. Moreover, on 20 November 1985, several hundred students in Beijing demonstrated in celebration of the victory by China's women's volley ball team over the Japanese team.

A case of disputed ownership involving a dormitory in Kyoto claimed by both Taiwan and China became an issue of high tension between China and Japan in 1987. When the Osaka High Court decided the *kokaryo* (*guanghua*) case, as it is known, in favour of Taiwan, China was incensed. It mounted a press campaign attacking the judicial decision and charging Japan with pursuing a 'Two Chinas' policy. The Chinese openly asked the Japanese authorities to intervene in the judicial ruling and to annul the court decision. Japan promptly responded that the ruling could not be reversed by the executive branch of the administration. China continued its media campaign, insisting that Japan's 'One China' policy was in jeopardy. Japanese public opinion showed signs of increasing resentment of China's renewed interference into a domestic Japanese problem. In 1988, China indicated that it was prepared to accept the legal argument of the division of powers and would not interfere in Japan's internal affairs.[28]

After 1978, China encouraged Japan to increase its military expenditures and publicly supported the US–Japan Mutual Security Treaty. Only in 1982, when the 'hawkish' Nakasone government was inaugurated, did it begin publicly to air its concern about 'resurgence' of Japanese militarism. China openly questioned the foreign policy goals put forward by the new Prime Minister, who proposed to turn Japan into a 'political power' and to use economic aid as a means to raise Japan's international position. By September 1983, China reversed its position after a large economic aid package had been offered by Japan and the Nakasone government had initiated several plans to tie China economically closer to Japan. This goal seemed to have been accomplished by 1984, when China and Japan enjoyed close political ties. These were largely the result of Nakasone's 'personalised diplomacy' and his links with China's top leadership – especially Hu Yaobang, then General Secretary of China's Communist Party and considered China's second most powerful man until his fall from power in January 1987.

When, at the end of 1986, Nakasone increased the defence budget above the 1 per cent limit, self-imposed in 1976, Chinese leader Deng Xiaoping again criticised Japanese military spending. Japan assured China of the defensive nature of Japan's military capabilities. Nonetheless, Japan's defence policy and military budget have remained controversial issues in Sino–Japanese relations and are frequently evoked in the public dialogue between the two countries.[29]

Economic Conflict

In addition to the open political rows over Japan's history textbooks, the 'Two Chinas policy' and 'resurgent militarism', there is much veiled political conflict over economic issues. These include the trade imbalance, Japanese restrictions on technology transfers to China and Japan's lack of enthusiasm for investing in China. The beginning of economic conflict in Sino–Japanese relations is usually identified with the crisis surrounding the Baoshan Steel Complex near Shanghai in 1981.

In the Baoshan incident, China unilaterally cancelled or suspended Japanese contracts worth about ¥300 billion. The Chinese charged that the plant's location was faulty and they were not satisfied with the project's progress. After difficult high-level political negotiations, Japan agreed to provide for ¥300 billion in commodity loans to complete the project. According to Japanese sources, China was simply unable to pay for the import of equipment needed to finish the project; it had also threatened to turn to alternate sources of supply.[30] This unilateral cancellation severely strained the Sino–Japanese economic relationship, and greatly affected the Japanese business community's perception of China as a business partner.

A second major crisis in bilateral economic relations erupted in 1985 when Japanese exports to China shot up by 40 per cent to reach $12.45 billion and China suffered an unprecedented trade deficit of $6.1 billion. The 1985 import boom was fuelled primarily by large imports of cars and consumer durables. It was also associated with gross abuse by Party organs and cadres, which led to numerous scandals as widespread corruption throughout China was uncovered. The over-heating of the economy eventually forced the Chinese government to restrict or cancel a great many import contracts, most of which were with Japanese exporters.

The Chinese justified their actions by blaming Japan for inflicting a massive trade deficit on China. Japanese exporters felt victimised, not for the first time, by China's failure to honour contracts. Retrospective analysis indicates that China's staggering trade deficits from 1984–6, amounting to more than $12.5 billion and representing more than half of China's total cumulative trade deficit, were primarily the result of the unbalanced structure of Sino–Japanese trade. Although the trend has since been substantially reversed, the issue of 'equality and reciprocity' figures high on the Chinese agenda, as China seeks to balance the trade account by expanding exports to Japan. To that end China, like so many others among Japan's trading partners, repeatedly applied political pressures after 1985. In May 1986, Japan responded by dispatching a MITI-sponsored trade mission to explore Chinese export potential. Moreover, Japan formed the Sino–Japan Trade Expansion Consultative Council to promote imports from China, thus setting up a formal organisational structure to deal with this important issue. These measures combined with other policy measures by the Chinese authorities and the depreciation of China's currency against the rapidly rising yen helped to alleviate the trade imbalance. Since 1986, China's deficit with Japan has diminished sharply. Over the same period China's world-wide exports have been on the rise and have generated a surplus. In this process, numerous Japanese small and medium-sized enterprises engaged in the China trade have gone bankrupt, which has added more strain to Sino–Japanese economic relations.[31]

China has also complained about Japan's lack of enthusiasm for direct investment in China. As shown in Table 7.4 Japanese FDI has in fact grown from a mere $100 million in 1985 to $1.2 billion in 1987. Yet China points out that Japanese investment in China is still only about 1 per cent of Japan's total overseas investments.[32] As noted earlier, most Japanese enterprises find little attractive in China's investment environment and prefer to invest elsewhere. At the highest political level, the Japanese have repeatedly urged China to improve its legal system, business infrastructure and foreign exchange management. In 1987, Japan formed yet another Blue Ribbon panel, under former Foreign Minister Saburo Okita, to devise a plan to attract Japanese investment to China. An important political step toward increasing Japanese investment in China is the Sino–Japanese Investment Protection Agreement, signed by the two countries on the occasion of Prime Minister Noboru Takeshita's visit to China in August 1988.[33]

Japanese technology transfer to China and Chinese technological dependence on Japan are also contentious issues in Sino–Japanese relations.[34] Chinese complaints focus mainly on the efficacy of Japan's technology transfer and its high introduction costs. More specifically, the Chinese claim that Japan is unwilling to transfer advanced technology and attempts to sell dated technology in fear that Japan's technology transfer could result in a back flow of exports from China to Japan – the so-called 'boomerang effect'. The Japanese tend to argue that China seeks 'frontier' technology inappropriate for China's level of development. Many Japanese engineers argue that China cannot absorb more advanced technology. The Chinese are very concerned about the high costs of technology transfer from Japan, and identify 'just' compensation as a major source of contention. The Japanese counter that China has little experience in pricing of technology transfer and is getting used to receiving 'free' Japanese economic assistance, grants and technical co-operation and thus may find it difficult to accept the idea of compensation for technology transfers.

Finally, many Japanese with extensive experience in the China market argue that inadequate conditions in China are impeding effective and efficient technology transfer.

There is a security dimension to the lingering technology transfer issue. Like those of other members of the Western Alliance, Japanese exports to socialist countries are subject to control standards set by the Coordinating Committee for Export Control (COCOM), of which Japan is a member. The notorious 'Toshiba Affair' had a most detrimental spill-over effect on China because Japan revised its COCOM checking procedures in the wake of the incident, which caused serious delays in technology transfers to China. This slowed down the pace of several ongoing projects. Chinese authorities, most irritated by Japan's time-consuming control procedures, urged MITI to speed up the process and charged that Japanese embargoes against China were discriminatory and incompatible with China's status as a friendly nation. Japanese business faced a dilemma: it was concerned about the US retaliation for the Toshiba incident, but at the same time worried that the strict application of COCOM rules would lead to more Western competition in the Chinese market. Under pressure from its business community, and after long consultations with the United States, the Japanese government eventually relaxed some of its restrictions. This had the effect of restoring Japanese technology transfer to China.[35]

Japanese corporate strategies and business policies on technology transfer have been very mixed, making generalisations difficult. The Japanese government has very little influence over individual enterprises in this area and would find it extremely difficult to entice Japanese firms to step up technology transfer to China, for reasons that range from fear of the 'boomerang effect' to general lack of enthusiasm for China as a place to invest. As a result, China continues to complain about the low volume of technology transfer and related Japanese foreign investment.[36]

CRISIS MANAGEMENT THROUGH POLITICAL AND ECONOMIC ACCOMMODATION

A distinctive pattern of crisis management seems to have evolved in Sino–Japanese relations since 1978: a political and/or economic incident of bilateral concern occurs, the incident triggers a 'crisis' in Sino–Japanese relations, the crisis is highlighted by the mass media and may lead to public demonstrations and is followed by protracted diplomatic negotiations. The crisis is eventually resolved at the highest political level, state to state, and leads to increases in Japanese financial aid and assistance to China. The pattern is acknowledged in a recent statement by a Japanese commentator: 'implicit in China's criticisms of Japan are its high expectations for Japanese economic cooperation ... the assumption seems to be that to atone for past aggression, Japan is obligated to assist China's economic development in every way possible ... and Japan has consistently fallen back on increases in economic aid as a way of silencing its Chinese critics'.[37] The following examples illustrate this pattern.

In the Baoshan Steel incident, the major reason for China's unilateral plant cancellation was not, as was first claimed, Japan's alleged faulty plant location, but China's inability to produce and export crude oil as foreseen in the LTTA. The resulting revenue loss and growing budget deficits forced the Chinese authorities to cut back investment plans. The Baoshan incident was widely covered by the Japanese press which also registered the outrage of the Japanese business community over China's breach of commercial contracts. Top level diplomacy, involving Saburo Okita, Deng Xiaoping and Vice Premier Gu Mu brought political and economic accommodation, with China declaring its willingness to honour some of the suspended contracts and provide compensation for others if Japan could provide long-term loans or participate as partner in joint ventures. Japan provided ¥300 billion for commodity loans to resolve the first conflict in Sino–Japanese economic relations.

The ¥470 billion Nakasone loan package of 1984 served well to alleviate Chinese discontent over the first textbook crisis and Chinese fears about 'resurgent' militarism in Japan. It also created goodwill for Nakasone's ODA-driven global political aspirations.

The ¥810 billion Takeshita Aid Package of 1988 was intended to satisfy Chinese requests in the light of several political incidents that had recently strained Sino–Japanese relations, including the second textbook crisis, the Okuno affair and the *kokaryo* case.

These repeated political conflicts in Sino–Japanese relations and ensuing political and economic accommodations affect public attitudes and perceptions in both countries. Chinese student demonstrations and editorials focusing on Japan's war guilt, 'resurgent' militarism and political aspirations are clear manifestations of China's latent nationalism and increasing anti-Japanese sentiment. The Japanese public, which has taken a very active interest in China affairs since 1972 and is polled frequently on its feelings about China, is increasingly apprehensive about developments between the two countries. For example, the 1988 survey by the Prime Minister's Office registered an increasing discontent with Sino–Japanese relations.[38] As propagated in the popular press and communicated on many public and private occasions, there is now a widespread feeling that the Japanese government is too easily giving in to Chinese demands and pressures. Many Japanese feel that China resurrects the spectre of Imperial Japan for political purposes when in need of concessions, funds or aid.

These observations support the argument that political considerations determine economic relations between China and Japan. The repeated, and thus far successful, management of recurring political and economic bilateral crises highlight the recognition of 'mutual interdependence' between the two. The supply effect of trade, investment and aid is maintained because both China and Japan are willing and capable of political accommodation in times of crisis, a fact that must be explained in terms of the benefits that both derive from the supply effect of economic relations. Given the asymmetrical capabilities of China and Japan, political and economic conflict will erupt periodically and focus on specific disputes. However, there is a fair chance that such disputes may be resolved through negotiations, presuming a continued convergence of interests in the stability of Northeast Asia.

CONCLUSION

This study confirms that Hirschman's theory of the influence effect of trade and investment is of great relevance for an analysis of Sino–Japanese economic relations. China and Japan must maintain their bilateral political and economic relationship to obtain goods desired or needed by both. The 'supply effect' provides China and Japan with a more plentiful supply of scarce goods and in turn enhances the national power of both. In situations where China and Japan have been willing to accommodate specific political demands and requests from each other to obtain or maintain the flow of such supplies, the 'influence effect' comes into play, as evinced by the LTTA of 1978, the 1981 Baoshan bailout and the aid packages of 1984 and 1988.

China depends on the stable supply of Japanese capital, capital goods and machinery as well as financial flows and technological co-operation. There can be no doubt that any kind of interruption in the flow of these supplies would greatly harm China's economic development and little doubt that social and political stability would also suffer. In that sense, Sino–Japanese economic relations confirm Hirschman's theoretical propositions of the supply and influence effect of trade. A related analytical question is why Japan structures its foreign economic relations with China as it does. The practice of post-war Japan's foreign relations should provide useful clues here.

Post-war Japan has not attempted to maximise power through the use of force. Instead, Japan has opted for an economically-based foreign policy and operated and supported what the international relations literature has described as 'interdependence' or 'mutual dependence', in which states are influenced by each other, and in which the use of force is recognised as largely ineffective and often unusable.[39] Japan's interdependence at the global level may be a partial explanation of its status and behaviour as a 'reactive' state which muddles through with a mix of strategy, pragmatism, and reluctance.[40]

Interdependence in Sino–Japanese relations does not necessarily imply equality and mutual benefit. On the contrary, given the vast differences in resource endowments – as well as industrial, economic, technological, and scientific capabilities – inequality persists. Sino–Japanese economic relations narrow the gap between the two nations. Japanese economic relations with China have in effect embodied a policy designed to link China to an interdependent Northeast Asian political economy, albeit one dominated by Japan. Current practice stands in stark contrast to that of Imperial Japan, which was exclusively driven by power maximisation through the use of force.

It is instructive here to refer to Hirschman's schematic outline of German trade policies of the 1930s designed to foster 'influence' in Eastern Europe, and a certain analogy with current Sino–Japanese economic relations is difficult to dismiss.[41] Intentionally or unintentionally, Japan has consistently pursued policies which in effect tie China to the Japanese economy. Japan has increased China's gain from trade and exported a wide range of goods. It has also fostered certain patterns of consumption and emphasised relations on a bilateral basis. All these factors make it exceedingly difficult for China to dispense with Japanese trade, investment and ODA. The highly differentiated exports to China, including consumer goods, machinery, plants and equipment, have already made way for the development of Chinese production facilities under joint venture arrangements with Japanese firms. Moreover, Japan has also fostered a bilateral trade base which is characterised by China's dependence on Japanese imports rather than on the Japanese market. For the time being, China appears locked into a dependency relation with Japan, and chances to 'escape' from Japanese economic influence, dependence and domination seem slim indeed. On the other hand, given the reciprocal effects of Sino–Japanese political relations, exerted through the skilful manipulation of political conflict, China has managed to create a degree of mutuality in the relationship.

Is Japan's influence in China the result of deliberate policy or an unintended consequence of Sino–Japanese economic relations? There can be no doubt that a stable and friendly China is in Japan's interest, especially given that Japan is very much concerned about perceived Soviet expansion into the Pacific. Peace and stability on the Korean peninsula also figure high on Japan's agenda. Therefore, starting with the Sino–Soviet rift, and especially since 1972, Japan has 'courted' China in an attempt to construct a more favourable environment in Northeast Asia. Through economic relations and influence Japan seems to have linked or 'tied' China to Japan, and in the process established a degree of political convergence on some of the problems facing the region.

Consolidating China's ties to the Japanese economy carries potential benefits for Japan. If these ties persist, Japan should be able to secure a supply effect from China in the form of markets for its products and a predictable source of supply for its petroleum and raw materials needs. Many of these benefits have yet to be realised. Japan–China trade as a proportion of Japan's foreign trade is still very low.[42] However, China represents enormous possibilities for Japanese trade and investment, given its technological and material needs and the size of its population. As Japan participates in and assists China's economic modernisation, it is laying a basis for the future supply of Japanese capital goods, spare parts, replacement units, consumer goods and joint ventures. On the other hand, China's raw material reserves, petroleum and coal holdings are of strategic interest to Japan's industrial economy. The record shows clearly, however, that China can increase its oil and coal production only with Japanese technological and financial assistance – an additional illustration of convergent interests.

Since 1978, Sino–Japanese interdependence has undergone several tests and challenges which were accommodated because of the political intervention of vested interests in both countries, and the prevailing recognition of mutual dependence of the two economies on the supply effect of trade, investment and aid. Those with vested interests in Sino–Japanese relations seem to view Sino–Japanese economic ties from a long-term perspective and appear little disturbed by the past vicissitudes and perennial conflicts that have afflicted Sino–Japanese bilateral relations. Ostensibly, China's top political leadership and Japan's economic decision-makers remain firm in their commitment to maintain economic exchanges between the two countries because both are painfully aware of the high political stakes and the economic costs that diminished Sino–Japanese economic relations would entail for them both. In short, Hirschman's trade and investment influence effect allows us to view Sino–Japanese economic relations from a dependency perspective, and shows that Japan does indeed exert a disproportionate economic influence effect on China. This is a fact with which China will have to live for the time being. The study confirms that 'mutual dependence' has a propensity to create asymmetrical costs and benefits, which stands in stark contrast to China's professed foreign trade principle of equality and mutual benefit. Thus, in the future, Sino–Japanese political and economic conflict is likely to increase rather than subside. Much will hinge on the skill and flexibility of both parties in accommodating future conflicts.

Notes and References

The research for this chapter was carried out over a one-year period from 1987–8, including two months of interviews in Japan and China. The author is grateful to numerous officials, businessmen, and scholars in both China and Japan, as well as to Miami University for financial support in the form of a Grant to Promote Research and Scholarship and a Summer Research Appointment. This chapter was written prior to the tragic events in China of May–June 1989.

1. See J. E. Spero, *The Politics of International Economic Relations* (New York: St Martin's Press, 1984) pp. 1–25; and Bruno S. Frey, *International Political Economics* (Oxford: Basil Blackwell, 1984) pp. 1–12.
2. The Chinese have complex views about dependency associated with major trading partners. Although they welcome trade, investment and technology transfer, they are often quick to suspect that they are not getting just benefits. As one analyst noted, to sustain the interest and concern of the one on whom they are dependent, they may feel the need to be provocative. See Lucian Pye, *Chinese Negotiating Style* (Santa Monica, CA: The Rand Corporation, 1982) pp. 48–9.
3. See Albert O. Hirschman, *National Power and the Structure of Foreign Trade* (Berkeley, CA: University of California Press, 1945) pp. 3–81.
4. The difficulty for country B, C, D, etc. of dispensing with the trade conducted with A seems to depend on three main factors: (1) the total net gain to B, C, D, etc. of their trade with A; (2) the length and the painfulness of the adjustment process which A may impose upon B, C, D, etc. by interrupting trade; (3) the strength of the vested interests which

A has created by its trade within the economies of B, C, D, etc. Hirschman, *National Power*, p. 18.

5. The number of Japanese companies moving production abroad has been increasing rapidly, but not the overseas production ratio, i.e. the sales of goods manufactured overseas to sales of goods domestically manufactured. See *Japan Economic Journal* (18 June 1988) p. 3.

6. For an excellent discussion of theories of foreign aid see John White, *The Politics of Foreign Aid* (London: The Bodley Head, 1974).

7. On the controversy in Japan as to whether or not ODA is a strategic means, see Juichi Inada, 'Japan's Aid Diplomacy: Increasing Role for Global Security', *Japan Review of International Affairs*, 2(1) (1988) pp. 91–112.

8. See Taifa Yu, 'Progress, Problems, and Prospects of Sino–Japanese Economic Relations: Bi-lateral Trade and Technological Cooperation', *Asian Perspective*, (2) (Fall–Winter 1987) pp. 218–47. Yu's article discusses how bilateral economic relations are inextricably bound up with politically motivated factors. See also Chalmers Johnson, 'The Patterns of Japanese Relations with China, 1952–1982', *Pacific Affairs* (Fall 1986) pp. 402–28. Johnson elaborates on the relative success of Japan's China policy in view of Chinese politico-economic manipulations. Also see Robert Taylor, *The Sino–Japanese Axis* (New York: St Martin's Press, 1985); Chae-Jin Lee, *China and Japan: New Economic Diplomacy* (Stanford, CA: Hoover Institution Press, 1984); Robert E. Bedeski, *The Fragile Entente* (Boulder, CO: Westview Press, 1983); Harry Harding, *China's Foreign Relations in the 1980's* (New Haven, CT: Yale University Press, 1984); Reinhardt Drifte, 'China and Japan', in Harish Kapur, (ed.), *The End of Isolation: China After Mao* (Dordrecht: Martinus Nijhoff Publishers, 1985) pp. 24–46.

9. See Richard Rosecrance, *The Rise of the Trading State: Commerce and Conquest in the Modern World* (New York: Basic Books, 1986).

10. Kent Calder, 'Japanese Foreign Economic Policy Formation: Explaining the Reactive State, *World Politics* (July 1988) pp. 517–41. This basic theme has been discussed in the *Wall Street Journal* and the *New York Times* for most of 1988 and well into 1989.

11. Sino–Japanese relations are officially governed by four principles enunciated by China and accepted by Japan: (1) Peace and Friendship, (2) Reciprocity, (3) Mutual Trust and (4) Long-term Stability.

12. On equality and mutual benefit in China's foreign trade see, C. Liu and L. Wang, *China's Foreign Trade* (Hong Kong: China Translation and Printing Services, 1980) p. 8.

13. For example, Japan's ODA has been closely tied to China's Seventh 5-Year Economic Plan (1986–90) and Sixth 5-Year Economic Plan (1981–5) which emphasised energy development, transportation and communication.

14. This point was made by Dennis T. Yasutomo, *The Manner of Giving: Strategic Aid and Japanese Foreign Policy* (Lexington, MA: Lexington Books, D.C. Heath, 1986) see especially pp. 120 ff.

15. For an excellent and detailed discussion of political and economic motives leading to the 1978 agreement see Bedeski, *The Fragile Entente*.

16. On the average during the 1978–86 period, 23.7 per cent of China's exports went to Japan, while 3.8 per cent of Japan's exports went to China. (Author's own calculation.)

17. See Ryosei Kokubun, 'The Politics of Foreign Economic Policy-Making in China: The Case of Plant Cancellations with Japan, *China Quarterly* (March 1986) pp. 19–44.

18. For an interesting discussion of China's vulnerability and interdependence see Yohng Hai Shi, 'Riben dui hua jingji zhanlue chu tan', *Yatai Jingi* (April 1986) pp. 22–4.

19. For more detail see, *Japan Economic Journal* (4 June 1989) pp. 1 and 6.

20. For a Chinese view on Japanese FDI in Asia see Chuanbi Wang, 'Riben dui Ya-Zhou zhi jie tou zi de ge ju yu qian jian', *Xiandai Guoji Guanxi* 1 (1987) pp. 9–13.

21. Akira Ariyoshi, 'Japanese Capital Flows', *Finance and Development* (September 1988) pp. 28–30.

22. For a widely propagated success story of Sino–Japanese economic cooperation see the China Otsuka case in *Beijing Review* (24–30 October 1988) pp. 20–3.

23. One can reasonably argue that there are functional equivalent vested interests for FDI and ODA.

24. In China we identify as 'vested interests' China's designated Special Economic Zones, elements in the foreign trade and economic relations bureaucracy, and numerous regional, provincial and city authorities who have established very close working relationships and commercial contacts with the Japanese. On the Japanese side we identify powerful interests in heavy industry, commercial/trading, and financial circles, as well as economic peak associations located in both the Kansai and Kanto regions and, of course, the national bureaucracy, especially MoF and MITI.

25. See Zhang Shubao, 'Does China Face a Debt Crisis?', *Beijing Review* (1–7 August 1988) p. 23.

26. See *Beijing Review* (19–24 September 1988) pp. 30–1, 43.

27. For a detailed discussion of the PFT and possible linkages to the LTTA see Bedeski, *The Fragile Entente*.

28. It is of interest to note, that the *kokaryo* verdict, now under appeal, was taken off the list of pending Sino–Japanese issues for the 1988 Sino–Japanese summit. This could mean that the issue has been shelved until the lengthy appeal process is completed. Nonetheless, the *kokaryo* case may very well become a test case for the resilience of Sino–Japanese relations.

29. For more recent Chinese views on Japan's defence, see Liu Jun, 'Military Budget a Blow to Peace', *Beijing Review* (18–24 January 1988) p. 14, and Lui Wenyu, 'Paving the Way to Send Troops Abroad', *Beijing Review* (2–8 May 1988) p. 15.

30. Author's interview with Mitsubishi official, Tokyo (21 July 1988).

31. For a good general and detailed discussion of Sino–Japanese trade from a Japanese perspective see Seizo Matsumura, 'Japan–China Trade in Retrospect – The 15th Anniversary of Normalizing Relations', *JETRO China Newsletter*, 72 (January–February 1988) pp. 19–23.

32. See Chuanbi Wang in *Xiandai Guoji Guanxi*.
33. Following nine rounds of negotiations since 1981, the agreement was welcomed by the Japanese business community, and containing guarantees of reciprocal 'national treatment', the pact is expected to boost Japanese investments and technology transfers to China. Based on *Japan Report* (December 1988) p. 2, and *Japan Times* (25 August 1988) pp. 1 and 3.
34. This discussion is based on extensive interviews by the author in Tokyo and Shanghai which included many Japanese businessmen, foreign trade officials, and Chinese Party officials, bureaucrats, academics, managers and engineers at the plant level.
35. Based on author's interviews in Japan and China (June–July 1988) and *Japan Economic Journal* (7 November 1987) p. 3 and *Beijing Review* (19–25 September 1988) p. 43.
36. For a Chinese view see Dencong Zeng, 'Zhong-ri jingji jishu hezuo de ji ge wenti', *Yatai Jingji* (June 1987) pp. 53–6.
37. See Nakae Yosuke, 'China and Japan: Differences between Friends', *Japan Quarterly*, 35(3) (July–September 1988) pp. 317–21.
38. According to *Seiron Chosa* (Tokyo: Sorifu, April 1988) p. 28. Japanese perceptions of China as a country seem consistently positive. However, the number of respondents that feel the relationship is not good has increased from 14.1 per cent in 1987 to 19.3 per cent, and the proportion who feel the relationship is very good has decreased from 76.1 per cent in 1987 to 70.2 per cent in 1988.
39. See, for example, Robert O. Keohane and Joseph S. Nye, *Power and Interdependence* (Glenview, IL: Scott, Foresman, 1989) 2nd edn, and David A. Baldwin, 'Interdependence and Power: A Conceptual Analysis', *International Organization*, 34(4) (Autumn 1980) pp. 471–506.
40. See Calder, 'Japanese Foreign Economic Policy'.
41. Hirschman, *National Power*, pp. 34–5.
42. Trade with China accounted for the following proportions of Japanese trade in the years indicated:

Year	(%)	Year	(%)
1980	3.4	1984	4.2
1981	3.4	1985	6.1
1982	3.2	1986	4.8
1983	3.6		

8 Japan's Security Policy After US Hegemony

Tsuneo Akaha

The ongoing debate on US hegemonic decline has far-reaching implications for US security relations with Japan. Some argue that both the sagging US economic performance relative to the burgeoning economies of Japan, Western Europe, and even some of the newly industrialising economies, and Washington's deteriorating ability to sustain its political and security commitments overseas, have caused a precipitous and probably irreversible decline in the US global leadership.[1] Others contend that the 'declinist' proposition is more imagined than real or that the decline is only a relative and temporary phenomenon, reversible through effective policy measures.

The declinist thesis has become a popular proposition in Japan and is fuelling Japanese debate on their role in the world after the Pax Americana.[2] This is an ominous sign for the stability of future US–Japanese security relations. This chapter will examine the impact of the post-hegemonic proposition on the security debate in Japan, with an emphasis on the cornerstone of Japan's security policy: its ties with the US.

THE DECLINE OF US HEGEMONY

To be hegemonic, a state must 'found and protect a world order that was universal in conception, i.e., not an order indirectly expressing the interest of one state but an order that most other states could find compatible with their interests given their different levels of power'.[3] Less powerful states learn to live with that order even if they cannot change it. In this system of relations, the hegemon exceeds all others in 'efficiency, scope, salience, and in sense of task'.[4] The important thing is that the supremacy of the dominant global power must not only manifest itself in concrete indicators of power, such as GNP, military spending, financial assets, foreign investment, energy production and consumption, and technological capabilities; it must also be perceived as the most dominant power. Other actors in the international system must respond to it accordingly.

The United States was indeed able to establish and maintain a hegemonic system of international relations in the post-war period. Japan's national interests were largely defined and pursued within the framework of the US-dominated Western, capitalist system. Despite the heated debate and sometimes violent division in Japan over its political and ideological identity in the 1950s and 1960s, the nation's security needs and policies during those decades were largely framed within the confines of the system of US alliances. However, maintaining the position of global dominance is an expensive proposition. It requires the existence of a continuing economic surplus which is used for the purposes of consumption, production and protection. The US economic surplus has largely disappeared in the 1980s and the once unchallenged global superpower is now caught between its many commitments and decreased capabilities.[5]

Recognition of the need to control defence spending to reduce the federal budget deficit has gained strength in the post-Reagan years. Three former Defense Secretaries (Harold Brown, Melvin R. Laird and James Schlesinger), two former Treasury Secretaries (Michael Blumenthal and William Simon), former Secretary of State Cyrus Vance, and former Chairman of the Federal Reserve Paul Volcker agreed that rates of growth in military spending in the early 1980s could no longer be sustained. Brent Scowcroft, the National Security Advisor to President George Bush, acknowledged the need to cut at least $300 billion from the Reagan Administration's military spending plans for 1990–4 as part of a broad effort to reduce the Federal deficit.[6]

One broad consequence of the US budget constraints has been mounting US pressure on its allies to increase their burden of national and collective defence. A 1988 congressional report on burden sharing among US allies concluded that 'the next administration should work hard to shift some of the current US defence burdens to other developed allies in order that the United States can be better prepared in the future to meet its responsibilities with the same or possibly lower level of defense spending'. The same report criticised Europe and Japan for 'not contributing or producing security resources and capabilities commensurate with their economic ability to pay or their vital interest in keeping their homelands free'. The report then declared:

> Alliances as a whole should play a larger role in deciding whether they view US troops and bases in their territories as necessary for defense and, if so, should share or pay for all of the additional costs incurred by the United States in stationing its forces overseas.[7]

The following analysis will examine Japan's perception of US power and security commitments, the actual level of the US military presence and support in Japan and the Asia–Pacific region, and Japan's perception of threats against its national security. These three factors affect Japan's expectations regarding US security commitments to Japan and its own defence requirements. The stronger the Japanese perception of US hegemonic decline, the greater will be Japan's propensity to redefine its security ties with the United States and move from one-sided dependence toward mutual interdependence. As the perception of the gap between threats to Japan's national security and the US security guarantees widens, the more serious will be Japan's effort to increase its resource commitment to burden sharing and/or self-help. Ironically, the more Washington calls for burden sharing and the more positive the Japanese response, the greater will be the loss in Japanese eyes of US credibility as a hegemon and defender of the Western alliance. This will be particularly problematic if Washington openly and publicly links economic issues and security issues.

JAPAN'S PERCEPTIONS OF US POWER

Japan's conception of its role in post-war international security affairs has evolved through several phases. In Phase 1, Japan moved from total disarmament to a self-imposed, internally directed security role during the US Occupation from 1945 to 1952. In Phase 2, through the end of the 1960s, Japan became a compliant follower of the US bilateral and global dominance, bent on domestic economic development. Phase 3 saw a gradually awakening junior partner in bilateral security relations with the United States coming to acknowledge, in the mid-1970s, that the US–Japan relationship was an 'alliance'. During the tenure of Yasuhiro Nakasone as prime minister, in the early to mid-1980s, Japan entered its fourth phase as a member of the 'Western alliance', with an increasingly significant impact on regional politics and security. In the current phase, Japan is a global economic power with an unmistakeable role in the political, economic, and security arenas of international relations.

The relationship between the victorious United States and defeated Japan in the immediate post-war period was determined by the overwhelming economic and military power and strategic interests of the United States. Initially, the US-led occupation forces undertook sweeping reforms to construct a demilitarised and democratic society and a capitalist economy in Japan. Under US protection, Tokyo pursued what has come to be known as the Yoshida Doctrine, named after the first post-war Japanese prime minister. The doctrine held, in summary, that Japan's foremost national goal should be economic rehabilitation accompanied by political-economic co-operation with Washington; that Japan should remain lightly armed and avoid involvement in international political-strategic issues; and that Japan's long-term security depended on a US military presence in the country.[8] These basic tenets of post-war Japanese policy were in accord with the US world-view of the period.[9]

However, the Cold War and US strategic interests in Asia put a halt to the demilitarisation process in occupied Japan. Two weeks after the outbreak of the Korean War in June 1950, the National Police Reserve was established in Japan. The internal security force was enlarged and reorganised into the Ground, Maritime and Air Self-Defense Forces in July 1954. At the same time, the United States provided millions of dollars in aid to the weak Japanese economy and also slowed down the break-up of the nation's powerful business concerns. Furthermore, Washington provided support to the conservative, pro-American political forces in Japan, which were united in 1955 under the banner of the Liberal Democratic Party (LDP).

Japan's re-entry into the international political system during this period was also largely determined by US strategic interests in Asia. Politically, Japan's sovereignty was restored with the 1952 San Francisco Peace Treaty. The Soviet Union and its allies did not sign the treaty, thus preventing Japan from settling the status of the Soviet-occupied territories to the northeast of Japan (the 'Northern Territories'). The United States continued to administer the Bonin Islands until 1965 and the remainder of the Ryukyu Islands, including Okinawa, until 1972. By the time Okinawa was returned, it housed one of the largest US forward bases in the world.

The 1952 Security Treaty between Washington and Tokyo further placed Japan in the US strategic orbit. The treaty provided for the US bases and facilities and the stationing of American forces in Japan. Reflecting the overwhelming US dominance in military power, the treaty obligated the United States to defend Japan against aggression but did not require a reciprocal commitment. In 1960, over the vehement and violent objection from the opposition forces in Japan, a new bilateral treaty, the Treaty of Mutual Cooperation and Security, was signed. The treaty obligated both parties to take action to assist each other in case of armed attack on territories under Japanese administration, although it was understood that Japan would not come to the defence of the United States because the Japanese Constitution prohibited dispatch of armed forces abroad. Notes accompanying the treaty required prior consultation between the parties before Washington undertook major changes in its troop deployment or equipment stockpiling in Japan. The treaty was also made subject to a one-year notice of revocation after 1970. These changes reflected the gradual increase in Japan's assertion of sovereignty, and US accommodation to it.

Japan's relations with its Asian neighbours were also largely determined by the US policy of keeping Japan in its strategic orbit and bringing Japan into the capitalist economic system. One example was the delay in the normalisation of diplomatic relations between Tokyo and Beijing until 1972. Likewise, the signing of a peace and friendship treaty waited until 1978.

In the 1950s and 1960s, Japan was gradually allowed to become a full-fledged member of the US-led international capitalist economic system. Japan joined the United Nations, the IMF, the World Bank, the Economic Commission for Asia and the Far East (ECAFE), GATT, the International Atomic Energy Agency, the OECD, and the Asian Development Bank (ADB). In the 1960s, Japan achieved the highest levels of domestic economic growth in the post-war world. Economic growth provided the wherewithal for the consolidation of political support for the ruling Liberal Democratic Party. As a result, Japan–US security relations remained relatively stable. By the end of the 1960s, Japan had become the dominant regional economic power. At the same time, a majority of the Japanese had come to accept the bilateral security treaty and the Self-Defense Forces as part of the status quo.

Japan's 'economic miracle' in the 1960s shielded the country against some major external disturbances that were to take place toward the end of the 1960s and in the early 1970s. Japan survived several external shocks: the Nixon Doctrine (announced at Guam in 1969), the 1971 US–Chinese rapprochement, the 1971 'New Economic Policy' of the US, the 1973–4 oil crisis, and the US withdrawal from the Vietnam War. Following these major disturbances, Japan emerged a confident junior partner in the bilateral relationship.

At the same time, Japan began to question Washington's political leadership. On the one hand, improved US–Chinese relations since the 1970s have been welcomed in Japan as an important factor contributing to the reduction of tension in East Asia in general and on the

Korean Peninsula in particular. On the other hand, the manner in which Washington pursued its policy of reconciliation with Beijing in the early 1970s generated much resentment in Japan. As is well known, the Nixon Administration decision to effect a rapprochement with the People's Republic of China came as a surprise – even as a shock – to Tokyo. Despite the pro-Beijing sentiments that had grown in Japan over the years and significant trade and other commercial relations that had developed between Japan and the People's Republic of China in the 1960s, the official policy of Japan was to follow the US lead in blocking Beijing's bid to replace Taipei in the United Nations and in not giving diplomatic recognition to Beijing. Many in Japan simply felt betrayed by Washington's 1972 decision.

A few years later, in 1978, President Carter's reversal of his decision to withdraw US ground troops from Korea in 1978 also weakened the credibility of US security commitments in the region. Washington's inability to extract itself from the Iranian hostage crisis the next year further reduced Washington's credibility as a global political leader. After the Soviet invasion of Afghanistan in 1979, Tokyo began to realise that Washington needed its allies' support to counter the growth of Soviet military power and political ambitions under Brezhnev. It was in these circumstances that Tokyo came to acknowledge its relationship with Washington as an 'alliance'.

Although President Reagan's major defence build-up through the mid-1980s seemed temporarily to halt the erosion of US military capabilities, Japanese leaders remained uncertain about the future of nuclear deterrence and the US–Soviet military balance. Moreover, the continuing pressure for greater defence burden sharing cast doubt on the will or ability of the US to underwrite its security commitments to Japan. It was under these circumstances that Yasuhiro Nakasone emerged as Japan's prime minister in 1982. A new type of Japanese leader, Nakasone was willing to speak in unequivocal terms about Japan's importance as a member of the 'Western alliance' and about Japan and the United States sharing a 'common destiny'. During his premiership, which lasted until Autumn 1987, Nakasone undertook major efforts to increase Japan's defence capabilities and to intensify its security co-operation with the United States.

This took place against the background of steeply rising US federal budget deficits, brought on by President Reagan's combined policies of tax reduction and military build-up: by 1986, the budget deficit had reached $221.2 billion, and the outstanding federal debt was $2.1 trillion.[10] As a result, the United States became heavily dependent on

Japanese capital to finance its trade and current account deficits – and remains so although the deficits have come down somewhat. The deterioration of US industrial competitiveness, reflected in its huge current account deficits, seemed a mirror image of Japan's growing strength in trade and finance.

The visible signs of US decline in financial power and trade have caused an increasing number of Japanese to question the US leadership in the Western system of alliances. The most articulate expression of Japanese apprehensions about the decline of US power is found in Japan's debate on comprehensive security in the early 1980s. The 1980 report by a task force appointed by the late Premier Masayoshi Ohira declared:

> In considering Japan's security, the most fundamental change that took place in the international situation in the 1970s is that the clear US superiority, in both military and economic dimensions, came to an end.[11]

Militarily, the report said, since the mid-1960s the United States had refrained from an arms build-up while the Soviet Union continued its arms expansion and as a result, the military balance changed globally and regionally. As a consequence, the report asserted, 'US military power can no longer provide the nearly sufficient security it once did to its friends and allies' and 'it has become necessary for US friends and allies to strengthen their self-help efforts particularly in the area of conventional forces, and the credibility of the US "nuclear umbrella" can no longer be maintained without their co-operation with the United States'. The report concluded that the 'Pax Americana is over', and the age of 'peace through burden-sharing' had begun.[12] Another report, prepared in 1985 by a private advisory group to Prime Minister Nakasone, presented a virtually identical view of the change in US power and its consequences for international peace and security.[13]

'Relative decline in US power' has more recently become part of the official vocabulary of the Japanese government. The 1988 diplomatic Blue Book of the Foreign Ministry declared that US power had suffered a relative decline in recent decades and stated:

> In today's international society characterized by increased interdependence, the United States and the Soviet Union still maintain great influence supported by their gigantic military power, but the relative weight of Japan, Western Europe, and China is also steadily

increasing. In the economic field, there has been a decline in the relative position of the United States, which has possessed overwhelming economic power and contributed to the formation and maintenance of international order since the end of the Second World War, and the free trade regime and the international currency regime based on the dollar as the key currency is facing a new dimension.

... To maintain a smooth operation of the present international order and to ensure the world peace and prosperity requires that each major free, democratic nation meet its commensurate international responsibility and role, and it is increasingly important that mutual dialogue and policy cooperation be strengthened.[14]

Japanese scholars, almost without exception, share the same assessment of US decline.[15] They generally echo the theme developed by Paul Kennedy in *The Rise and Fall of the Great Powers* (1987) about excessive military commitments and their consequences for hegemonic decline.[16] In fact, Kennedy's work itself has become a popular topic of discussion, and meets with widespread approval.[17]

By the time Noboru Takeshita succeeded Nakasone as Japanese prime minister, the Japanese had accepted a global, activist role for their nation. No longer were the Japanese satisfied with the traditional bilateral, US–Japanese framework in which to define their international role. Nor were they content with passively following US leadership. Takeshita's foreign policy was based on four basic principles: ensuring continuity in Japan's diplomacy, developing Japan's foreign policies on its own will and initiative, placing the highest priority on developing the Japanese–US relationship, and making Japan a 'nation contributing more to the world'.[18] During Takeshita's premiership, Tokyo substantially increased its multilateral initiatives, particularly in the area of foreign economic assistance.

In pursuit of the fourth goal, Takeshita announced in 1988 what he called an 'International Cooperation Initiative'.[19] The Initiative was based on three pillars: expansion of ODA, promotion of international cultural exchange, and strengthening of Japan's contribution to international peace.[20]

Expansion of Japan's ODA was adopted as the goal of its fourth medium-term (1988–92) ODA programme. The government planned to disburse ODA funds of over ¥50 billion during the five-year period – more than double the sum disbursed in the preceding five years – making Japan the largest ODA provider in the world. The aid programme also called for an expansion of the grant components of aid and debt relief measures, the strengthening of co-operation with international governmental organisations and nongovernmental organisations, the improvement of yen-denominated loans and the expansion of totally untied aid.[21]

The cultural component of the Initiative called for an expansion of the Japan Foundation; the establishment of a new trust fund in the United Nations Education, Scientific, and Cultural Organisation (UNESCO) for the preservation of the world's cultural heritage and relics; an expansion of the Japan Exchange and Teaching (JET) Program; the establishment of a Japan–ASEAN Cultural Exchange Centre and the implementation of special exchange projects between Japan and Europe.

Japan's contribution to international peace was to be enhanced by an active diplomatic role in resolving regional disputes, such as those in Afghanistan and the Gulf. Japan planned to provide funding and personnel for UN peacekeeping activities. Tokyo would also increase its assistance to refugee programmes and reconstruction programmes for post-conflict situations. To accomplish these goals, Tokyo pledged $259 million, which represented an increase of 180 per cent. The budget included $134 million in assistance for the voluntary repatriation of Afghan refugees and contributions to the Palestine support project under the UN Development Programme and to the cost of maintaining the Multinational Force and Observers (MFO) on the Sinai Peninsula. Furthermore, Tokyo assigned government officials to the UN Good Offices Mission in Afghanistan and Pakistan (UNGOMAP) and the UN Iran–Iraq Military Observer Group (UNIIMOG). Japan studied the assignment of personnel to the UN Transition Assistance Group (UNTAG) in Namibia and to assist in the settlement of the Kampuchean conflict.[22]

The non-military and largely financial contribution that Tokyo is committed to providing overseas complements Japan's continuing adherence to a defence policy whose mission is 'strictly defensive'. In this connection, Tokyo has carefully balanced the rate of increase in its ODA spending and defence spending over the last decade. This pattern is likely to continue.

US MILITARY PRESENCE AND SECURITY COMMITMENTS IN THE ASIA–PACIFIC REGION

The 1969 Nixon Doctrine marked the single most important turning point in the post-war US military policy toward the Asia–Pacific region. As US troop deployments were reduced globally (by 1.2 million between 1969 and 1972) and in the Asia–Pacific region (by 600,000), the United States increased its security assistance to its friends and allies in the Asia–Pacific region. There was a conscious effort in Washington to increase various forms of security assistance to make troop reductions possible and to compensate for reduced troop presence in the region.[23] More recently, however, US security assistance to Asian–Pacific countries has generally been reduced.

Although direct US military support has increased globally in recent years, the amount of various types of military support for Asia–Pacific nations has either declined markedly or remained steady – with the visible exception of US economic support for the Philippines, which has substantially increased. In the aftermath of Vietnam, Washington consistently assigned lower priorities to the Asia–Pacific region.[24] US foreign policy makers today realise that declining US foreign aid levels in the Asia–Pacific region have added to the growing fear that budgetary pressures will compel the United States to pull back from involvement in the region's affairs.[25]

In contrast to the declining US military presence and assistance in the Asia–Pacific region, the United States has stepped up its military sales to Asian–Pacific nations since the 1970s. Between 1977 and 1981, the US transferred $34 billion in arms globally, of which arms transfers to Asian–Pacific countries amounted to $6.7 billion. For the 1982–6 period, these figures rose to $51.4 billion and $11.9 billion respectively.[26] US arms sales have various objectives: to supplement its security assistance programme, assist its friends and allies in improving their defence capabilities, maintain US military ties with regional powers, reduce the economic burden of security commitments in the region, and promote commercial arms export.

PERCEPTIONS OF SECURITY THREATS TO JAPAN

The reduction of the US military presence in the Asia–Pacific region in the 1970s and of security assistance in the 1980s would not have concerned the Japanese security and foreign policy makers as much as it did if during the same period the Soviet Union had not attempted to increase its military presence in the region through a major force build-up. Had Moscow not taken the military-orientated foreign policy in the region during the period of US retrenchment, the reduction of tension following the reduced US presence would indeed have been an ideal scenario for the Japanese, who remained quite reluctant to increase their defence spending.

This was not to be, however. Japan in the first half of the 1980s found itself in a considerably less friendly security environment, with the credibility of its protector across the Pacific significantly eroded and with its perennial adversary to the north bent on altering the 'correlation of forces' in its favour.

A major Soviet military build-up in the Asia–Pacific region began in the mid-1970s. By 1982 the Soviets had deployed in the region almost one-third of their strategic missiles, including ICBMs and SLBMs; almost one-quarter of total naval strength, assigned to the largest of their naval fleets, the Pacific Fleet; and about 360,000 ground troops in 39 divisions, including a division stationed on Japanese-claimed 'Northern Territories', just off the eastern coast of Hokkaido.[27]

Recognising the 'drastic' US force reduction in the Western Pacific region following the end of the Vietnam War, defence policy makers in Tokyo wrote in 1982:

> In such a context of international relations, it is considered that a potential threat to this nation's [Japan's] security has considerably increased because of the constant Soviet military buildup in the Far East in terms of both quality and quantity.[28]

General Secretary Mikhail Gorbachev's diplomatic initiatives, including a call for naval arms control, withdrawal of US and Soviet bases in the Philippines and in Vietnam respectively, confidence building measures in the Pacific and establishment of a collective Asian security system, have been met largely with scepticism in Tokyo. Rather than improving bilateral relations, Japan's response has shown, in Chalmers Johnson's words, a 'pattern of confused assessments and conflicting priorities'.[29] The Toshiba fiasco (in which a subsidiary of that Japanese company sold sensitive equipment to the Soviet Union, provoking US wrath), Japan's decision to participate in SDI research and development, and above all Tokyo's insistence that the return of all Soviet occupied islands to Japan is a prerequisite for a peace treaty, all stand in the way of a significant improvement in the bilateral relations. The reluctance on the part of Japanese business concerns to participate in Soviet-initiated developmental projects in the Soviet Far East as aggressively as they had in the 1960s–1970s, dampens the otherwise opportune moment for improved relations.[30] Barring a breakthrough on the territorial issue, substantially improved Japanese–Soviet relations are unlikely.[31]

If Japan's geographical proximity to the Soviet Union is one of the fundamental strategic problems that Tokyo must face, another permanent strategic problem that haunts it is the nation's continuing dependence on foreign sources of raw materials and on access to export markets abroad. The 1973–4 oil crisis heightened Japanese fear of major disruptions of their economic ties to the rest of the world and forced them to seek ways to reduce their vulnerability.[32] Japan's search for 'economic security' has included concerted and continuing efforts to reduce tensions in regions vital to its largely economic interests, namely, the Middle East and Southeast Asia. However, such efforts are necessarily long-term and their effects are uncertain.

BROADENING US–JAPAN SECURITY CO-OPERATION AND BURDEN SHARING

Following the defeat in the Second World War, a broad national consensus emerged in Japan on the nation's immediate goals and priorities. The consensus, though it was not without significant opposition, maintained that under US security protection and political leadership, Japan should concentrate first on the economic recovery from the immediate effects of the Second World War and second on the establishment of a democratic political system. Under these circumstances, the mainstream view asserted that Japan should forego foreign security commitments or independent political obligations overseas. This was the general thrust of Tokyo's foreign policy throughout the 1950s and 1960s.

By the early 1970s, when domestic opposition had lost much of its significance for the nation's security policy, the dominant mainstream view held that Japan's security above all else depended on its close political, economic, and security ties with the United States, that Japan's military capabilities should be strictly defensive within the framework of Article 9 of its Constitution, and that the nation should eschew development or possession of offensive weapons including nuclear weapons.

Partly because of these factors, and partly in reluctant response to Washington's calls for burden sharing, bilateral security consultation has grown closer over the years. Since 1978, joint defence studies and planning have been instituted and today are an important part of security co-operation between Washington and Tokyo. Topics of joint studies have included joint defence planning, sea-lane defence, the Japan–US defence co-ordination centre, the exchange of intelligence, common operational preparation, inter-operability, and Japanese facilities assistance to the US Forces in the case of a situation in the Far East outside Japan which will have an important influence on the security of Japan.[33] Joint military training between Japanese and US forces has also become more frequent and extensive over the years.[34]

Since 1979, Japan has also stepped up its support of the US forces in Japan. In accordance with the agreements between the Japanese and US Governments under the terms of the Status of Forces Agreement, Japan is obligated to furnish facilities and areas without any expenses to the US Forces, Japan (USFJ).[35] In FY 1988, Tokyo budgeted something in excess of 300 billion yen for such things as the rental of and improvements to USFJ living quarters and other facilities, wages and other costs of Japanese employees of USFJ and the expenses of maintaining the environment surrounding US military facilities.

Throughout the 1970s, discussion of defence burden sharing between Washington and Tokyo was confined to the issue of Japanese defence spending. The United States generally complained that Japan was not spending enough to take up an appropriate share of the burden of national defence. In response to the persistent US calls for increased defence spending, Tokyo gradually increased its defence spending and in 1984 decided to abolish its eight-year-old policy of keeping its defence budget below 1 per cent of the nation's GNP. As a result, Japan's defence spending slightly exceeded 1 per cent of GNP in FY 1988 (see Table 8.1).

As Washington came to recognise and appreciate Tokyo's willingness to increase its spending at rates far exceeding most other spending items, the discussion on burden sharing turned increasingly to a possible division of missions and roles between the two countries for the defence of Japan and of the US strategic interests in the Western Pacific. For example, the congressional defence sharing panel mentioned earlier stated that the Japanese government should 'at a minimum, accelerate its ability to perform the self-defence, "1000-mile" and "closing of the straits" missions and prepare to carry out these missions if needed without direct U.S. assistance'.[36]

As Tokyo gradually realised the limits of its ability to translate its economic prowess into political influence in its effort to reduce its economic vulnerability in the 1970s, its interest in peacetime defence

Table 8.1   Japan's defence spending, FY 1955–1988

Year	Defence spending (billion yen)	Ratio to GNP (%)
1955	134.9	1.78
1960	156.9	1.23
1966	301.4	1.07
1970	569.5	0.79
1975	1327.3	0.84
1980	2230.2	0.90
1981	2400.0	0.91
1982	2586.1	0.93
1983	2754.2	0.98
1984	2943.5	0.99
1985	3137.1	0.99
1986	3343.5	0.99
1987	3517.4	1.00
1988	3700.3	1.01

Source: Japan: An International Comparison, 1987 and 1989 (Tokyo: Keizai Koho Center, 1988 and 1989) p. 86 and p. 85 respectively.

measures to protect its maritime trade routes increased. In part to reduce a feared major disruption of shipping to and from its ports and in part in response to US prodding for greater defence burden sharing, Prime Minister Zenko Suzuki decided in 1981 that Japan should undertake to improve its maritime defence capabilities to protect its sea lines of communication to a distance of 1,000 nautical miles from its shores. At about the same time, defence policy makers in Tokyo began talking about the possibility of closing Japan's strategic straits (Soya, Tsugaru, and Tsushima) against the Soviet Union in times of crisis. Given Japan's substantially strengthened maritime defence capabilities and gradually improving air defence capabilities, it might be tactically possible to carry out such a mission. However, whether such a move would be in Japan's security interests is still debated.

Critics of Japan's expanded maritime defence argue that a straits blockade against the Soviet Union would surely invite a massive Soviet attack. Others counter the criticism by pointing out that Japan would be unlikely to resort to such an extreme military move unless and until US–Soviet confrontation had escalated to such a level that Japan's direct support for US forward-deployed forces in the Western Pacific became necessary. Critics assert that in such an eventuality, when a direct and massive exchange of US and Soviet forces (including strategic forces) would most likely have taken place, Japan's straits blockage would have little military meaning. Yet others, including defence officials, maintain that Japan should be prepared to meet any contingency, including closure of the straits, if only to improve the deterrence credibility of US–Japan security planning. Without a national consensus, Japan's ability to deliver on its pledge remains uncertain.

The search for economic security that had led to the problematic consideration of sea lane and straits defence also generated increasing enthusiasm about the concept of 'comprehensive security' as a general direction for Japan's security policy. The concept, first introduced toward the end of the 1970s, looks at Japan's security needs in a multi-dimensional and multi-level framework. Potential threats to Japan's security are thought to include not only military developments (such as the Soviet force build-up) but also political events (such as the Iran–Iraq conflict or the Arab–Israeli conflict) and economic developments (for example, an economic crisis in Southeast Asian countries).[37] Although 'comprehensive security' remains an ambiguous concept, its appeal among the Japanese is considerable.

Parallel to the development of the concept of comprehensive security was a growing recognition that Japan's security and prosperity contributed to regional and international peace and security and vice versa. It was through the development of this awareness and through the discussion of the comprehensive approach to national and international security during the early 1980s that a national consensus emerged on the need to expand Japan's economic assistance as part of Japan's broadly conceived security policy. The consensus held that Japan's economic assistance, including what one Western observer has called 'strategic aid',[38] should be considered a part of its contribution to international peace and security.

Washington has recently accepted the idea of considering Japan's ODA as part of its defence burden. For example, the congressional burden sharing panel referred to earlier called upon Japan to 'increase its official development assistance budget substantially' and to 'target more untied aid to countries with both economic need and strategic importance to Japan and the United States [i.e. Turkey and the Philippines]'.[39]

Although Tokyo denies that Washington wants Japan to play a military role as part of its defence burden,[40] Japan's expanded ODA is clearly conceived of as the nation's contribution to regional and international security. An example of US–Japan co-operation on economic assistance for a strategic US ally is the Multilateral Assistance Initiative (MAI) for the Philippines. President Bush and Prime Minister Takeshita have twice expressed their joint support for a successful multilateral programme, which is designed to support economic reforms and provide needed infrastructure to enhance the investment climate in the Philippines. The US Administration is seeking $200 million for FY 1990 as the first US contribution.[41] Japan has recently pledged a $1 billion contribution in FY 1990, with a grant component of about 15 per cent.[42] The World Bank and the IMF have pledged their co-operation for the development and administration of the programme.

Yet another development that has moved Japan and the United States toward more equal sharing of the defence burden is in the area of arms technology transfer.[43] As a former US science official at the US Embassy in Tokyo put it, '[T]he bilateral technological relationship between Japan and the U.S. is the most extensive and intensive existing between any two countries'.[44]

Weapons transfer between the two countries has been based on the 1954 Mutual Defense Assistance (MDA) Agreement. The agreement provided the basis for US grant-aid (terminated in 1964), Foreign Military Sales (FMS), and co-production (since the mid-1950s) of US-developed weapon systems under licensing arrangements. In recent years Japan has produced the P-3C maritime patrol aircraft, F-15 fighter aircraft, and the Patriot surface-to-air guided missile.

Until recently, weapons and weapons technology transfer had been totally one-sided, from the United States to Japan. This was in line with Tokyo's 1967 policy prohibiting arms export. In response to US prodding, Prime Minister Nakasone decided in January 1983 to exempt the transfer of dual-purpose technologies to the United States from the 1967 policy. Accordingly, an Exchange of Notes was concluded in November 1983, followed by the conclusion in November 1983 of Detailed Arrangements concerning the transfer of such technologies. By 1988 Tokyo had approved the transfer to the United States of SAM-related technology, technology related to the construction of naval vessels, and technology related to the modification of US naval vessels.

In March 1985, Washington asked Tokyo to participate in the Strategic Defense Initiative (SDI).[45] Tokyo announced in September 1986 that it would co-operate with Washington and in July 1987, Tokyo and Washington concluded an 'Agreement on Japan's Participation in the SDI Research', establishing a framework for future co-operation.

The defence industry in Japan is small but is improving fast in both quality and sophistication. Defence production represents only 0.5 per cent of Japan's total industrial output. For even the top defence contractors, defence sales constitute an insignificant share of their total sales. In certain sectors, however, defence contracts are important. In the aerospace industry, for example, 83.8 per cent of the value of Japanese aircraft production in 1985 went to the Self-Defense Forces (SDF). The top ten defence contractors account for about 80 per cent of the total SDF outlays. Procurement of advanced electronics for defence intelligence and surveillance is becoming an attractive outlet for private companies with potential in this fast advancing field.

The Japanese Defense Agency has emphasised domestic procurement, spending more than 80 per cent of its fund domestically each year. Profit and market motivations favour domestic production, as does the private sector's desire to diversify technology and other defence-related products.

Important in this connection is the October 1987 US–Japan agreement concerning a \$1.2 billion project to produce a new generation of fighter support aircraft (dubbed FSX for 'fighter support experimental') to replace the outdated F-1s and F-4s. After long and difficult negotiations over the selection of the model aircraft, Tokyo decided in October 1987 to opt for co-production, using the F-16 design developed by General Dynamics as the basis for the new plane's design; but to include a miniaturised active phased-array radar designed by Mitsubishi Electric and to build the wings from a single piece of composite material, developed in Japan, that is radar-absorbent to give the plane stealth characteristics. Six prototypes of the plane are scheduled to be built by 1993.

The Japanese government was both embarrassed and disturbed when in early February 1989 opposition in the US Congress and in the Bush Administration prompted the National Security Council to order an interagency review of the agreement. Tokyo saw the co-production agreement as a political compromise since domestic arms manufacturers had preferred to build the new plane on their own. Tokyo had also quickly authorised \$80 million for initial design work on the aircraft. Japanese Defense Agency Director-General Kichiro Tazawa publicly stated: 'It is unfair that the U.S. is raising objections to the project just because its administration has changed. I expect the U.S. to act as a superpower'.[46]

President Bush and the Departments of Defense and State were in favour of proceeding with the project.[47] Critics of the project in the United States warned that the deal was a technological 'give-away'.[48]

The Commerce Department was concerned, for example, that at a time of huge US trade deficits, the project would help Japan's nascent aircraft industry eventually compete against US aircraft manufacturers. Faced with concerted opposition, Bush decided to seek 'clarifications' from Japan that US participation in the production of the FSX would represent a minimum of 40 per cent, that the United States could prevent the transfer to Japan of such defence technology as would strengthen Japanese aircraft and space industries to the detriment of US industries, and that US participants would have full access to any and all Japanese technology used in the project.[49] Tokyo eventually acquiesced and agreed in April that the US side would perform 40 per cent of the production work and that Japanese technology used in the project would be shared with the United States.[50]

TROUBLING DEFENCE–TRADE LINKAGES

Of the FSX episode, retired Japanese Vice Admiral Naotoshi Sakonjo, now a defence analyst in Tokyo, told reporters, 'The U.S. government has taken the trade issue into the defense cooperation issue'.[51] As Japan continues to emphasise the economic and commercial dimensions of bilateral technology transfer, the United States has a growing concern about the national security implications of Japan's aggressive drive for technological development and acquisition. A number of recent developments are quite telling in this regard.

In 1985, a Japanese ball-bearing producer, Minebea, sought New Hampshire Ball Bearings Inc., but the Pentagon blocked the transfer of defence-related products out of New Hampshire. Also in the mid-1980s, the late Commerce Secretary Malcolm Baldrige successfully objected to the takeover of the Fairchild Semiconductor Corporation by Fujitsu of Japan. In the most recent development involving attempted Japanese takeover of a US firm, the Bush Administration decided in April 1989 to block temporarily a proposed Japanese purchase of General Ceramics Inc., a New Jersey company that is involved in a nuclear weapons contract using critical technology.[52] The 1988 Omnibus Trade and Competitiveness Act gives the White House authority to seek court injunctions against mergers or takeovers that imperil national security by transferring vital technology overseas.

How did the defence–trade linkage develop in US–Japanese relations? The question of issue linkage first surfaced as the US trade deficit with Japan grew to historically unprecedented levels in the first half of the 1980s and as the perception deepened in the United States that its products were losing out to their Japanese competition not only in international markets but in the United States as well. As the US pressure on Japan to open its domestic market to US and other foreign products and Japan's reluctant agreement to implement market liber-alisation measures did not produce immediate results, frustrations built up among US Congressmen and industrialists. At the same time, Japan responded only grudgingly to US pressure to increase its defence spending.

Some analysts in the United States openly advocated linkage. Galenson and Galenson, for example, noted that the 'importance of the American market to Japan gives the United States considerable lever-age in defence discussions with Japan, and it might not be unreasonable to require a *quid pro quo* from Japan in return for the maintenance of relatively free trade between the two countries'.[53] Most analysts in Japan warned that if Washington should link the defence and trade issues, generally favourable attitudes of the Japanese people toward the United States would turn sour.[54] By the mid-1980s, the possible linkage had become a highly visible concern in Tokyo and in Washington. Caspar Weinberger said in 1986, for example:

I have been objecting to linking them [defence and trade issues] together up until now because these two are entirely separate problems ... This year is an election year, and Congress may try to link the trade and defense problems together. The Government, however, will oppose such moves.[55]

In 1987, Japanese Prime Minister Nakasone declared that the 'widening of our [US–Japanese] bilateral trade imbalance has escalated into a serious problem which could threaten the very foundations of our otherwise excellent relations'[56] – a sentiment that was later echoed by President Reagan.[57] The concern about defence–trade issue linkage is most likely to intensify during the Bush Administration because, as it is generally acknowledged, Bush is substantially more conciliatory to the Congress than was Reagan and because the bilateral trade gap is likely to continue at politically unacceptable levels.

CONCLUSION

Tokyo's 1984 decision to eliminate the defence spending ceiling of 1 per cent of GNP was domestically controversial. It is unrealistic to expect the defence budget to increase much faster than it has (about 5 per cent annually). There are several constraints on Japanese defence spending. First, the nation's economy is expected to grow at only modest, albeit respectable rates, significantly lower than in the 1960s and 1970s. Second, as was demonstrated by the maritime defence debate, there is no consensus as to the exact nature of the division between Japan and the US of defence missions in the Western Pacific. Third, sustained increases in defence allocation can at best be achieved when seen as balanced by similar or faster increases in the nation's resource commitment to foreign economic co-operation.

A fourth constraint emerges from the fact that the Japanese government's revenues are not expected to grow sufficiently to allow substantially expanded defence spending, as signalled by the unprecedented political crisis that befell the ruling Liberal Democratic Party in 1989. Prime Minister Takeshita was forced to resign in May 1989 in part due to the unpopular 3 per cent consumption tax that the Takeshita government introduced and in part because of Takeshita's involvement in an influence-buying scandal involving the Recruit Company. His successor, Sosuke Uno, was also forced to resign because of the disastrous results of the upper house election in July, in which the Liberal Democrats lost their majority in the 252-seat House of Councillors.[58] Following the elections, the Socialist party has introduced legislation in the Upper House to rescind the tax – a move which would put a revenue squeeze on the government.

Across the Pacific, US demands for Japan to take a greater defence burden are likely to grow. The federal budget deficit, threatened cuts in domestic programmes, and increasing dependence on foreign sources of investment capital cause this author to doubt seriously Washington's ability to maintain its extensive security commitments in the Asia–Pacific region. As an American observer has pointed out,

> public support for the arms buildup has eroded, and the financial capacity of the United States to maintain the arms buildup is fast running out. The choices must now be faced of raising taxes, running a large budget deficit or substantially cutting social programs. None of these choices commands much support.[59]

In the Asia–Pacific region, this means that the United States must increasingly turn to Japan and other allies to share the burden of regional security, particularly in Southeast Asia, where the continuing Kampuchean conflict and political instability in the Philippines pose a serious challenge to the development of a Western-orientated regional political economy. However, Tokyo faces formidable constraints, domestically and externally, on its regional security role.

What are the prospects for an expanded regional security role for Japan? Some ongoing developments point in the direction of reduced tensions in the Asia–Pacific region, thus diminishing the need for a regional security role to match Japan's economic role. The dynamic economic growth throughout the region and the growing confidence among the region's political leaders augur well for the construction of a stable post-hegemonic order in the Asia–Pacific region. Reduction in superpower tensions cannot but facilitate this process. In addition, there is a growing realisation in the region that economic security is an essential but often neglected part of national security and its pursuit through military means is often counterproductive. On the other hand, many of the rivalries and conflicts in the region (such as those in North–South Korea, China–Vietnam, Vietnam–ASEAN, Indonesia–China) as well as domestic sources of instability (such as in the Philippines) are deep-rooted and are unlikely to disappear in the foreseeable future.

What, realistically, can Japan be expected to do? In this author's view, Japan's direct sharing of military responsibilities in regional security is and will remain for quite some time an unrealistic option. Obstacles against Japan's military role are overwhelming. Popular support for Article 9 is unshakeable and the mainstream consensus on the strictly defensive national security policy is generally accepted by the public. Any unrestrained foreign attempt to pressure Japan into assuming a militarily-based regional security role would be counterproductive. It would further erode the troubled LDP's credibility as the defender of the increasingly self-assured and confident Japanese populace who by and large continue to be quite pacifist in their world outlook. It would encourage the opposition forces, on the left or right, to exploit the LDP's unabashedly pro-American stance. This would be destabilising in the present Japan where nationalist sentiments, both healthy and unhealthy, are clearly on the rise. Furthermore, uncontrolled US pressure on Japan would further expose the declining US leadership.

Finally, Japan's neighbours to the West and the Southwest would be extremely apprehensive of any discussion in Tokyo of Japan's regional military role. They would see it as a resurgence of Japanese militarism. Other Asian countries would accept more readily Japan's financial support for their economies, which would help reduce their defence burdens. Although Tokyo does not explicitly acknowledge such a direct linkage between Japan's economic assistance and its recipients' defence needs, it openly hopes that its economic aid will promote economic development and help produce political stability in the area.

In contrast to the stable but nonetheless circumspect support for continuing increases in defence spending, there is in Japan a much more favourable outlook on foreign economic assistance. Japan is now being challenged by outside observers to expand its ODA commitments from the current level of slightly above 0.3 per cent of GNP, to levels comparable to defence spending, or about 1 per cent of GNP.[60] While this may not be an immediate prospect, there is no question that Tokyo plans to respond positively to such calls within its fiscal constraints. The government has recently announced that its ODA funding will increase by more than 9 per cent from FY 1989 to FY 1990. In comparison, its defence budget is expected to increase by slightly more than 6 per cent.[61] These increases, in summary, are the most reliable indicators for the foreseeable future of domestic support for Japan's contribution to its broad comprehensive concept of national and international security.

Notes and References

1. For proponents of the US hegemonic decline thesis, see, for example, David Calleo, *Beyond American Hegemony; The Future of the Western Alliance* (New York: Basic Books, 1987); Robert Gilpin, *The Political Economy of International Relations* (Princeton, NJ: Princeton University Press, 1987); Paul Kennedy, *The Rise and Fall of the Great Powers* (New York: Random House, 1987).

2. Chalmers Johnson, 'The End of American Hegemony and the Future of U.S.-Japan Relations', *Harvard International Review*, 10th anniversary issue, *American Foreign Policy: Toward the 1990s* (1989) pp. 127–31.

3. Robert Cox, 'Production and Hegemony: Toward a Political Economy of World Order', in Harold K. Jacobson and Dusan Sidjanski (eds), *The Emerging Industrial Economic Order* (Beverly Hills, CA: Sage Publications, 1982) p. 45.

4. Torbjon Knutsen, 'Hegemony in the Modern International System', paper prepared for the 1986 Annual Meeting of the American Political Science Association (Washington, 28–31 August 1986) p. 15.

5. Robert Gilpin, *War and Change in World Politics* (Cambridge: Cambridge University Press, 1981) pp. 17, 156, 187.

6. *New York Times* (3 June 1988; 28 November 1988).

7. *Interim Report of the Defense Burdensharing Panel of the Committee on Armed Services*, House of Representatives, 100th Congress, 2nd Session (August 1988) (Washington, DC: US Government Printing Office, 1988) pp. 4–7.

8. See Kenneth B. Pyle, 'Japan, the World, and the Twenty-first Century', in Takashi Inoguchi and Daniel I. Okimoto, *The Political Economy of Japan, Vol. 2, The Changing International Context* (Stanford, CA: Stanford University Press, 1988) pp. 454–6.

9. Stephen D. Krasner, 'Japan and the United States: Prospects for Stability', in Inoguchi and Okimoto, *The Political Economy of Japan*, pp. 401–2.

10. *Japan: An International Comparison, 1989* (Tokyo: Keizai Koho Center, 1989) p. 81.

11. Sogoanzenhosho Kenkyu Gurupu, *Sogoanzenhosho Senryaku* (Comprehensive security strategy) (Tokyo: Okurasho Insatsukyoku, 1980) p. 7.

12. *Sogoanzenhosho Senryaku*, pp. 7–8.

13. Heiwamondai Kenkyukai, *Kokusaikokka Nihon no Sogo Anzenhosho Seisaku* (Comprehensive security policy of an international nation Japan) (Tokyo: Okurasho Insatsukyoku, 1985) pp. 24–9. The four major developments identified by that report were: (1) the rough parity between the US and Soviet strategic capabilities, (2) the decline in US economic power and the problems of budget deficits in the advanced countries and debt accumulation in the developing nations, (3) the growing trends toward a multilateral international system caused by the rise of China as an independent force on the international scene and by the increasingly assertive Third World and (4) the first signs of the 'Pacific Age' due to the advancement of the nations in the Pacific region.

14. Gaimusho, *Showa 62-nenban, Gaiko Seisho, Wagakuni Gaiko no Kinkyo* (Diplomatic Blue Book, recent developments in our nation's diplomacy, 1988) (Tokyo: Okurasho Insatsukyoku, 1988) p. 2.

15. See, for example, Takashi Inoguchi, *Kokusai Kankei no Seiji-keizaigaku: Nihon no Yakuwari to Sentaku* (The political economy of international relations: Japan's role and choices) (Tokyo: Tokyo Daigaku Shuppankai, 1985); Takashi Inoguchi, *Tadanori to Ikkokuhaneishugi o koete: Tenkanki no Sekai to Nihon* (Beyond free-ride and unilateral prosperity: The world and Japan in a transitional period) (Tokyo: Toyo Keizai Shimposha, 1987); Takashi Inoguchi, 'Beikoku: Ajiansenryaku Minaoshi Hitsuyoni' ('The United States: Asian strategy review has become necessary'), *Nihon Keizai Shimbun* (18 March 1989) p. 21; Kuniko Inoguchi, *Posuto-haken Shisutemu to Nihon no Sentaku* (The emerging post-hegemonic system: Choices for Japan) (Tokyo: Chikuma Shobo, 1987); Tadashi Kawata, *Kokusaikankei no Seiji-keizaigaku* (The political economy of international relations) (Tokyo: Nihon Hoso Shuppan Kyokai, 1987); Tadashi Kawata, *Kokusai Seiji-keizaigaku o mezashite* (Toward international political economy) (Tokyo: Ochanomizu Shobo, 1988).

16. Paul Kennedy, *The Rise and Fall of the Great Powers*. As soon as Kennedy's book came out in the United States, it was translated into Japanese and became an instant best-seller in Japan. Kennedy has since been invited by numerous publishers and professional associations in Japan. This attests to the widespread acceptance among Japanese intellectuals of the theme of US hegemonic decline.

17. See, for example, Chihiro Hosoya, 'Riijonarizumu no Taito to Nihon no

Sentaku' ('The rise of regionalism and Japan's options'), *Gaiko Forum* (Diplomatic forum) (October 1988) pp. 26–33; Terumasa Nakanishi's interview with Paul Kennedy, 'Watashi wa naze "Taikoku no Kobo" o Kaitaka' ('Why did I write the "Rise and Fall of the Great Powers"?'), *Gaiko Forum* (October 1988) pp. 62–77; Kuniko Inoguchi's interview with Paul Kennedy, 'P. Kenedi Kyoju Nihon o Kataru' ('Professor P. Kennedy talks about Japan'), *This Is* (November 1988) pp. 136–55; 'Paul Kennedy Kyoju ga Kataru: "Gunjika wa Suitai Hayameru"' ('Professor Paul Kennedy speaks: "Militarization quickens decline"'), *Asahi Shimbun Weekly AERA* (21 March 1989) pp. 58–9.

18. These principles were presented in Takeshita's speech at the National Press Club in Washington on 14 January 1988. The speech is reproduced in full as 'A Nation Contributing More to the World: Japan's Commitment to Global Prosperity', *Speaking of Japan*, 9(89) (May 1988) pp. 27–32.

19. This was first announced during Takeshita's trip to London in May 1988 and reiterated as part of his speech before the third special session of the UN General Assembly on disarmament. The latter speech is reproduced in full as *Speech by Noboru Takeshita, Prime Minister, at the Fifteenth Special Session of the General Assembly (Third Special Session Devoted to Disarmament), United Nations, New York (1 June 1988)*, Policy Speech Series, 25 (Tokyo: Ministry of Foreign Affairs).

20. An outline of these components appears in Gaimusho, 'Kokusai Kyoryoku Koso: 'Sekai ni Kokensuru Nihon" no Gutaizo' ('Framework for international co-operation: A concrete image of "Japan contributing to the world"), *Toki no Ugoki* (15 July 1988) pp. 26–8.

21. An English summary of the budgetary allocations for the new initiative is found in Ministry of Foreign Affairs, 'International Cooperation Initiative (Contributing to the Peace and Prosperity of the World)' (January 1989) (mimeo).

22. 'International Cooperation Initiative'.

23. The then Defense Secretary, Melvin Laird, admitted there was a tradeoff between troop reductions in the region and security assistance increases. See *Final Report to the Congress of Secretary of Defense Melvin R. Laird before the House Armed Services Committee* (8 January 1973) pp. 5–6.

24. John M. Collins, *U.S.–Soviet Military Balance, 1980–1985* (Washington, DC: Pergamon-Brassey, 1985) p. 139.

25. For an expression of this realisation, see for example the statement by William Clark, Jr, Acting Assistant Secretary for East Asian and Pacific Affairs, before the Subcommittee on Asian and Pacific Affairs of the House Foreign Affairs Committee (27 February 1989). The statement is reprinted as William Clark, Jr, 'FY 1990 Foreign Assistance Requests for East Asia and the Pacific', *Current Policy*, 1150.

26. Daniel Gallik (ed.), *World Military Expenditures and Arms Transfers, 1987* (Washington, DC: US Arms Control and Disarmament Agency, 1988).

27. *Defense of Japan, 1982* (Tokyo: Japan Time, 1982) pp. 31–3.

28. *Defense of Japan, 1982*, p. 30.

29. Chalmers Johnson, 'Japanese–Soviet Relations in the Early Gorbachev Era', *Asian Survey*, 27(11) (November 1987) pp. 1147–52.

30. For an explanation of the Japanese reluctance, see Kazuyuki Kinbara, 'Nisso–shiberiya Kaihatsu Kyoryoku no Kaiko to Tembo' ('A relection and prospects of Japan–Soviet Siberia development co-operation'), in *Tokyo Kokusai Shimpojumu: Tenkaiki no Soren* (Soviet Union in Transition) (Tokyo: Nihon Kokusaimondai Kenkyujo, 1986) pp. 300–22.

31. For the same view, see Robert A. Scalapino, 'Asia's Future', *Foreign Affairs*, 66(1) (Fall 1987) p. 106. During the recent working-level discussions between Moscow and Tokyo, for example, Moscow emphasised that the conclusion of agreements on principles of economic co-operation, protection of Japanese investment in the Soviet Union, and reciprocal opening of bank offices, environmental protection, tourism, and peaceful space development would pave the way toward Gorbachev's visit to Tokyo. Tokyo countered that the political climate is not ripe for such agreements to have a positive effect on the bilateral relations, *Asahi Shimbun* (21 March 1989) p. 2.

32. See Tsuneo Akaha, 'Japan's Response to Threats of Shipping Disruptions in Southeast Asia and the Middle East', *Pacific Affairs*, 59(2) (Summer 1986) pp. 255–77.

33. Boeicho, (ed.), *Boeihakusho* (Defence White Paper) (Tokyo; Okurasho Insatsukyoku, 1988) p. 184.

34. The description of US–Japan joint military exercises is based on *Boeihakusho*, pp. 199–202; Melinda W. Cooke, 'National Security', in Frederica M. Bunge (ed.), *Japan, a Country Study* (Washington, DC: US Government Printing Office, 1983) p. 377.

35. The description of Japanese support for US forces in Japan is found in *Boeihakusho*, pp. 206–13.

36. *Interim Report of the Defense Burdensharing Panel of the Committee on Armed Services*, House of Representatives, 100th Congress, 2nd Session (August 1988) (Washington, DC: US Government Printing Office, 1988) pp. 8–9.

37. For a discussion of the concept of 'comprehensive security' in English, see Robert W. Barnett, *Beyond War: Japan's Concept of Comprehensive National Security* (Washington, DC: Pergamon-Brassey, 1984); J. W. M. Chapman, R. Drifte, and I. T. M. Gow, *Japan's Quest for Comprehensive Security: Defense, Diplomacy, and Dependence* (New York: St Martin's Press, 1982). Discussions in Japanese can be found in: Gendai Sogo Kagaku Kenkyujo, *80-nendai Nihon no Sogoanzenhosho* (Japan's comprehensive security in the 1980s) (Tokyo; Kyoikusha, 1979); Heiwa-mondai Kenkyukai, *Kokusaikokka Nihon no Sogo Anzenhosho Seisaku* (Comprehensive security policy of an international nation Japan) (Tokyo: Okurasho Insatsukyoku, 1985); Sogo Anzenhosho Kenkyu Gurupu, *Sogo Anzenhosho Senryaku* (Comprehensive security strategy) (Tokyo: Okurasho Insatsukyoku, 1980).

38. Dennis T. Yasutomo, *The Manner of Giving: Strategic Aid and Japanese Foreign Policy* (New York: Lexington, 1986).

39. *Interim Report of the Defense Burdensharing Panel*, p. 9.

40. See for example Prime Minister Takeshita's press conference with

Japanese reporters in Washington on 3 February 1989 in *Asahi Shimbun* (5 February 1989) p. 1.

41. David F. Lambertson (Deputy Assistant Secretary for East Asian and Pacific Affairs), 'Future Prospects for the Philippines', *Current Policy*, 1157, pp. 5–7.
42. *Asahi Shimbun* (4 July 1989) p. 3.
43. For a detailed discussion of the security implications of bilateral technological issues between Japan and the United States, see Reinhard Drifte, *High Technology in Japanese–American Relations*, forthcoming.
44. Justin Bloom, 'The US–Japan Bilateral Science and Technology Relationship: A Personal Evaluation', in Mitchell B. Wallerstein (ed.), *Scientific and Technological Cooperation Among Industrialized Countries; The Role of the United States* (Washington, DC: National Academy Press, 1984) quoted in Drifte, *High Technology*, pp. 28–9.
45. For a detailed study of Japan's decision to participate in the SDI research and development, see Peggy L. Falkenheim, *Japan and Arms Control: Tokyo's Response to SDI and INF*, Aurora Papers, 6 (Toronto: The Canadian Centre for Arms Control and Disarmament, 1987).
46. *The Christian Science Monitor* (4 April 1989) p. 6.
47. *New York Times* (4 March 1989) pp. 1 and 4.
48. *New York Times* in its editorial on 18 March 1989 called on Bush to cancel the project.
49. *Asahi Shimbun* (7 April 1989) p. 4.
50. *New York Times* (12 April 1989) p. 21.
51. *The Christian Science Monitor* (4 April 1989) p. 6.
52. *New York Times* (18 April 1989) pp. 33 and 47.
53. Walter Galenson and David W. Galenson, 'Japan and South Korea', in David B. H. Denoon, (ed.), *Constraints on Strategy: The Economics of Western Security* (Washington, DC: Pergamon-Brassey, 1986) p. 157.
54. See, for example, Hisahiko Okazaki, *A Grand Strategy for Japanese Defense* (Lanham, MD: University Press of America, 1986); Kenichi Ito and Fuji Kamiya, 'Mazakon Kokka Nihon no Katsuro' ('The way out for the nation with a mother complex, Japan'). *Shokun* (October 1985) pp. 44–59.
55. *American Foreign Policy, 1986* (Washington, DC: US Department of State, 1986) p. 532.
56. Nakasone's speech at the National Press Club in Washington on 1 May 1987, in *JEI Report* (8 May 1972) p. 2.
57. Ronald Reagan, *National Security Strategy of the United States* (Washington, DC: Pergamon-Brassey, 1988) p. 87.
58. The precipitous decline in the LDP's popular support to unprecedented low levels (25.6 per cent) prior to the elections and the public revelation of Uno's involvement with a geisha girl both contributed to the disastrous results of the election. The Liberal Democrats won only 36 seats out of the 126 seats for election and were clearly defeated by the Socialists who won 46 seats. As a result, the LDP controlled only 109 seats in the 252-seat House of Councillors, *Asahi Shimbun* (25 July 1989) p. 1.
59. Harold Jacobson, 'Eroding Hegemony and National Tolerances for

Security Responsibilities', in Ronald A. Morse and Shigenobu Yoshida (eds), *Blind Partners: American and Japanese Responses to an Unknown Future* (Washington, DC: University Press of America, 1985) p. 90. Jacobson notes that economic conflicts with Japan have had no apparent impact on the public's willingness to use US military forces to defend Japan.

60.   Such an appeal has come from former West German Chancellor Helmut Schmidt and former US Defense Secretary Robert McNamara, *Asahi Shimbun* (3 July 1989) p. 3 and (5 July 1989) p. 10.

61.   *Asahi Shimbun* (11 July 1989) p. 1.

9 Stuck in a Mould: The Relationship between Japan and the Soviet Union
Wolf Mendl

In the midst of all the ferment created by Soviet General Secretary Gorbachev's domestic and foreign policies, the relations between Japan and the Soviet Union remain stuck in a pattern, apparently little affected by the winds of change. The fact that their shared interests – and there are some – are outweighed by the issues that divide them, may be one explanation of the stalemate in post-war Japanese–Soviet relations. Another may be that each has given low priority to the other. For the Soviet Union, Japan has occupied fifth place in the focus of its attention, after the United States, Europe, China and the Middle East. Conversely, Japan was not greatly attracted to the Soviet economy, preferring instead to give priority to China in its economic relations with the nearby Asian mainland.

These characteristics of the relationship can be traced back to the earliest encounters between the two nations. However, since 1945 it has been influenced by additional factors: the circumstances of the Soviet Union's entry into the war against Japan; the dispute over the Northern Territories; and the American-dominated occupation of Japan, leading to the subsequent close association with the United States. Of these three, the territorial issue has become the symbol and the substance of Japan's relationship with its giant northern neighbour.

THE LEGACY OF HISTORY

Three elements have dominated the encounter between Japan and Russia since the beginning of the eighteenth century.[1] The first was the commercial/economic interest. Next came the problem of territorial delimitation. The third was the impact of the international environ-

174

ment, especially the behaviour of third parties, including the United States, China, Britain, France and Holland.

The commercial impulse came mainly from the Russians, knocking at the door of a Japan that showed no interest in foreign trade. Later in the nineteenth century, with the expansion of the Japanese empire and the need for sources of energy and raw materials to feed its industrialisation and militarisation, Japan became interested in Sakhalin, though the main thrust was towards Korea, Manchuria and China. Japanese commercial interest in Russia was negligible, although it increased somewhat after the opening of the Suez Canal and the completion of the Trans-Siberian railway.[2] Russo–Japanese exchanges amounted to a small proportion of Japan's total foreign trade, especially when compared with the share taken by China, the United States and Southeast Asia. For the Russians, the economic nexus was more important, both for meeting the needs of the population scattered along the shores of the Sea of Okhotsk and the Japan Sea and for the development of Siberia. The main bones of contention between the two countries were control over the coal and oil deposits of Sakhalin and fishing rights in the surrounding seas.

Russia had been supplied by Japan with great quantities of material and food during the First World War and had become its principal customer. In the aftermath of the Revolution and during the years of Japanese intervention in Siberia, trade continued on a large scale. After the Bolsheviks had consolidated their power, the volume of trade declined and, although it increased again at the end of the 1920s, economic relations were beset by the same problems as in the years after the Second World War, such as Soviet shortages of foreign currency and disputes over fisheries.[3]

The question of territorial delimitation and sovereignty led to a succession of treaties which defined and redefined the boundary between the two empires.[4] Until the end of the Second World War, the main focus had been on the economically and strategically important island of Sakhalin. The Kurile Islands had originally been stepping-stones for the Russians in their search for contact with Japan. The four territories (Etorofu, Kunashiri, Shikotan, and the Habomai group of very small islands) that are at the centre of the dispute today have been regarded as Japanese territory since the mid-nineteenth century. Indeed, Shikotan and the Habomais were not mentioned in the Treaty of Shimoda (1855), which was the first formal delimitation of the frontier between the two states. Nor had the Russians ever laid claim to those smaller territories. The same applies to Kunashiri. Etorofu, on the other hand, had been a source of dispute in the sixty years before the Treaty of Shimoda. In the negotiations leading up to that treaty, Admiral Putiatin had originally insisted that Etorofu was Russian territory and had then suggested partitioning the island as a compromise. During the negotiations preceding the Treaty of St Petersburg (1875), in which Japan acquired the remainder of the Kuriles up to Kamchatka in exchange for recognising Russian sovereignty over Sakhalin, the Japanese had initially offered to hand Etorofu and half of Kunashiri to Russia in return for Japan's sovereignty over Sakhalin.[5]

However, these were little more than bargaining postures. The Japanese case for considering Etorofu and Kunashiri as part of the national territory rests firmly on the provisions of the Treaty of Shimoda. All that had gone before conveys

> the impression that a Russo–Japanese frontier developed almost imperceptibly over a period of years, during which national boundaries in the modern sense of the word did not exist. Until the nineteenth century, neither Russia nor Japan had a clear conception of how far its sovereignty extended in the Kuriles.[6]

As for the international environment – the third element in the encounter – Japanese and Russian policies were influenced from the beginning by rivalry among the Great Powers. The leaders of Tokugawa Japan were much concerned over the approaching threat from the north, east and south. Some welcomed the Russian advance as an opportunity to increase the wealth of Japan through commerce and because they no longer believed in the wisdom of the seclusion policy. Others were conscious of the Russian threat and called for the construction of a powerful navy, for coastal fortifications and for certain preventive measures such as the colonisation of Hokkaido and territorial expansion in Sakhalin and the Kurile Islands.[7]

Once Japanese isolation had been forcibly ended, Japan vacillated between two policies. One aimed at playing off the foreign powers against each other. The other sought alignment either with Russia or with the maritime powers of the Pacific. The first of these emerged with the attempt to obtain pledges of protection from Commodore Perry against the Russians and from Admiral Putiatin against the Americans.[8]

The rivalry between the United States and Russia in the northern Pacific was both a threat and an opportunity for Japan. (After 1945, the Cold War brought nothing new, apart from its ideological content.)

Commodore Perry had envisaged a 'fierce and final encounter' between 'the Saxon and the Cossack' on which 'the freedom or the slavery of the world' would depend.[9] The German Minister in Washington wrote to Bismarck in 1874, that:

> the United States regards Japan as an appendage of America ... And although the Yankee feels strongly enough to be able to hope that sooner or later he will be in a position to paralyse the influence of all European powers in Japan, the Asiatic proximity of Russia yet fills him with a secret fear.[10]

Similarly, the Russians were worried by American or British advances in the region. In March 1852, the Governor-General of Siberia reported his fear that China and Japan were falling under British and American influence and that the American opening of Japan might extend to Sakhalin.[11] Suspicions of American intentions and fear of Japanese–American collusion were heightened by ideological perceptions after the Revolution of 1917 and only mitigated by the belief that the contradictions among the capitalist powers might be exploited in the Soviet interest.[12]

The tangled skein of animosities did not mean, however, that Japan and Russia (and later Japan and the Soviet Union) were locked in implacable hostility throughout the two centuries prior to the end of the Second World War. There is much historical evidence that the Japanese were favourably disposed towards the Russians and sometimes clearly preferred them to other foreigners.[13] Even when the clash of rival imperial ambitions sharpened in the last quarter of the nineteenth century, there were periods during which Japan and Russia sought accommodation and collaboration in managing the affairs of Northeast Asia.

Feelings of dislike on the Japanese side were mixed with a sense of superiority which antedated their victory in the war of 1904–5 and had been fostered by an awareness of Russia's economic backwardness.[14] There were statesmen, such as Ito Hirobumi and Goto Shimpei, who were inclined to pursue a pro-Russian policy – a tendency which continued into the Soviet era.[15] But there were others – Yamagata Aritomo, Katsura Taro and Nitobe Inazo among them – who entertained negative feelings towards Russia.[16] Those feelings were readily reciprocated by the Russians after the war of 1904–5 and as a result of the Japanese occupation of the Soviet Far East (1918–22).

ISSUES IN THE POST-1945 RELATIONSHIP

All the elements of the bilateral relationship before 1945 reappeared in the post-war era. However, their content and relative importance had changed. From the Japanese perspective, the territorial question was to become the most important issue. Having failed to gain a foothold in Japan under the occupation or by exploiting the newly revived Japan Communist Party (JCP), the interest of the Soviet Union centred first on weakening Japan's association with the United States and later on the benefits to be derived from tapping Japan's economic strength. The international environment had also changed and brought with it new problems of security for both countries.

In some respects, the bilateral relationship seemed to come full circle after 1945. It was reminiscent of earlier encounters in at least three ways. First, until the late nineteenth century, it had been Russia that had 'pushed' towards Japan. From the 1890s onwards, Japan had done the pushing. Now the Soviet Union took advantage of Japan's defeat to advance its interests. Second, the economic motive had been the principal if not the sole reason for the Russian advance. Later, it provided a strong impulse behind the Japanese advance against the Tsarist Empire and the Soviet Union. That interest all but disappeared from the Japanese side in the early post-war years. Finally, the relationship had begun when Japan tried to stand outside the arena of power rivalries and found itself buffeted by the aggressive behaviour of the Western states. After the middle of the nineteenth century Japan rapidly became the most aggressive of the competing powers in the region. Following the Pacific War it reverted to a more passive role, which it is only now beginning to shed.

The Northern Territories

In tracing the origins of the current dispute over the Northern Territories, we have to distinguish between the positions of the three powers most concerned. The point of departure is the secret agreement among the Allies at Yalta in February 1945. According to this document, the Kurile Islands were to be handed over to the Soviet Union as one of the conditions for Russia's entry into the war against Japan. Moreover, it was stated that Russia's claims should be 'unquestionably fulfilled' after Japan's defeat.[17]

The Soviet Union declared war on 8 August, six days before the surrender of Japan, and began occupying the Kuriles on 18 August, taking one island after another until its forces reached Uruppu, which lies to the north of Etorofu. They stopped there and temporarily retreated northwards, assuming that the Americans would receive the surrender of the Japanese forces to the south.[18] This understanding was based on an agreement between the American and Soviet chiefs of staff over the boundary line between their respective areas of operation within which each was to receive the enemy's surrender.[19] Eventually, however, the Soviets occupied all the Kuriles as well as Shikotan and the Habomais.

Stalin had cabled Truman on 16 August, making the 'modest suggestion' that the area in which Soviet forces were to receive the surrender of the Japanese, should include 'all' the Kuriles and the part of Hokkaido north of a line from Kushiro in the east to Rumoi in the west. Truman rejected the request for a zone of occupation on Hokkaido, but acceded to the demand over the Kuriles. In subsequent exchanges between the two leaders, Truman referred to the Kurile Islands as 'Japanese territory, disposition of which must be made at a peace settlement', but added: 'I was advised that my predecessor agreed to support in the peace settlement the Soviet acquisition of these Islands'. Truman had not considered it 'offensive' when Stalin asked him to 'confirm that agreement'.[20] He thus expressed the basic position subsequently to be assumed by the United States and also an ambivalence between the commitment to support the Soviet claim and a refusal to confirm it without a peace treaty.

Leaving on one side the circumstances under which the Kuriles were occupied and an element of confusion over the proper recipients of the Japanese surrender,[21] the American position over the territorial issue has been beset by the contradiction between the promise made to Stalin in Yalta and the policy of turning Japan into a friend and ally. That policy was activated by the onset of the Cold War and in response to the cost of what had become a prolonged occupation. Until then, the United States had acted very much in line with its commitment to the Soviet Union.

On 8 November 1945, the Basic Initial Post-Surrender Directive to the Supreme Commander Allied Powers (SCAP) for the Occupation and Control of Japan had provided for the complete governmental and administrative separation from Japan of certain Pacific islands, including Formosa, the Pescadores, and Karafuto (Sakhalin), and 'such other territories as may be specified in future directives'. In a directive to the Japanese Government, dated 29 January 1946, the territories were defined as the Kurile Islands as well as the Habomai group and Shikotan. This obviously played into the hands of the Soviet claim. It also revealed another weakness in the American position, for the agreement at Yalta had included no definition of the Kurile Islands.

In the later stages of preparations for the peace treaty with Japan, the Americans held that if the Soviet Union became a party to the treaty, the United States had no alternative but to support the transfer of South Sakhalin and the Kuriles to it. On the other hand, it is also clear from the official records that the chief negotiator of the treaty, John Foster Dulles, hoped that the Russians would not sign it. At first he wanted any reference to these islands omitted from the draft proposal for a treaty, confining himself to giving oral assurances to the Soviets of American support if the Soviet Union signed the treaty. Reference to Sakhalin and the Kuriles was eventually included under pressure from the allies, although it was emphasised that 'the precise definition of the extent of the Kurile Islands should be a matter for bilateral agreement between the Japanese and Soviet Governments or for judicial determination by the International Court of Justice'.[22]

It became American policy to draft the treaty of peace in such a way that the United States could not be accused of reneging on the Yalta agreement, while ensuring that its terms would make it unacceptable to the Russians because it did not transfer sovereignty over the Kuriles to the Soviet Union. Later, when the Japanese claim for the return of the Northern Territories was formulated, the United States supported the position that 'Kuriles' meant only the islands north of Etorofu.[23]

The Soviet position on the Northern Territories was perfectly straightforward. The islands were to be annexed and Russified. In February 1947, the territories were incorporated into the Russian Soviet Federated Socialist Republic and by 1949 there were no Japanese left on the islands.

Several arguments are advanced in support of the Soviet position – some specious, others more substantial.[24] The historical claims, based on exploration and territorial control, can be dismissed fairly easily, especially as Russian historians before 1945 had conceded Japanese rights to the Southern Kuriles. Soviet apologists argue that the Treaty of Shimoda was invalidated by Japan's subsequent acts of aggression. The list usually begins with the attack in 1904 (which was, however, excused in a Soviet note to the League of Nations in May 1924, as 'an act caused by the aggressive policy of the Tsarist Government towards Japan, who, in order to forestall the danger struck the first blow at her adversary'[25]); other examples include the occupation of Siberia, incidents on the Manchurian/Mongolian border in the 1930s, and the indirect support given to Nazi Germany after 1941.

The decision taken at Yalta is considered to be final, with the occupation of the territories seen as a natural outcome of Japan's defeat. Indeed, all the territorial arrangements made by the allies at Yalta are regarded by the Soviet Union as definitive, having the force of an international treaty. The Proclamation to Japan issued at Potsdam on 26 July 1945, by Truman and Churchill with the approval of Chiang Kai-shek, which was signed by the Soviet Union upon its entry into the war, had set out the allied terms and warned: 'We will not deviate from them. There are no alternatives. We shall brook no delay' (Article 5). The territorial dispositions were included in Article 8: 'The terms of the Cairo declaration shall be carried out and Japanese sovereignty shall be limited to the islands of Honshu, Hokkaido, Kyushy, Shikoku, *and such minor islands as we determine*' (emphasis added).[26]

The Cairo Declaration, signed by Roosevelt, Churchill and Chiang Kai-shek on 17 November 1943, stated that the allies 'covet no gain for themselves and have no thought of territorial expansion'. It went on to say that Japan would be stripped of all Pacific islands that it had seized and occupied since the beginning of the First World War and listed the 'stolen' territories to be returned to China. It concluded that 'Japan will also be expelled from all other territories which she has taken by violence and greed'.[27] Stalin gave full support to the Declaration at the Teheran summit with Churchill and Roosevelt at the end of November.

In the Soviet view, ignorance of the secret agreements reached at Yalta does not provide a basis for questioning the post-war territorial settlement. By surrendering unconditionally and accepting the Potsdam Proclamation, Japan had also accepted the principle that its postwar boundaries were to be determined by the allies, who were acting on the basis of their previous agreements, including the one reached at Yalta.[28] The Soviets have never ceased to remind the Japanese that they lost the war and must accept the consequences.

No distinction is made by the Soviets between the Kuriles and the Northern Territories or between Kunashiri and Etorofu, on the one hand, and the Habomais and Shikotan, on the other, although the smaller islands are referred to as the 'Little Kuriles'. The argument that Japan had given up its rights to the Kuriles but had not ceded sovereignty to the Soviet Union under the terms of the Treaty of San

Francisco, is dismissed as a manoeuvre of the United States and Japan, since they had made it virtually impossible for the Soviet Union to subscribe to the Treaty.[29]

Behind the historical, political, legal and moral attempts to justify the Soviet position lies the view that the post-war frontiers should be regarded as inviolate. Such a view is of great importance for the Soviet Union, surrounded as it is by a host of states with irredentist claims. Furthermore, declaring the post-war arrangements to be sacrosanct is an essential ingredient of the Soviet preoccupation with security, a preoccupation readily understood in the light of Russian and Soviet history, which was illustrated in Stalin's statement on the day on which Japan signed the Instrument of Surrender:

> Henceforth, the Kurile Islands shall not serve as a means to cut off the Soviet Union from the ocean or as a base for a Japanese attack on our Far East, but as a means to link the Soviet Union with the ocean and as a defence base against Japanese aggression.[30]

After the onset of the Cold War it was only necessary to substitute 'American' for 'Japanese' in the statement in order to have an accurate reflection of the Soviet Union's twin objectives: the security of its East Asian territories and the desire to strengthen its strategic position in the region. The acquisition of the Kuriles was the first of many steps whereby the Soviet Union sought recognition as a major power in the Pacific, which General MacArthur had called an 'Anglo–American Lake'.

Japan is, of course, the chief protagonist in the quarrel over the Northern Territories, although it required time to clarify its position. Until the start of discussions about a peace treaty, it could do little to influence Allied policies. Nevertheless, in early planning for a treaty, the Foreign Ministry stressed the importance of the territorial question and put forward a strong case for the retention of sovereignty over the Kuriles.[31]

The Northern Territories featured in Diet debates from 1947 onwards. At first the interest focused almost exclusively on the grave effect that the Soviet occupation was having on Japan's fishing industry. The fate and livelihood of the Japanese population expelled from the Islands was another concern that exercised the parliamentarians. The territorial question began to occupy the centre of attention from 1949 onwards. Nakasone Yasuhiro, then a young, strongly nationalist and anti-communist member of the Democratic Party, insisted that while Japan was bound by the Cairo and Potsdam Declarations, which had not mentioned the Kurile Islands, it was not bound by the secret agreement of Yalta. Prime Minister Yoshida, on the other hand, evaded the challenge and explained that it was the American view that Japan was bound by the Yalta agreement[32] which had been made public by the United States Department of State on 11 February 1946.

In the many subsequent exchanges, only the JCP urged acceptance of the Yalta decisions. The Director of the Foreign Ministry's Treaty Bureau stated shortly after the signature of the Treaty of San Francisco: 'As to the range covered by "the Kurile Islands", as used in the Treaty, I believe that both the Southern and Northern Kurile Islands are included'.[33] The statement was repudiated four months later by the Vice-Minister of Foreign Affairs, but it hinted faintly at a certain ambivalence in the Japanese position which has persisted to the present day. It indicated a possible willingness to move toward some compromise by separating Etorofu and Kunashiri from the Habomai Islands and Shikotan. However, the same Director of the Treaty Bureau, Nishimura Kumao, also insisted that if the Soviet Union did not sign the Treaty of San Francisco within three years, Japan could be regarded as retaining its sovereign rights over the Kuriles.[34] Although Japan had been anxious to avoid all mention of the northern islands in the peace treaty, the United States could not wholly escape its obligation to the Soviet Union, even at the height of the Cold War and with a 'hot war' raging in Korea.

The final version of the Treaty met the Japanese position in three respects. While Japan renounced 'all right, title and claim to the Kurile Islands' and to South Sakhalin in Article 2(c), there was no indication that sovereignty had passed to the Soviet Union. This left the issue open to be decided either in a separate agreement or through a ruling of the International Court of Justice. Secondly, the wording of Articles 25 and 26 of the Treaty was such that by its refusal to accede to it, the Soviet Union forfeited any rights to benefit from its terms.[35] Lastly, the definition of the Kuriles was vague, thus leaving it open for Japan to claim that the definition should be that which was contained in the Treaty of St Petersburg.[36] Reference to the Kuriles in the Treaty of San Francisco could also be taken to imply the exclusion of the Habomais and Shikotan, which had never been mentioned in international agreements concerning the Kuriles. It thus presented the possibility of some interim compromise over the territorial issue, as emerged in the Soviet–Japanese negotiations of 1955–6.

Two other factors are noteworthy: Japan's exploitation of power rivalries in the region and the increasing importance of the military/ strategic element in relations with the Soviet Union. As the Japanese tried to press the Americans for an early conclusion of the peace treaty, they sought advantage from the policy of playing off the powers against each other, although the political leadership was convinced that the country's future prosperity and security required a close alignment with the United States. The Minister of Finance, Ikeda Hayato, played the Russian card when he hinted in a conversation with the Financial Adviser to SCAP, that the Soviet Union 'may offer a peace treaty in advance of the United States and might include in that offer the return of Sakhalin and the Kuriles'.[37]

The question of Japanese security had surfaced early in American calculations. In June 1946, Truman's special envoy to the Far East reported that the Soviet entrenchment in Korea could be interpreted as part of a strategy:

> To provide ... encirclement of [the] jaw of a pincer against Japan in the event that Japan was built up by some foreign power to use as a base against the USSR. The other jaw of the pincer would be the Valdivostok peninsula, Karafuto, and the Kurile Islands.[38]

The problem of Japan's security was also raised in an internal memorandum of the American Occupation authorities. It argued for the return of the Northern Territories to Japan because continued Russian occupation would bring 'Soviet power within exceedingly close proximity of metropolitan Japan, a situation which the Japanese cannot help but regard as a grave strategic liability'.[39] The Japanese may not have stressed that part of the problem under the Occupation, being more immediately concerned with the threat from within posed by the JCP, but the arguments deployed in the memorandum form part of the argument used by those who worry about the Soviet 'threat' today.

The emergence of the territorial issue cannot be separated from a deep-seated feeling of grievance and betrayal which coloured Japanese perceptions. The Soviet entry into the war was seen as a stab in the back and a violation of the Neutrality Pact which the two states had signed on 13 April 1941. The duration of the Pact was for five years and it was renewable. The intention not to extend it for a second five-year term had to be announced one year before expiration. In April 1945, the Soviet government gave notice that it would not renew the Pact. Since it was not due to expire until April 1946, the Japanese regard Russia's entry into the war in August as a violation of this treaty.[40] Further-more, the Soviet Union began hostilities a week before Japan's surrender and after Japan had sought its good offices to mediate an end to the conflict. Even if Japan accepted the right of the Allies to settle its frontiers, the Cairo Declaration had stipulated that it would be driven out of territories acquired 'by violence and greed'. This could be taken to apply to South Sakhalin, but not to the Kurile Islands. Soviet participation in the war is, therefore, interpreted as an act of aggression whose purpose was to seize territory at the expense of a gravely weakened opponent on the verge of surrender.

This detailed discussion of the genesis of the dispute over the Northern Territories has been necessary not only to understand subsequent developments and the significance of the issue today, but because the main issues in Japan's relations with the Soviet Union have clustered around it. The long and involved story of the Japanese–Soviet dialogue – and its absence at certain periods – can be summarised fairly briefly.

Negotiations for a Soviet–Japanese peace treaty in 1955–6 failed largely because of the territorial issue. It was exploited by the opponents of Prime Minister Hatoyama within the Liberal Democratic Party (LDP) and by the United States, which had no interest in a Japanese–Soviet rapprochement at that time. Although the Soviets had initiated the negotiations and had caught the Japanese unprepared[41] they began on the basis of a seven-article memorandum presented by the Japanese side. It referred to the territorial issue in the following terms:

> The Habomais, Shikotan, the Kurile Islands and southern Sakhalin are historically Japanese territory, but upon the restoration of peace we propose a frank exchange of views regarding future disposition of those areas.[42]

The Japanese Ambassador had instructions that the unconditional return of the Habomais and Shikotan would be a satisfactory basis on which to conclude a peace treaty and that the return of the Southern Kuriles was demanded for historical reasons but was not essential for an overall settlement. The rest of the Kuriles and South Sakhalin had been mentioned only for bargaining purposes. The Russians countered with a draft treaty which would have led to the abrogation of the US–Japan Security Treaty and Japanese recognition of Soviet sovereignty over South Sakhalin and the Kuriles.[43]

By August 1955, the Soviets had offered a compromise which dropped the demand for the abandonment of the US–Japan Security Treaty and expressed a readiness to return 'the Little Kuriles'. There came a point when the Japanese Foreign Minister, Shigemitsu Mamoru, seemed to be on the verge of concluding a treaty on the basis of an immediate return of Shikotan and the Habomais, but he was overruled by the government in Tokyo.[44] Accordingly, the Japanese position reverted to the demand for a return of all four Northern Territories. The final Declaration of 19 October 1956, which restored diplomatic relations but left the parties without a peace treaty, included a statement in Article 9, that the Soviet Union would 'transfer to Japan the Habomai Islands and the island of Shikoton [*sic*], the actual transfer of these islands to Japan to take place after the conclusion of a Peace Treaty'.[45]

From the start, the Japanese position had been confused. It fell victim to the personal rivalry between Hatoyama and Yoshida, which was further aggravated by the tension between those who gave priority to the relationship with the United States, who included Yoshida, and those like Hatoyama, who were inclined towards a more independently orientated foreign policy. In addition, Mr Dulles had intervened in August 1956, with a warning that if Japan accepted the Soviet proposals (i.e. the return of the 'Little Kuriles' with the virtual cession of Etorofu and Kunashiri to the Soviet Union), the United States would regard this as granting a 'greater advantage' under the terms of Article 26 of the San Francisco Treaty – and that might lead to a 'permanent' American occupation of Okinawa.[46] Scholars and observers are divided over the degree to which the American intervention was influential in preventing a treaty on the basis of a territorial compromise, but there can be no doubt that it was an attempt by the United States to influence the negotiations.[47]

The history of the negotiations underlies the potential for flexibility on both sides as well as the importance of domestic politics, the international environment and the role of third parties. These are significant points to remember as we survey the course of events since then and note the apparent *dialogue des sourds* which has taken place since 1960. The Soviets have vacillated between denying the foundation of any Japanese claim at all and hinting that the problem can be discussed. The Japanese side has remained adamant that no peace treaty can be signed without the return of all four territories. As of mid-1989, the Soviet Union has adopted the 'hint' position and the Japanese, while sticking to the 'all or nothing' position, express their satisfaction that a dialogue over the issue has been resumed after many years. Nearly all the other issues between the two countries are directly or indirectly related to the dispute over the Northern Territories.

Security: The Military Dimension

The existence of a Soviet military 'threat' to Japan was first raised by the United States in preliminary and informal discussions with the Japanese over the shape of an eventual peace settlement. It was heavily influenced by the emerging US confrontation with the Soviet Union and was based on the assumption of an American withdrawal from Japan after a peace treaty had been signed. Until then, the Japanese authorities had regarded Soviet–American rivalry as a manifestation of normal tensions between great powers and not as a fundamental obstacle to a co-ordinated Allied policy over the shape of a peace settlement. This, presumably, would include a continued Allied (i.e. American) military presence in Japan to ensure that its terms were carried out.

The prospect that an American withdrawal would expose Japan to Soviet pressures was raised by General Robert Eichelberger, Commander of the US Eighth Army, when he warned that Soviet forces based on Sakhalin and the Kurile Islands might capture airfields in Hokkaido. This theme of Russian military power and the weakness of Japan, especially the existence of a potential fifth column in the shape of a powerful JCP, was an element in the debate among American policy makers about the post-war settlement with Japan. The fear was shared by Prime Minister Yoshida and led to the 1951 Security Treaty with the United States.[48]

The military dimension of security, especially as it related to the Russian occupation of the Northern Territories, subsided in the 1960s, after the Soviet Union had withdrawn most of the troops stationed on Etorofu and Kunashiri. It revived with a new build-up of Soviet forces on those islands in the spring of 1978, when negotiations for the signature of a Sino–Japanese Treaty of Peace and Friendship were nearing their conclusion. At present, a force of division strength, including the most modern equipment and with a substantial infrastructure of bases and some forty Mig-23 fighters, is stationed on the larger two islands. In addition, a number of divisions are deployed on Sakhalin, around the Sea of Okhotsk, and in the Maritime Province of the Soviet Far East. All this has to be set against the background of an impressive development of naval and air power, the fruit of long-term planning since the 1960s.[49]

Any comparison between Soviet and Western forces in the region has to take into account deployment strategies and missions as well as technological and geographical factors. The Soviet Union has created in the Sea of Okhotsk a bastion for its nuclear ballistic missile submarines (SSBN), which are capable of targeting large areas of the Western United States. The Central and Southern Kuriles provide the most secure, ice-free passage Soviet naval forces into and out of the Pacific Ocean. Japanese military planners express concern over a potential Soviet capability to land substantial forces in key areas of Hokkaido, primarily to seize control of the Soya–La Perouse Strait linking the Sea of Japan with the Sea of Okhotsk.[50]

Making due allowance for some exaggeration, Soviet armed strength in the region is nonetheless formidable. The trend of the Soviet build-up and the Japanese–American response are perfect illustrations of the law of mutual insecurity; the perceived requirements of one party's security become the ingredients of the other party's insecurity.

Russian military planning proceeds from the assumption of a potential multiple threat to its vulnerable East Asian position from China, the United States and Japan. The list of vulnerabilities is long. It includes extended and precarious lines of communication, a population thinly scattered over vast territories, seaports which are icebound for part of the year and exits to the China Seas and the Pacific that can be blockaded by the enemy. From this perspective, the stationing of the best and most heavily armed divisions of the Japanese Ground Self-Defence Force (GSDF) in Hokkaido, the formidable air power concentrated at the American base of Misawa in Northern Honshu, the planned expansion of the Japanese Maritime Self-Defence Force (MSDF) and the deployment of powerful units of the US Seventh Fleet in the Sea of Japan, are all seen as 'threatening'. The allies have justified their deployment not only as a response to a steady increase of Soviet military power, but also to Soviet expansionism in the 1980s, especially the acquisition of basing facilities at Danang and Cam Ranh Bay, and the supply of military hardware to North Korea in return for overflying rights and the possible use of ports.[51]

Security: The International and Political Dimensions

The military aspect of security cannot be separated from its political aspect, which has been dominated by Japan's close alignment with the

United States. In the first decades following the restoration of Japan's sovereignty, the overall direction of Japanese policy was greatly influenced by US relations with the Soviet Union. Since its *aide-memoire* of September 1956 (see note 23), the United States has maintained its formal support of the Japanese position over the Northern Territories, though this may not have been as vigorous as the Japanese would have liked. From time to time, the Japanese Government has asked the American President to raise the issue with Moscow.[52]

By and large, Japan has rather faithfully, if not always enthusiastically, endorsed the general US line towards the Soviet Union, in contrast to the more nuanced position it has taken on the China question.[53] The Soviets encouraged dependence on the United States by making it all too obvious that their objective was to undermine and eventually remove American protection and thus pull Japan into their own sphere of influence. In January 1960, following the signature of the revised security treaty between the United States and Japan, they stipulated that Shikotan and the Habomais would be returned only after all American forces had been withdrawn from Japan.

The change in the international environment brought about by the hostility between the Soviet Union and China, and by the restoration of American and Japanese relations with China, opened a wider field of manoeuvre for Japanese diplomacy. Yet, despite protestations about an 'equidistant' policy towards China and the Soviet Union in the 1970s, the choice had already been made at the beginning of the decade. To be sure, Japan was very reluctant to include the anti-hegemony clause (aimed at the Soviet Union) in the Treaty of Peace and Friendship with China, but that was more out of fear of its exploitation by China than out of any intention to pursue an equidistant policy.

Japan's *immobilisme* towards the Soviet Union has several causes. The first and most obvious one is the territorial dispute in which the Japanese regard themselves as the aggrieved party. Next is the fact that the only conceivable military threat to Japan comes from the Soviet Union. A third is the dominance of the Yoshida policy line in post-war Japan, which laid primary stress on economic reconstruction, a low-key diplomatic posture and reliance on the Japan–US security system.[54]

Only two prime ministers of the post-war era have displayed a tendency to break with this line: Hatoyama and Nakasone. It is possible that the former wanted to normalise relations with the Soviet Union as an initial step towards a more independent stance, which would have included an element of balancing between the superpowers. His opposition to the Yoshida line was reinforced by personal antipathy and anti-American sentiment.[55] It may seem strange to regard Nakasone as the other deviant, given his excellent personal relationship with US President Reagan during his term of office and his staunch support of the Western Alliance. Nakasone, an intelligent nationalist, sees Japan's close association with the United States and the West as a necessary first stage in the achievement of a more independent role in world politics. During the last years of his term as Prime Minister, he began to cultivate a personal relationship with Mr Gorbachev, which has continued since Nakasone became an 'elder statesman'. There can be little doubt of his ambition to be instrumental in bringing Gorbachev to Tokyo and to make a contribution to a settlement of the territorial dispute.[56]

Miki Takeo might be regarded as the third prime minister to have stepped out of line. An article in *Foreign Affairs* by one of his advisers was seen as a trial balloon for a possible 'two-tier' approach to solving the territorial issue. It suggested the conclusion of a peace treaty on the basis of the return of the Habomais and Shikotan and an agreement to shelve the problem of the reversion of Kunashiri and Etorofu for twenty-five years.[57] This proposal provoked a storm of protest in Japan. Miki's political power base within the LDP was weak and whatever his intentions, they remained unfulfilled. His and many other examples illustrate the extent to which foreign policy initiatives in Japan depend on personal ambition and on domestic politics, especially the personal and factional rivalries within the ruling party.

The Economic Interest

The economic dimension is usually seen as having a major bearing on any bilateral relationship. This is all the more true of an economic power like Japan, whose external policies seem to be almost exclusively governed by economic considerations – at least until now. Yet, in its relations with the Soviet Union, the focus has been on historical, security, political and diplomatic factors. Several reasons account for the lack of emphasis on economic factors.

In spite of loose talk about 'Japan Inc.', detailed analyses have revealed that business interests rarely speak with one voice and frequently pull in opposite directions.[58] While the fishing lobby and, at times of recession, the steel industry have shown a strong interest in an improvement of Japanese–Soviet relations, large sectors of industry and commerce – especially the dominant service industries like banking and insurance – are much less interested.

Part of the explanation lies in the structure of Japanese–Soviet trade, which is more like that between a developed and a developing economy than between two highly developed societies. Japan's principal exports by category have been capital equipment and manufactured goods. The main Soviet exports have been sources of energy and raw materials. Of course, the relative importance of various items has changed over time.[59]

In terms of value, Japan's trade with the Soviet Union has never amounted to much more than 2 per cent of its total foreign trade. Fluctuations in the level have depended more on the status of contracts under the system of compensation agreements than on the prevailing political climate. Thus, Soviet–Japanese trade fell by about a quarter in 1983, compared with the previous year, partly because the procurement of Japanese goods for the Urengoi–Uzhgorod gas pipeline had come to an end and there was no major new contract in the offing.[60] At the height of the 'Siberian boom' in the 1960s and early 1970s, the proportion of trade with the Soviet Union in relation to Japan's overall trade never exceeded 3 per cent. Between 1950 and 1974, there was only one year (1962) in which the balance of trade was in Japan's favour. In every year since then, Japan has had a surplus.[61] It is one of the Soviet Union's major trading partners. On the other hand, the Soviet Union occupies a much lower position among Japan's trading partners. For instance, in 1988 the value of Japan's China trade was three times that of trade with the Soviet Union.[62]

Fishing rights and investment constitute the other two main themes in the economic relationship. The issue of fishing zones is, of course, directly related to the territorial issue and has been the subject of many post-war agreements, varying in duration from one to five years, which regulate the catches and *modus operandi* of the two parties. We may note several characteristics of the relationship, without going into detail. The Soviets claim that they are more concerned with the economic and technical aspects than with the political implications.

From the Japanese perspective, the political dimension is of great importance because they are the *demandeurs* in this respect. Their fishing industry depends on the ability to operate in waters under Soviet control and to harvest kelp (*konbu*) along the shores around the Northern Territories. The Soviets have used their strong position to put pressure on Japanese fisherfolk, granting them benefits and favours in return for consumer goods and useful information. Failure to comply has meant harassment and arrest with long periods of imprisonment. The Japanese authorities are particularly anxious to prevent a de facto recognition of the Soviet occupation of the Northern Territories through collaboration between Japanese and Soviet fishing concerns. A recent example of this was the case of an Ainu Fishing co-operative, which planned to establish a trout hatchery off Kunashiri as a joint venture with the Soviets. The Ainu were the original inhabitants of the Kurile Islands and a new assertiveness among them raises the intriguing prospect of further complications in the territorial dispute.[63] Soviet support for various Japanese–Soviet friendship associations is also seen as part of the effort to penetrate and influence public opinion.[64]

Finally, there remains the question of Siberian development. The potential of that region is not in dispute, but its attraction is heavily outweighed by adverse considerations. The enormous geographical and technical difficulties of extracting the resources of Siberia and of developing a solid industrial infrastructure require massive investments with long time horizons. The Soviet Union is short of hard currency as a result of the decline in the price of oil and natural gas, which account for some 80 per cent of its foreign earnings. It cannot, therefore, afford to buy the necessary equipment and technology. It would take several years to compensate for the shortage of capital by developing export-orientated manufacturing industries on the Chinese model and with the help of foreign investment. Similarly, to develop the potentially large domestic market for consumer goods in collaboration with foreign enterprises would require a convertible rouble, which remains a long-term prospect and may not be achieved until the turn of the century.

In contrast to Japan's economic relations with China, those with the Soviet Union are often restricted for political reasons. When the interest of Japanese industry in the China market flags MITI may step in to keep it alive.[65] With the Soviet Union, on the other hand, the government acts as a restraint. The decision not to participate in the construction of the Baikal–Amur Railway was taken following Chinese pressure against an enterprise with strategic implications. Japanese firms sometimes slip the leash, as when they assisted in the construction of a dry dock of obvious benefit to the Soviet Pacific Fleet, or when the Toshiba Machine Corporation sold milling machines to the Soviet Union which indirectly would make it easier for submarines to elude acoustic detection. The latter incident caused serious difficulties with the United States. On the whole, however, political and strategic considerations dominate Japan's economic relations with the Soviet Union.

Popular Images

The Soviet Union usually competes with Korea and, occasionally, a Southeast Asian state for top place among the 'least-liked' countries in Japanese public opinion surveys. This contrasts with popular attitudes towards Japan in the Soviet Union. In spite of the extreme hostility of the Soviet media through most of the post-war era, the public, especially young people, have a favourable image of Japan as a country of advanced technology with much-admired cultural traits. One reason for this view is the absence of memories of Japanese 'aggression'. The war of 1904–5 and the occupation of Siberia have passed into history, although the party and government did their best to keep the memory alive.[66] On the other hand, the circumstances of the Soviet entry into the Pacific War, the cruelties committed by the Red Army in Manchuria, the appalling treatment meted out to Japanese prisoners of war and their long captivity, as well as the seizure of the Northern Territories have powerfully influenced Japanese perceptions of the Soviet Union.[67]

Public opinion is, however, fickle. The fact that Russia has a negative image does not necessarily mean that it will persist for all time. One need only refer to the dramatic changes in the mutual perceptions of the French and Germans since 1945 or the rather more favourable view of the Russians held by many Japanese in the mid-nineteenth century. Nonetheless, popular feelings about the Soviet Union are complex and deeply rooted in history. Racialism may not be as important a feature as is commonly supposed; it is a variable which becomes salient under certain economic and political conditions, when it is often exploited for ulterior motives. There has been equal racialism on the European side, as expressed in fears of the 'Yellow Peril' (primarily directed against China) which found such strong expression in Russia at the turn of the century and is still latent today.[68] Historical influences help to explain the aversion for the northern neighbour, but the post-war experience is a more important factor. It has been strengthened by an antipathy to communism, which is regarded as an alien ideology like other Western systems of thought.

The occupation of the Northern Territories has played its part in perpetuating the generally hostile attitude towards the Soviet Union. Although the interest of the average Japanese in the issue is aroused only when he is reminded of it, as on Northern Territories Day (7 February – the anniversary of the Treaty of Shimoda), the sense of injustice is deeply ingrained. Schoolchildren are taught about the issue in the same way that all Argentine children learn about the Malvinas being wrongfully occupied by the British. It is possible that Mr Gorbachev and his policies may eventually reduce the negative image. In early 1988 there were some signs of a more favourable public attitude towards the Soviet Union. One-fifth of the respondents to a poll thought that the Soviet Union was peace-loving. Five years earlier, only 2.1 per cent subscribed to that view.[69] But to lay more enduring foundations for good Japanese–Soviet relations, there will have to be more substantial changes.

THE GORBACHEV PHENOMENON

It is too early to assess the significance and implications of Soviet policies since 1985. If they persist, they will have a profound impact on the pattern of world politics. Already there have been substantial changes in the atmosphere and substance of East–West relations, but the effect on Japan's relations with the Soviet Union has remained rather limited.

Within a year of Gorbachev's assumption of power, there was a new ambassador in Tokyo. Unlike his predecessors, he had not been a member of the Party's Central Committee, but he was a career diplomat with a knowledge of Japan and Japanese.[70] The appointment did not signify any rise in the status of Japan in Soviet eyes but, at least, here was a genuine 'Japan hand' who could be counted upon to understand Japanese feelings and report them back to his superiors.

Gorbachev's first four years have also seen some agreements. One, on fishing, was signed in December 1986, and signalled an improvement in bilateral relations both in the short time it took to negotiate and in its terms. Following Foreign Minister Shevardnadze's visit to Tokyo in December 1988, documents were exchanged on cultural relations as well as a treaty for the protection of 287 kinds of migratory birds. Japan had taken fifteen years to ratify the treaty because the Soviets had listed two species as inhabiting only the Northern Territories. Acceptance of this would have been tantamount to a Japanese recognition of Soviet sovereignty over the islands. Only after the Soviet Union had omitted one and admitted that the other was also resident elsewhere in the Soviet Union, could the treaty be ratified.

A similar problem arose over the visits by former Japanese residents to ancestral graves on the Northern Territories. They had ceased in 1976, when the Soviet Union required visas for such trips. Compliance, again, would have implied recognition of Soviet sovereignty. Under a new agreement, visits are allowed without passports and visas, but with identification papers issued by the Japanese Government. Similar arrangements apply to Russian visits to the graves of servicemen who died in captivity during the 1904–5 war. However, since that would have appeared to be purely reciprocal and therefore an implied Japanese recognition of Soviet sovereignty over the Northern Territories, the same right of visits to Japanese graves was extended to Sakhalin, Moscow and other places. The Japanese side could thus maintain the fiction that reciprocity was granted only in return for Japanese visits to the Russian mainland.[71]

Other examples of an improvement in bilateral relations include the establishment of a joint working group at vice-ministerial level to continue discussions over a peace treaty; Japanese aid following the Armenian earthquake in December 1988, and after the gas explosion and rail disaster in the Urals in June 1989; the establishment of a working party by the Hokkaido prefectural government and the authorities in Sakhalin and Khabarovsk to examine the feasibility of a Hokkaido–Sakhalin Ferry Service and of a freight service between Otaru and the terminal of the second Siberian railway. Agreement has also been reached that Mr Gorbachev should visit Japan some time in 1991.

The sum total of developments since 1985 add up to several minor agreements, an intensified dialogue at different levels and on different subjects, expressions of goodwill and good intentions and, most important of all, a Soviet readiness to listen, if not to respond, to Japanese territorial claims. However, these developments trace only the periphery of the realtionship, though they may be a necessary preparation of the ground for more substantial progress, which will have to include measures that deal with the central issue.

CONCLUSION

The two countries remain deadlocked over the Northern Territories. As the status quo power, the Soviet Union hopes that, for Japan, the attraction of Siberian development and the fear of being shouldered out by other Western rivals will push the territorial question into the background. It might be impossible to abandon it altogether, but it could become a formal rather than a real issue, just as Chinese claims to large tracts of Soviet East Asia and the Japanese-controlled Senkaku

Islands or the Japanese claim to the Korean-occupied Takeshima Islands have become formal issues without impairing the development of bilateral relationships. Japan, on the other hand, insists that the Soviet Union should pay the price for friendly relations and economic co-operation by accepting the legitimacy of its demands and negotiating seriously over the territorial issue.

Each party may overestimate the strength of its position and underestimate the determination of the other. With the choice of alternative partners from Western Europe, South Korea, and possibly the United States, it is doubtful whether the Soviet Union would be prepared to exchange the strategically important southern Kuriles for Japanese capital and technology. Japan's generally weak economic interest in the Soviet Union and doubts about the success of the new Soviet policies make it unlikely that it would allow the territorial issue to subside or that it would accept a 'separation of economics from politics'.

Two questions remain: what is it that makes the issue so important in the bilateral relationship, and how might it be resolved? After all, Japanese–Soviet relations since 1956 have not been so different from those of other Western countries with the Soviet Union, where there are no territorial problems. Relations have fluctuated under the influence of tension and detente between the superpowers and according to changing economic interests. The Northern Territories issue has been more forcefully stressed at times of general tension, but it seems to have been the excuse for, rather than the cause of, tension.

This may be the Soviet perception. Bearing in mind the way in which other territorial disputes in the region have been put into cold storage, the Russians have sought to bypass the issue by proposing the signature of a treaty of 'co-operation and good neighbourliness' or some such formula, thus avoiding the seemingly intractable problem of a formal treaty of peace. However, to make comparisons with other bilateral arrangements in Northeast Asia is misleading. China and the Soviet Union had not been at war with each other and had been allies. Japan did sign a Treaty of Peace and Friendship with China in 1978, which made no mention of the Senkaku Islands.[72] Japan and the Republic of Korea signed a Treaty on Basic Relations in 1965 and agreed to leave the dispute over Takeshima to be negotiated separately in the future.[73] The Soviets might think that a settlement on the lines of the Sino–Japanese Treaty would be the ideal solution. Failing that, the Japanese–Korean Treaty could be a useful model.

Neither of these solutions would satisfy Japan's present position.

The territorial question was not the central or most important issue in the relationship between China and Japan or between South Korea and Japan. In the former, China is the claimant and decided to shelve the issue in favour of more important objectives. In the latter, Japan is the claimant, but was under strong pressure from its business community and the United States not to allow this obstacle to stand in the way of making a new start in relations with its former colony. A peace treaty with the Soviet Union would be the fourth attempt to settle the frontier between the two states. The previous delimitations were in 1855, 1875 and 1905, when Japan acquired South Sakhalin.

In theory, at least, it is possible to envisage progress in resolving the dispute along the lines of Article 9 of the Joint Declaration of October 1956 or of Hirasawa's proposals in 1975. This approach would include the immediate and unconditional return of Shikotan and the Habomais and some formula to safeguard the Japanese position over Etorofu and Kunashiri, without their immediate evacuation by the Soviet Union. The territorial arrangements might be buttressed by a number of agreements over fishing rights, commerce, economic co-operation, and other related issues. Further variations have been suggested since then, such as a lease-back proposed by anonymous Soviet officials; an idea which may owe something to similar proposals that have been made from time to time about the Falkland Islands.

In practice, there are formidable obstacles in the way of any progress. The Soviet Union might agree to hand over Shikotan and the Habomais as promised in 1956. Furthermore, since Gorbachev has had no difficulty in abandoning or reversing Stalinist policies, it should be possible for him to do the same with Stalin's legacy over the Northern Territories. The argument that the Soviet Union would never surrender territory is dubious. The 1984 border treaty with North Korea,[74] which included territorial concessions, and recent changes in Eastern Europe make it harder to insist on the inviolability of the post-war status quo.

However, the Russians are not ready to give up the military/strategic advantage conferred by their control over the Northern Territories without substantial changes in the region's strategic environment. In two major policy speeches on East Asia, Gorbachev resurrected earlier proposals for an Asian collective security system.[75] They contain major differences from previous blueprints. The objective of encircling and isolating China has disappeared and there have been minor but significant concessions over the boundary in the Amur River. Most important, there will be substantial troop withdrawals and cuts. Nevertheless, the basic objective of confirming post-war political and territorial settlements remains. Probably the biggest obstacle to progress on the Soviet side is the continued neglect of Japan. Gorbachev's two speeches gave no indication that this attitude had changed. Apart from some condescending words about its post-war achievements, Japan is urged to forget the past and to concentrate on economic cooperation.

The difficulties on the Japanese side are, if anything, more serious. The formal position of the Japanese government has hardened into a demand for the return of *all* four territories. A prime minister who accepted anything less would be in trouble on two fronts. Rivals in his party as well as the opposition would seek to exploit the 'sell-out' for their own political advantage. All parties accept the justice of the territorial demand, although there are considerable variations among them about its extent (only the four territories or all of the Kuriles) and the method by which it might be achieved (a step-by-step approach or an all-embracing settlement, perhaps leading to a fundamental change in Japanese foreign policy). In addition, those who out of ideological or other motives want to revive patriotic and nationalist feelings in a civilian mass-consumer society, have an interest in blocking any accommodation and in emphasising the 'threat' from the north.

In spite of the obstacles on both sides, strong hints from Soviet leaders that they are prepared to take the territorial question seriously and Japan's expressed willingness to work for an improvement in the bilateral relationship without making settlement of the territorial dispute a precondition, point toward the possibility of a compromise. Until recently, there was no immediate prospect of a breakthrough in the current negotiations because of Soviet preoccupations elsewhere. It is noteworthy that during his visit to China in May 1989, Gorbachev expressed a strong desire for improved relations with Japan. Having made his settlement with China, it may be that he is now ready to devote greater attention to Japan. The decision to visit Tokyo in 1991 may indicate that the Russians, at least, calculate that by then they will have achieved a breakthrough in their relations with Japan.

The impulse that will propel both sides towards an agreement is therefore likely to arise from a favourable international environment which would make an accommodation appear to be highly desirable. The United States has a key role to play in this respect. Since the origins of the territorial dispute lie in Soviet–American relations during and after the war, one could say that the United States has a moral responsibility to work for a resolution. Most of the post-war era has been dominated by the confrontation between the two superpowers. As a friend of the United States, Japan has been in the forefront of the confrontation. The territorial issue also served to show the United States and the rest of the world that Japan, too, could be tough and stand up to the Soviet Union. However, an American involvement that took the form of a US–Soviet *diktat* would be wholly unacceptable to Japan. The US could act constructively only in an indirect manner.

A wide-ranging arms control regime in Northeast Asia would have the effect of reducing the strategic importance of the Northern Territories. Thus, a successful START agreement might reduce the importance of the Sea of Okhotsk as a base for Soviet SSBNs. Reductions in Soviet and American naval and air forces would be another step in that direction. The demilitarisation of all the Kurile Islands, Sakhalin, and Hokkaido would change the strategic environment even more dramatically. Gorbachev's overall policies point in this direction. The co-operation of the United States, the entry of China into the process of detente and current moves towards a dialogue in Korea are also helping to create an environment in which it would be easier to make progress over the Northern Territories. The international climate would be further improved if the evolution of a mutual security system were reinforced by a gradual economic integration of the whole region, including the Soviet Union, China, Japan and Korea; something foreshadowed in Sino–Soviet calls for trilateral co-operation.[76]

A quite different course of events might lead to a dramatic shift in power relationships, in which Japan and the Soviet Union were drawn into close co-operation for one reason or another. Implausible as such a scenario may seem today, it has historical antecedents and would, of course, provide a strong incentive to remove any obstacles in the way of a rapprochement. Another possibility is the sharpening of Japanese–Soviet antagonism through a renewed Cold War or some other form of big-power rivalries in the region. In that event, the friction in the bilateral relationship would grow and any settlement of the Northern Territories issue would become much more intractable.

In the short term, the willingness of both parties to negotiate patiently and persistently and the existence of a favourable climate of international relations in the region will be indispensable to the search for a solution to the problem of the Northern Territories. The issue of territorial rights and sovereignty remain central to the dispute. Historical experience tells us that they can linger for centuries. An accelerating movement towards global economic integration, in which Japan is a leader and the Soviet Union a would-be participant, and the rapid emergence of global environmental problems may eventually make questions of sovereignty and territorial control seem less central. But it will take time.

Notes and References

The author would like to express his thanks to the Japan Foundation for enabling him to study this subject on one of its fellowship awards and to his wife for help with material in the Japanese language.

1. The classic study of the first two centuries of Russo–Japanese relations is George A. Lensen, *The Russian Push Toward Japan: Russo–Japanese Relations, 1697–1875* (Princeton, NJ: Princeton University Press, 1959).
2. Lensen, *The Russian Push*, pp. 417–18, 422–4.
3. George A. Lensen, *Japanese Recognition of the USSR: Soviet–Japanese Relations 1921–1930* (Tokyo: Sophia University and Tallahassee, FL: The Diplomatic Press, 1970) pp. 5–6, 322–32.
4. In addition to the work of Lensen, which contains the full texts of the Treaties of Shimoda and St Petersburg (in Lensen, *The Russian Push*, pp. 475–7 and 501–6), the territorial question is most comprehensively treated in two books by John J. Stephan, *Sakhalin: A History* (Oxford: Oxford University Press, 1971) and *The Kuril Islands: Russo–Japanese Frontier in the Pacific* (Oxford: Oxford University Press, 1974). In this article, all references to Stephan are from the 1974 book. For a very brief summary of the historical background to the Northern Territories issue, see Wolf Mendl, 'Japan's Northern Territories: An Asian Falklands?', *The World Today*, 43(6) (1987) pp. 99–100. The Japanese perspective is to be found in Kimura Hiroshi (ed.), *Hoppo Ryodo o Kangaeru* (Sapporo: Hokkaido Shimbun, 1982).
5. Stephan (1974) pp. 92–3.
6. Stephan (1974) p. 61.
7. Lensen, *The Russian Push*, pp. 177–9, 182–3.
8. George A. Lensen, *The Strange Neutrality: Soviet–Japanese Relations during the Second World War 1941–1945* (Tallahassee, FL: The Diplomatic Press, 1972) pp. 214–16.
9. Lensen, *The Strange Neutrality*, p. 214.
10. Quoted in Lensen, *The Russian Push*, p. 441.
11. Lensen, *The Russian Push*, pp. 277–82.
12. In 1920, Lenin had referred to the struggle between Japan and the United States for control over the Pacific and its coastline, which made 'war between America and Japan inevitable'. V. I. Lenin, *On the Foreign Policy of the Soviet State* (Moscow: Progress Publishers, no date) p. 303.
13. See Lensen, *The Russian Push*, pp. 316–18, 355–68, 444–5, 448–52.
14. Lensen, *The Russian Push*, p. 424.
15. Lensen, *Japanese Recognition of the USSR*, pp. 85–6, 145–6.
16. 'For Russia the Japanese have had no reason to entertain a very favourable feeling. The Kurile Islands, which had belonged to Japan, were slowly and silently wrested from our territory, or, as the native phrase is "were motheaten". The constant boundary disputes in Saghalien [*sic*], which it was a policy becoming the aggressive temper of Russia to evoke, only terminated in the exchange of that island in 1875, for a comparatively useless group of the Kuriles', Inazo Nitobe, 'The Intercourse between the United States and Japan: an historical sketch', originally published in 1891 (Baltimore, MD: Johns Hopkins Press),

reprinted in *The Works of Inazo Nitobe: Vol. II* (Tokyo: University of Tokyo Press, 1972) p. 338. For a good discussion of the 'pro-Russian' and 'pro-British' elements in the Japanese leadership at the beginning of the century, see Ian H. Nish, *The Anglo–Japanese Alliance: the Diplomacy of two Island Empires, 1894–1907* (London: The Athlone Press, 1968) pp. 167–8.

17. For the Kurile Islands and the Yalta accord, see *Foreign Relations of the United States* (hereafter referred to as *FRUS*), *The Conference at Malta and Yalta 1945*, pp. 379–83, 984.

18. *Japan's Northern Territories* (Tokyo: Northern Territories Issue Association, 1974) p. 5. The Association is a semi-official body supported by the Gaimusho. See Stephan (1974) pp. 158–65 for an account of the military operations in the Kuriles.

19. *FRUS 1945*, vol. 6, pp. 658–9.

20. *FRUS 1945*, p. 692. For Stalin's request and the subsequent exchanges with Truman, see *FRUS 1945*, pp. 668, 670, 687, 695–6, 698–9. There is a useful account of the Allied discussions about the plans for acceptance of the Japanese surrender, in Herbert Feis, *The Atomic Bomb and the End of World War II* (Princeton, NJ: Princeton University Press, 1971) pp. 151–4.

21. The Japanese claim that the USSR occupied Shikotan and the Habomais as the result of a procedural error. During the war, the military units stationed on these small islands were under the Chishima (Kurile) command, although Shikotan and the Habomais were a political subdivision of Hokkaido, separate from the local administration of the Kurile Islands. In August 1945, Imperial Headquarters had ordered units in the Kuriles to surrender to the Russians and the units in Hokkaido to capitulate to the Americans. The troops on Shikotan and the Habomais surrendered to the Soviets, presumably because they were under the Chishima command, although, so it is argued, they should have been counted among those in Hokkaido.

22. *Aide-Memoire* to the British Embassy (13 March 1951) in *FRUS 1951*, vol. 6, Part 1, p. 922.

23. 'The United States has reached the conclusion after careful examination of the historical facts that the islands of Etorofu and Kunashiri (along with the Habomai Islands and Shikotan which are a part of Hokkaido) have always been part of Japan proper and should in justice be acknowledged as under Japanese sovereignty'. *Aide-Memoire* on Yalta issued by the Department of State on 7 September 1956. Quoted in Stephan (1974) p. 246.

24. For a summary of the Soviet perspective, see Stephan (1974) pp. 203–8. Also, Yevgeni Prokhorov and Leonid Shevchuk, 'Japan's Territorial Claims to the USSR', *International Affairs* (Moscow) (February 1989) pp. 42–7.

25. Quoted in *Japan's Northern Territories*, p. 23.

26. *International Declarations* (London: National Peace Council, September 1945) pp. 27–8.

27. Stephan (1974) p. 240.

28. Prokhorov and Shevchuk, 'Japan's Territorial Claims', pp. 42–3, 45–6.

29. Among the many reasons advanced by Anatoly Gromyko for the inability to accede to the Treaty, were the refusal to invite the People's Republic of China, that the Treaty gave no guarantee against the revival of Japanese militarism or the recurrence of aggression, that it made no provision for the withdrawal of foreign troops from Japan, that it allowed Japan to join regional security pacts that were a threat to peace in East Asia, that the territorial provisions violated the rights of the Soviet Union and the People's Republic of China, and that the economic provisions ensured foreign privileges which had been obtained during the occupation. Hugh Borton, *Japan's Modern Century* (New York: The Ronald Press Company, 1955) p. 442. For Borton's own role and views, see Michael M. Yoshitsu, *Japan and the San Francisco Peace Settlement* (New York: Columbia University Press, 1983) pp. 3, 12–13.

30. Quoted in Fuji Kamiya, 'The Northern Territories: 130 Years of Japanese Talks with Czarist Russia and the Soviet Union', in Donald S. Zagoria (ed.), *Soviet Policy in East Asia* (New Haven and London: Yale University Press, 1982) p. 126.

31. Yoshitsu, *Japan and the San Francisco Peace Settlement*, pp. 7–9.

32. *Record of Debates in the House of Representatives (Shugiin)* (1950) (Showa 24) (4 November).

33. Quoted in Ito Kenichi, 'Hopporyodo Henkan eno Senryaku', *Voice* (March 1986) pp. 134–47. See also, Kamiya, 'The Northern Territories', p. 128.

34. *Record of Debates in the House of Councillors (Sangiin)* (1952) (Showa 26) (13 November).

35. *Article 25*: 'For the purposes of the present Treaty the Allied Powers shall be the States at war with Japan, or any State which previously formed a part of the territory of a State named in Article 23 [a list of the Allied powers that signed the Treaty, excluding, among others, the Soviet Union], provided that in each case the State concerned has signed and ratified the Treaty. Subject to the provisions of Article 21 [referring to China and Korea], the present Treaty shall not confer any rights, titles or benefits on any State which is not an Allied Power as herein defined; *nor shall any right, title or interest of Japan be deemed to be diminished or prejudiced by any provision of the Treaty in favour of a State which is not an Allied Power as so defined*' (emphasis added).

 Article 26: 'Japan will be prepared to conclude with any State which signed or adhered to the United Nations Declaration of January 1, 1942, and which is at war with Japan, ..., which is not a signatory of the present Treaty, a bilateral Treaty of Peace on the same or substantially the same terms as are provided for in the present Treaty, *but this obligation on the part of Japan will expire three years after the first coming into force of the present Treaty*. Should Japan make a peace settlement or war claims settlement with any State granting that State greater advantages than those provided by the present Treaty, those same advantages shall be extended to the parties of the present Treaty' (emphasis added).

 For a discussion of the Japanese position over the Kuriles during the negotiations for the Treaty, see Yoshitsu, *Japan and the San Francisco Peace Settlement*, pp. 7–9, 12–14, 17–18, 35, 44–5.

36. *Sakhalin–Kuril Islands (Karafuto–Chishima) Exchange Treaty (1875) Article II*: 'In exchange for the cession to Russia of the rights on the island of Sakhalin, ..., His Majesty the Emperor of all the Russias, for Himself and His descendants, cedes to His Majesty the Emperor of Japan the group of the Kuril islands which he possesses at present, ... This group comprises the following eighteen islands'. There follow the names of the islands, beginning with Shimushu and ending with Uruppu. Text of the Treaty of St Petersburg (English translation from the original text in French); Lensen, *The Russian Push toward Japan*, pp. 501–2.

37. Summary of Discussion between Hayato Ikeda and Joseph Dodge (2 May 1950) *FRUS 1950*, vol. 6, p. 1196. See also Yoshitsu, *Japan and the San Francisco Peace Settlement*, pp. 32–7.

38. *FRUS 1946*, vol. 8, p. 708.

39. *FRUS 1949*, vol. 7, Part 2, pp. 787–91.

40. Lensen, *The Strange Neutrality*, pp. 15–17, 277–9; O. Edmund Clubb, *China and Russia: The 'Great Game'* (New York: Columbia University Press, 1971) pp. 239–41, 345–7.

41. Kamiya, 'The Northern Territories', p. 129.

42. Kamiya, 'The Northern Territories', p. 130.

43. Savitri Vishwanathan, *Normalization of Japanese–Soviet Relations 1945–70* (Tallahassee, FL: The Diplomatic Press, 1973) pp. 72–3, 73–5.

44. Vishwanathan, *Normalization*, pp. 76, 79.

45. Stephan (1974) p. 247.

46. Vishwanathan, *Normalization*, pp. 79–80. See also, Nakamura Kenichi, 'Soren Kyoiron Karano Dakkyaku', *Sekai* (April 1985) pp. 56–73.

47. Vishwanathan and Nakamura attach considerable significance to American intervention. Kamiya omits any mention of it in his account of the negotiations in Kamiya, 'The Northern Territories', pp. 129–32. For a detailed description of the role of the United States, see the memoirs of Japan's chief negotiator Matsumoto Shunichi, *Mosukuwa ni kakeru niji* (Tokyo: Asahi Shimbunsha, 1966). For the influence of domestic politics and pressures, see Donald C. Hellmann, *Japanese Foreign Policy and Domestic Politics: The Peace Agreement with the Soviet Union* (Berkeley and Los Angeles, CA: University of California Press, 1969).

48. Yoshitsu, *Japan and the San Francisco Peace Settlement*, pp. 17–18, 25, 39.

49. Myles C. Robertson, *Soviet Policy Towards Japan: An Analysis of Trends in the 1970s and 1980s* (Cambridge: Cambridge University Press, 1988) pp. 113–17.

50. See the round-table discussion on the nature of the Soviet threat: 'Uchimura Gosuke vs. Kurisu Hiroomi Daitoron Soren no Nippon Senryo – sonotoki Tennosei ya Jieitai wa konaru', *Gendai* (2 February 1981) pp. 116–27.

51. Evidence of North Korean concessions to Soviet military requirements is hard to come by. The Russians are reported to have financed the construction of a port at Najin (25 miles from the Soviet border) in return for naval facilities and a link with the Soviet rail system. There have also been reports of the provision of substantial military aid in return for the use by the Soviet Pacific Fleet of naval facilities on the west

coast. Soviet warships visited Wonsan on the east coast in 1985 and 1986, but there is no confirmation that facilities have been made available. *The Economist* (5–11 May 1984, 28 September 1985); *Guardian* (7 and 8 June 1984, 1 October 1985, 3 December 1986). See also, Masashi Nishihara, *East Asian Security and the Trilateral Countries* (New York and London: New York University Press, 1985) pp. 46–7.

52. The most recent occasion was on President Reagan's visit to Moscow in May–June 1988. *Weekly Overseas Edition of The Japan Times* (hereafter referred to as *JTW*) (18 June 1988). Premier Sato had asked President Nixon to do the same on an earlier occasion. Stephan (1974) p. 220.

53. Wolf Mendl, *Issues in Japan's China Policy* (London: Macmillan for The Royal Institute of International Affairs, 1978) pp. 15–16, 122–3.

54. For a discussion of the development of this line, *Hoshu Honryu*, and its impact on the political economy of Japan, see Michio Muramatsu and Ellis S. Krauss, 'The Conservative Party Line and the Development of Patterned Pluralism', in Kozo Yamamura and Yasukichi Yasuba (eds) *The Political Economy of Japan, Vol. I: The Domestic Transformation* (Stanford, CA: Stanford University Press, 1987) pp. 516–54.

55. Hatoyama, a prominent pre-war politician, had been purged by the Occupation authorities in 1946 and did not return to politics until 1951. Haruhiro Fukui, *Party in Power: The Japanese Liberal-Democrats and Policy-making* (Berkeley and Los Angeles, CA: University of California Press, 1970), pp. 204–5.

56. Nakasone first met Gorbachev at Chernenko's funeral in March 1985 and was favourably impressed, describing Gorbachev as a 'man bestowed with energy and a modern sense', quite different from his predecessors, *JTW* (30 March 1985). He has been to Moscow on several occasions since his retirement, most notably in July 1988, when he met Gorbachev and secured from the Soviet leader an acknowledgement that the territorial dispute was an issue as well as a reference to the 1956 offer to return Shikotan and the Habomais, *JTW* (6 August 1988).

57. Kazushige Hirasawa, 'Japan's Emerging Foreign Policy', *Foreign Affairs* (October 1975) pp. 155–72.

58. See Mendl, *Issues in Japan's China Policy*, pp. 33–9. Also, Sadako Ogata, 'The Business Community and Japanese Foreign Policy: Normalization of Relations with the People's Republic of China', in Robert A. Scalapino (ed.), *The Foreign Policy of Japan* (Berkeley, CA: University of California Press, 1977) pp. 175–203.

59. Kazuyuki Kinbara, 'The Economic Dimension of Soviet Policy', in Gerald Segal (ed.), *The Soviet Union in East Asia* (London: Heinemann and Boulder, CO: Westview Press, 1983) p. 110; *JTW* (31 December 1988).

60. Robertson, *Soviet Policy Towards Japan*, pp. 54, 80.

61. Kinbara, 'The Economic Dimension', p. 104. Naotake Nobuhara and Nobutoshi Akao, 'The Politics of Siberian Development', in Nobutoshi Akao (ed.), *Japan's Economic Security* (Aldershot: Gower, 1983), p. 214. Vishwanathan, *Normalization*, pp. 92, 94, 98–9, 168; *Financial Times* (15 February 1983); *Japan Times* (5 March 1986); *JTW* (25 February and 3 March 1984, 15 August and 12 September 1987, 21 December 1988).

62. *JTW* (4 May 1985). Joachim Glaubitz, 'Zur Aussen- und Sicherheits

politik Japans', *Aus Politik und Zeitgeschichte*, Beilage zur Wochenzeitung, *Das Parlament* B 19/88 (6 May 1988) p. 42.

63. *Asahi Evening News* (23 and 31 August, 2 September 1988); *Yomiuri* (2 September 1988).

64. Murayama Masao, 'Nisso Shinzen Dantai nadono Doko', *Koan Joho* (October 1980) pp. 13–30. For the Soviet exploitation of trade for political purposes, see Fukuyama Hideharu, 'Soren no tainichi Seijikosaku', *Koan Joho* (April 1983) pp. 21–42. The Soviet version is to be found in M. Demchenko, 'Japan's Movement for Friendship with the Soviet Union', *Far Eastern Affairs*, 2 (Moscow) (1986) pp. 66–74. See also Robertson, *Soviet Policy Towards Japan*, pp. 192–7.

65. Wolf Mendl, 'Japan–China: The Economic Nexus', in Akao (ed.), *Japan's Economic Security*, p. 235.

66. See Uda Fumio, 'Sorenjin no Nihonimeiji wa naze warukunaika', *Chuo Koron* (April 1983) pp. 86–95.

67. An interesting analysis and interpretation of Japanese attitudes towards the Soviet Union is to be found in the article by Nakamura, 'Soren Kyoiron karano Dakkyaku'. See also Tsuyoshi Hasegawa, 'Japanese Perceptions of the Soviet Union: 1960–1985', in Tsuyoshi Hasegawa (ed.), *The Soviet Union Faces Asia: Perceptions and Policies* (Sapporo: The Slavic Research Center, Hokkaido University, 1987) pp. 37–70.

68. Clubb, *China and Russia*, pp. 125, 133. See also Allen S. Whiting, *Siberian Development and East Asia: Threat or Promise?* (Stanford, CA: Stanford University Press, 1981) p. 93. Whiting discovered that fear of the 'Yellow Peril' was most pronounced the further one was away from East Asia and least noticeable in Vladivostok or Khabarovsk. For a Soviet view of Chinese and Japanese 'racism' see M. I. Sladkovsky, *China and Japan: Past and Present*, Robert F. Price (ed. and trans.) (Gulf Breeze, FL: Academic International Press, 1975).

69. Gilbert Rozman, 'Japan's Soviet Watchers in the First Years of the Gorbachev Era: The Search for a Worldview for the Japanese Superpower', *The Pacific Review*, 1(4) (1988), pp. 418–19.

70. Nikolai Soloviev had been chief of the Foreign Ministry's Second Far Eastern Division and was an expert on Japanese affairs, having served in the Tokyo Embassy.

71. *JTW* (19 July 1986).

72. *Japan* (London: Japanese Embassy, 21, 16 August 1978).

73. Lazar Foscaneanu, 'Les Relations Nippo–Coréennes et les Traités de Tokio du 22 Juin 1965', *Politique Étrangère*, 4–5 (1965) pp. 369–409.

74. Nishihara, *East Asian Security*, p. 47.

75. Rede des sowjetischen Parteichefs Gorbatschow Über die Asienpolitik der Sowjetunion: 28 Juli 1986; *Europa Archiv*, 41. Jahr No. 16 (25 August 1986) pp. D457–66. Text of Gorbachev's speech at Krasnoyarsk (16 September 1988) *Summary of World Broadcasts* (SWB), Third Series SU/0260 (19 September 1988) pp. 14–15.

76. 'Attention has been paid in the Soviet Union to statements in the Chinese press on the possibilities of developing Chinese–Soviet–Japanese trilateral economic activity ... We share this approach', Gorbachev in speech at Krasnoyarsk (16 September 1988) SWB, Third Series SU/0260.

10 Four Japanese Scenarios for the Future

Takashi Inoguchi

Japan is in an era of transition. Behind a facade of confidence in their country's future, many Japanese feel adrift in the world of the late twentieth century.[1] The Japanese energy that is currently directed overseas is no longer based, as it was in the 1960s, on a nationally orchestrated strategy. Governments are no longer sure how to guide society, or with what goals. And Japanese society itself displays its loss of faith in the belief-system so dominant in the 1960s. Today the almost blind belief of that period in the loyalty to big business firms has lost its appeal. It is not an exaggeration to say that in the 1980s Japan had been improvising its responses to the unfamiliar challenges from within and without on an ad hoc basis, tenaciously adhering to time-honoured ways of doing things.

Bereft of a sense of direction, and uncertain about the future, Japan has been haunted by a vague angst about its future which has led it sometimes to hedge, and at least to limit, its commitment to the demands, requests and suggestions coming from overseas that Japan, now a global economic power, should take on more global responsibility.[2] As one observer aptly put it,

Japan, in fact, does not seem to be pursuing any reasoned search for a secure place in an uncertain world, much less a plan to dominate it, but rather an energetic, opportunistic drift reminiscent of the early 1930s, with freebooting individuals and companies out giving their country a bad name while native people back home believe, like the king of Spain, that hoarding gold will make them rich. Japan has had far too many eggs – defense, trade and technology – in one US basket, considering how uncertain the US seems to be about what to do next.[3]

One of the salient themes which emerged in the directionless Japanese society of the 1980s is an emphasis on traditional values: values such as perseverance, frugality, diligence, effort, family, community, sacrifice, humility, the spirit of harmony and deference for the elderly. This fact is instructive. The problem is that these traditional values cannot be the basis for Japanese principles in guiding Japanese global policy. Former Prime Minister Noboru Takeshita's favourite saying, 'When you do something, sweat by yourself and give credit to others', may be the epitome of humility, generosity and altruism, but it cannot be the sole organising principle of Japanese diplomacy. The same can be said about economic efficiency and profitability. They cannot dominate other considerations when the dollar's volatility could shake down the world economy or when the United States makes it imperative for its allies to implement tighter measures on technological transfer to communist countries.

Apart from these traditional values and economic criteria, which are too vague to allow one to fathom how the Japanese would like to see the world evolve, what are Japan's conceptions of its global position and its global roles? In other words, how is the country shaping its scenarios of the future worlds in which Japan will occupy a not unimportant position? This chapter addresses these and related questions, especially in relation to burden sharing and power sharing with the United States in the management of the world economy and international relations.

I will present below four Japanese scenarios of the world system in 25–50 years' time, making a clear distinction between the economic and the political and security arrangements envisaged in each scenario. In each scenario, Japan's role and the degree of burden sharing/power sharing with the United States will also be indicated. Next, the feasibility of the four scenarios will be discussed in terms of three major conditions, assessing the relative feasibility and desirability of each scenario. The United States and Japan will be the primary focus, though other major actors, no less important to Japan than the United States, will be touched upon as much as possible. Lastly, I will reflect on my findings in the light of the dominant aspirations and apprehensions of the Japanese.

But before these four scenarios are introduced, more straightforward, if somewhat prosaic opinion poll results will be presented. To know what opinion polls reveal is important since the scenarios of the future that follow are inevitably those conjured up largely by educated elites and do not necessarily represent the prevailing moods and sentiments of ordinary Japanese people.

JAPAN'S EXTERNAL ROLE: OPINION POLL RESULTS

A 1987 opinion poll provides useful data on how the Japanese people see Japan's external role. The Public Relations Department of the Prime Minister's Office commissions annual polls on Japanese diplomacy. The poll conducted in October 1987[4] contains one question relevant to our interest: 'What kind of roles do you think Japan should play in the community of nations? Choose up to two from the list below'. The list had five items:

1. Japan should make contributions in the area of international political affairs such as the improvement of East–West relations and the mediation of regional conflicts.
2. Japan should consolidate its defence capability as a member of the Western camp.
3. Japan should contribute to the healthy development of the world economy.
4. Japan should co-operate in the economic development of developing countries.
5. Japan should make contributions in scientific, technological and cultural exchanges.

Not surprisingly, the respondents overwhelmingly preferred roles outside the security and political realms. Item 3 registered 50.4 per cent; item 4, 34 per cent and item 5, 31 per cent, the three together adding up to 115.4 per cent out of a total of 162 per cent. By contrast, item 1 recorded 24.2 per cent, while item 2 registered only 7.8 per cent. It is very clear from these figures that the Japanese are disinclined to accept a major political or security role in the world.

Another poll (1986) conducted by an academic team permits us to compare the priorities attached by respondents to the domestic and international roles the government should play.[5] It allowed for multiple choices from among a list of priorities:

1. Preventing crime and securing people's safety (law and order).
2. Promoting technological innovation and raising productivity and production efficiency of the economy as a whole (economic power).
3. Increasing defence capability and consolidating national security.
4. Building roads, schools and hospitals and making life comfortable (standard of living).

5. Enhancing patriotism and strengthening the solidarity of the nation (national solidarity).
6. Promoting adjustment with foreign countries in economic fields and improving the world economy as a whole (global economic welfare).
7. Increasing taxes for those who can afford it and taking care of the poor and needy (social welfare).
8. Managing the economy to prevent inflation and unemployment (domestic economic management).

Instead of asking, 'To which task do you want to see the government attach its first priority?', the poll stated: 'There are many kinds of government policies nowadays. What do you think about the emphasis which government puts on each of them? Choose one of the following answers: (1) much more emphasis, (2) a little more emphasis, (3) keep as it is, (4) a little less emphasis, (5) no emphasis, (6) don't know and (7) no answer.

To make comparison simple, we will look only at responses for the first answer – much more emphasis. The following order of priorities emerges:

1. Domestic economic management (55.7 per cent).
2. Law and order (55.7 per cent).
3. Social welfare (45.2 per cent).
4. Standard of living (44.5 per cent).
5. Economic power (29.7 per cent).
6. Global economic welfare (27.8 per cent).
7. National solidarity (18.8 per cent).
8. National security (11.3 per cent).

In order to make comparison across different polls possible, I must make an admittedly crude assumption. If global economic welfare is said to correspond roughly to Japan's contribution in the economic field, and national security is said to correspond roughly to Japan's contribution in the security field, then two things are immediately clear: first, the overwhelming primacy of domestic priorities and, secondly, the overwhelming weight given to economic contributions compared to security contributions in Japan's desired role in the world. All this is not surprising. However, it is very important to keep in mind that, given the preoccupation with internal affairs and the avoidance of a commitment to security matters, public acceptance of the kind of world role for Japan that is envisaged by the Japanese government and expected by foreign countries can come only slowly.

It is true that overall public acceptance of Japan's greater role in the world, whether of an economic nature or otherwise, has been steadily increasing for the last few years, especially during the tenure of the Nakasone Cabinet (1982–7). But this has been largely a grudging acceptance, coming only after the government had made a series of carefully calculated incremental moves without arousing too much opposition.[6] We can recall the recent breakthrough in 1987 when the defence budget exceeded the limit of 1 per cent of GNP,[7] and also various measures enabling enhanced security co-operation with the United States, including the Japanese decision to allow participation in the US Strategic Defense Initiative (SDI) programme. But what is seen by the Japanese government as the barrier of public acceptance is still very much in evidence when it comes to Japan's security role in the world.

One recent event reinforces the impression gained from these polls. When the United States and many other NATO countries were sending naval boats to the Persian Gulf in 1987 under the US flag, the suggestion to send the Maritime Safety Agency's boats, put forward by the Prime Minister and the Foreign Ministry, was defeated in Cabinet discussions because of opposition from the Ministry of Transport (which has the Maritime Safety Agency under its jurisdiction). The Cabinet Secretary played a crucial role in siding with the Minister of Transport and with public opinion.[8] It is only against such a background that we can accurately assess Japan's conceptions of global roles, to which I now turn.

THE FOUR SCENARIOS

The following four scenarios of the world in the next 25–50 years are seen by the Japanese as 'visions of the future'.[9] Although in some respects they overlap, they represent differing views on the future of global development, the distribution of economic and military power, and institutions for peace and development. It should also be mentioned that these scenarios have not been sketched out by the Japanese alone; both Japanese and non-Japanese have articulated their preferences, given a future in which Japan will play an enhanced role.

Pax Americana, Phase II

This image of the future was first articulated by the Americans. It is the image of an America retaining its leading position in the world and making full use of its advantage in having created the institutions of post-Second World War order and security. This scenario depicts an America experienced in forging the 'balanced' or globalist view of the Western Alliance and deftly prodding and cajoling its allies into enlightened joint action. The outline of this scenario was first made during the latter half of the 1970s, when the post-Vietnam trauma was still strong and when Soviet global influence was somewhat exaggeratedly felt in the United States. In the parlance of American political scientists, the key word was 'regimes' – rules and practices in international interest adjustment – whereby the United States would retain its enlightened hegemony and control the direction of world development. Such phrases as 'after hegemony' and 'cooperation under anarchy' – both used as book titles – epitomise the primary thrust of policy and academic interest in articulating this model of the future.[10]

This image has been intermittently put forward in different forms. Confident in the retention of America's cultural hegemony in the Gramscian sense, Bruce Russett, a Yale political scientist, criticised the declaration of America's decline and imminent demise by likening it to the premature report of the death of Mark Twain. More directly and bluntly, Susan Strange of the London School of Economics has asserted that US hegemony has not yet gone; the lament on 'after hegemony' is the favourite habit of American self-indulgence, she says. More recently, Paul Kennedy of Yale has described the revival of American composure and confidence, combined with the sombre recognition of the inevitability of national decline in the longer term.[11]

In Japan, this image of America's future has been a consistent favourite. Naohiro Amaya, a former vice-minister in MITI was fond of talking about '*Go-Bei*' ('later United States'), as if the United States prior to Vietnam was called '*Zen-Bei*' ('earlier United States'). This is an analogy with the later Han dynasty of China, which was restored after 17 years of disappearance and survived for another two centuries. Similarly, Yasusuke Murakami, a well-known economist, has argued that the hegemonic cycle that has been observed for the last few centuries has ceased to repeat itself largely because the world economy has been transformed from something based on individual national economies to a much more integrated structure. His scenario delineates an America which is an enlightened and experienced *primus inter pares* in an increasingly multipolar world.[12]

This image has been a favourite one, not least because it encourages the basic retention of Japan's traditional concentration on an economic role with no drastic increase in its security role, which is largely delegated to the United States. Although Japan's profile in the world has changed a great deal in the 1980s, the Japanese preference for limiting the country's commitment to military matters, many of which are generally deemed to have dubious utility, has not been altered.

Japan's roles in Pax Americana Phase II are not significantly different from its present ones. Essentially, these are primarily of an economic nature, with the bulk of global security shouldered by the United States. Even if Japan–US security co-operation is accelerated, this basic division of labour is unlikely to change. Even if Japan were to enhance its out-of-area security co-operation by sending warships to the Persian Gulf to shoulder the cost of oil imports, it would be bolstering the US-dominated world rather than becoming a main security-provider in the region. Even if Japan were to increase its security-related assistance to some Third World countries like Pakistan, Turkey, Papua New Guinea and Honduras, the security leadership of the United States would remain strong. Needless to say, there are those who argue that Japan will start in due course to exert influence by accumulating credit in the United States and other countries. But in this scenario Japanese self-assertiveness will be restrained by various domestic and international factors.

Japan's regional roles in this scenario will be heavily economic. More concretely, Japan will become the vital core of the Pacific growth crescent, encompassing three areas: (1) northern Mexico, the Pacific United States and Canada; (2) Japan and (3) the Pacific – the Asian NICs, coastal China, the Association of Southeast Asian Nations (ASEAN) countries and Oceania.[13] The incorporation of the second and the third economic groups into the extended US economic zone will be a vital factor in a US revival. In short, Japan's role in this scenario will be to link the US economy with the Asian Pacific economies in a more balanced manner than today. In this scenario, the current US efforts to liberalise the Pacific Asian markets, revalue local currency–dollar exchange rates and promote burden sharing in development aid, finance and international security will be given further momentum. At the same time, Pacific Asian nationalistic anti-Americanism will be considerably restrained. Perhaps it is important to note that Pax Americana Phase II will need a no less vigorous Western

Europe. An enlarged and enhanced European Community (EC) will remain a pillar of this scenario. But if it degenerates into regional protectionism of the sort that can be glimpsed in the tougher EC anti-dumping policy on printing machines, through arrogance derived from an expected enlarged size and power, then it will elicit a negative reaction from the United States and Japan.

'Bigemony'

This second scenario for the future has been propagated by economists and businessmen, fascinated by the rapid development and integration of what Robert Gilpin, a Princeton political scientist, calls the *'nichibei* [Japan–US] economy'. That is to say, the economies of Japan and the United States have become one integrated economy of a sort. C. Fred Bergsten, an economist who worked as a senior bureaucrat in the Carter administration and is now Director of the Institute for International Economics, coined the word 'bigemony', which denotes the primordial importance of the United States and Japan in managing the world economy. Zbigniew Brzezinski, National Security Advisor to President Carter, coined the expression 'Amerippon' to describe the close integration of the American and Japanese manufacturing, financial and commercial sectors, and indeed the two economies as a whole. This image of the future has been enhanced by the steady rise in the yen's value compared to the US dollar, and the concomitant rise in Japanese GNP, now registering 20 per cent of world GNP.[14]

In Japan this image has been put forward most forcefully by former Prime Minister Yasuhiro Nakasone. In one of his meetings with President Reagan, he suggested that the two countries should forge a single community of the same destiny, although what he envisaged focused on security rather than on economic aspects of the bilateral relationship.[15] It must be noted that Japanese images of the future have tended to focus on Japan–US relations, to the dismay of Europeans and Asians, let alone other Third World countries. This tendency itself shows the strength of this second scenario.

Japan's roles in the 'bigemony' scenario may appear to some to be very similar to those envisaged in Pax Americana Phase II. However, economic power becomes military power almost inevitably, and Japan does not constitute the historic exception to this rule.[16] But the form in which Japan's economic power will be translated into military power needs close attention. Under 'bigemony' the technical, economic and strategic co-operation/integration between the United States and Japan will become formidable, and of the largest scale in history. It is therefore not difficult to foresee, for instance, advanced fighter aircraft being developed jointly and manufactured primarily for Japanese use, with Japanese finance, though with American know-how, and also sold to third countries under the label, 'Made in the United States'. The large-scale strategic integration between these two countries as developed in the Pacific in the 1980s will come to be seen as a good testimony of the bigemonic roles Japan can play in security areas.

Japan's regional role in 'bigemony' is an acceleration of the features presented in Pax Americana Phase II. A gigantic Pacific economic community will be forged, with Japan's role reminiscent of the role played by the corridor stretching from northern Italy through northeastern France, the Rhineland and the Low Countries to southern Britain in modern European economic development. Under this scenario, the potentially heated contest between the United States and Japan over the structural framework of Pacific Asia's economic relationship with the United States will be largely dissipated. Currently, Pacific Asia faces increasingly clear alternatives as to its economic framework: either a US-led free-trade regime established through a bilateral agreement with the United States, or a regional community with de facto Japanese initiatives, which would try to retain a free-trade zone even if North America and Western Europe fell into the temptation of protectionism and regionalism of a malign kind.[17] Furthermore, the strategic integration of many countries in the region may make it hard to accommodate the Soviet Union within an invigorated bigemonic structure, thus relegating it to a far less important status than it currently occupies, unless some other countervailing moves are continuously taken. In this scenario Western Europe, though large in size and high in income level, will be increasingly localised within Europe and its immediate vicinity. This picture reminds one of Immanuel Wallerstein's scenario of the future predicting the formation of two de facto blocs, one comprising the United States, Japan and China, and the other both Western and Eastern Europe.[18]

Pax Consortis

Japan's third scenario portrays a world of many consortia in which the major actors proceed by busily forging coalitions to make policy adjustments and agreements among themselves – a world in which no single actor can dominate the rest. This scenario resembles Pax Americana Phase II in its crude skeleton with its 'regimes' and 'co-operation under anarchy'. However, the major difference is that the thrust of the third scenario rests on the pluralistic nature of policy adjustment among the major actors, whereas that of the first conveys the desirability or necessity (or even the hoped-for inevitability) of 'administrative guidance' or 'moral leadership' by the state that is *primus inter pares* – the United States. This third image is favoured by many Japanese, not least because Japan is averse to shouldering large security burdens. It is also favoured because Japan is not completely happy about America ordering everyone around, especially when it only grudgingly admits its relative decline.

Kuniko Inoguchi, a Sophia University political scientist, articulates this scenario most eloquently and forcefully in the context of the American debate on post-hegemonic stability of the international system.[19] The image has also been put forward by former Vice-Minister Shinji Fukukawa of MITI, which favours minimising the role of military power. Recently, MITI and the Ministry of Foreign Affairs, conscious of the increasing intrusion by other ministries into foreign affairs, have been trying to use national security and the Western Alliance as a stick to discipline other ministries which might otherwise move in an 'irresponsible' direction (as in the Toshiba case, when it came to light in 1987 that the Toshiba company had sold equipment to the Soviet Union which the United States claimed was in breach of the COCOM agreement on technology transfer). The image of Pax Consortis accords on the whole with the pacifist sentiments of most Japanese.

Japan's role in the Pax Consortis scenario is two-fold. First, with the superpowers' strategic nuclear arsenals increasingly neutralised either by the de facto US–Soviet detente process or by technological break-throughs, Japan's primary role is that of quiet economic diplomacy in forging coalitions and shaping policy adjustments among peers, no one of which is predominant. Secondly, Japan's role is that of helping to create a world free from military solutions. That would include, if possible, the diffusion of anti-nuclear defensive systems to all countries and the extension of massive economic aid tied to ceasefire or peace agreements between belligerent parties. Japan's primary regional role in this scenario would be that of co-ordinator or promoter of the interests of the Asian Pacific countries which have not been fully represented either in the UN system or in the economic institutions of the industrialised countries, such as the OECD. Japan's secondary regional role is that of moderator, especially in security areas.[20] This might include acting as an intermediary and attempting to achieve reconciliation between North and South Korea, or the provision of neutral peacekeeping forces in Cambodia and/or Afghanistan in order to facilitate reconstruction through massive aid flows from such multilateral institutions as the Asian Development Bank (ADB). Western Europe will loom larger in this scenario than in the other three. In line with its role is such forums as the Western seven-power summits, Western Europe will continue to play an even larger role, having been traditionally quite adept in those situations where multiple actors adjust conflicting interests. The increasing economic ties between Western Europe and Pacific Asia will also encourage thinking along the lines of this scenario.[21]

Pax Nipponica

A fourth image of the future, 'Pax Nipponica', was first put forward by Ezra Vogel, a Harvard sociologist, who in 1979 published a book entitled *Japan as Number One*. It is a world in which Japanese economic power reigns supreme. This scenario has been propagated by those Americans who are concerned about the visible contrast between the United States' relative loss of technological and manufacturing competitiveness and Japan's concomitant gain. Ronald Morse of the US Library of Congress, for example, published an article entitled 'Japan's Drive to Pre-eminence'.[22] This view has also been gaining power in Japan, reflecting both the noticeable rise in the value of the Japanese yen compared to the US dollar and other currencies and Japan's leading position as a creditor country. The steady rise of Japanese nationalism, in tandem with what the Japanese call the internationalisation of Japan, is contributing to the strength of this scenario, because the intrusion of external economic and social forces into Japanese society stimulated nationalistic reactions against internationalisation.

Japan's role in this scenario is best compared to that of Britain during the nineteenth century, when it played the role of balancer among the continental powers, its global commercial interests presumably helping it to fulfil this role. As for Pax Consortis in its fullest version, a prerequisite for the advent of Pax Nipponica is either the removal of the superpowers' strategic nuclear arsenals or the development of an anti-nuclear defence system. Without the neutralisation of nuclear weapons, Japan's leading role in the security area would be minimised, and Pax Nipponica in its fullest form would not be realised. In this scenario, Japan's regional role will coincide with its global role, as its pre-eminent position will enable it to play the leading role in the Asian Pacific region as well.

These scenarios offer substantially different visions of Japan's future. I will now consider what conditions must prevail if they are to be realised.

REQUIREMENTS FOR THE FOUR SCENARIOS

To what extent are these scenarios feasible? Under what conditions will the scenarios come into being? In attempting to answer these questions, I will first identify three factors which seem to distinguish these scenarios from each other, and secondly, speculate on the feasibility of each scenario in the next 50 years.

There appear to be three major factors which are crucial in distinguishing these scenarios from each other – (1) the effective neutralisation of strategic nuclear arsenals, (2) scientific and technological dynamism and (3) the debt of history.

Neutralising the Nuclear Arsenals

It is the arsenals of strategic nuclear forces that have allowed the United States and the Soviet Union to retain their superpower status and global influence. Whether these weapons will become obsolete – in other words, whether they cease to be a crucial factor determining global development – remains to be seen. Whether the United States or the Soviet Union or any other country will be able to arm itself with a defensive weapons system which makes it immune to nuclear attack is another question which needs to be answered, and the American SDI and its Soviet counterpart are directly related to this factor. The Conventional Defense Initiative, in which the United States has recently proposed that Japan be jointly involved, may be included as a miniature version of a less ambitious yet more solid kind of effort. Ronald Reagan's fascination with the SDI and Japan's quiet effort to build the CDI may simply reflect what might be called a 'Maginot line' complex surfacing again years after its failure.[23]

If such a revolutionary weapons system is realised, strategic nuclear arsenals will be neutralised. Unless this happens, the fourth scenario,

Pax Nipponica, will have difficulty in emerging because while super-power status is based on ownership of strategic nuclear weapons, both the United States and the Soviet Union will remain superpowers despite all their economic difficulties. In a similar vein, the third scenario, Pax Consortis, will not materialise into a system comprising both economic and security regimes without a similar neutralisation of strategic forces. With the disarmament process between the United States and the Soviet Union slowly making progress, strategic nuclear forces may not make much difference in determining global develop-ments. There are those who, arguing in favour of Pax Consortis, maintain that nuclear weapons and even military power in general have already ceased to be a major factor in international politics and that economic interdependence has deepened sufficiently to make war an obsolete instrument for resolving conflicts of interests, at least among OECD countries and in direct East–West relations. Even granting that military power has become less important, I would argue that what is sometimes called the 'Europeanisation of superpowers', in Christoph Bertram's phrase, will progress so slowly as to make it hard to envisage the fully fledged scenarios of Pax Consortis or Pax Nipponica inside the twentieth century. Needless to say, those who argue for Pax Consortis talk about it in a somewhat nebulous future most of the time.

Scientific and Technological Dynamism

The second factor concerns the innovative and inventive capacity of nations – how vigorous they are in making scientific and technological progress and in translating it to economic development. Needless to say, forecasting technological development is not easy. However, even a cursory examination of the social propensity to innovate seems to tell us that the Americans have been the most innovative nation, with the Japanese following on steadily behind. Such conditions as open compe-tition, abundant opportunities, a strong spirit of individualism and freedom and high social mobility, which are observed in the United States, compare very favourably to conditions in Japan.

There is another argument, however, which completely opposes this: that is to say, that Japanese technological innovation has been making steady progress. The following evidence is adduced for the argument:

1. The number of licences obtained by Japanese companies and individuals in the United States has come very close to that of the

United States itself. In 1987, the top three companies were all Japanese firms – Canon, Hitachi and Toshiba (in that order).[24]
2. More articles by Japan-based authors have appeared in *Chemical Abstracts* than by authors from any other country for several years.
3. The United States in the first 30 years of this century produced as few as five Nobel Prize winners, which is about on a level with Japan's seven winners for the 40-year period since 1945.[25]

Yet as far as general innovativeness is concerned, the United States seems likely to enjoy its dominant position at least until the end of the twentieth century. If this argument is sufficiently strong, then the first scenario gains force.

The Legacy of History

The third factor is related to the memory of the peoples of the nations occupied in the Second World War of their treatment, primarily at the hands of the Germans and the Japanese. As the former Secretary-General of the Chinese Communist Party, Hu Yaobang, once said to Toyoko Yamazaki, a Japanese novelist, the memory of people who have suffered from war disappears only 80 years after the event. His evidence for this is the Boxer intervention in China in 1900, which has virtually been forgotten, whereas he argues that the memory of the second Sino–Japanese war of 1937–45 will not disappear from the memory of the Chinese for another 40 years. With the question of their wartime atrocities still a politically controversial issue, as shown by international reaction to Japanese official visits to the Yasukuni Shrine in Tokyo (which contained the remains of Japanese war criminals) and President Reagan's 1985 conciliatory visit to the Bitburg cemetery (which contained the graves of Waffe-SS men), Japan or West Germany cannot play a leading role without facing many barriers.[26] Pax Nipponica is inherently difficult because of this factor.

THE FOUR SCENARIOS RECONSIDERED

Let me now examine the four scenarios in the light of the three factors discussed above.

Pax Americana, Phase II

Whether Pax Americana Phase II is realised or not will critically depend on factor 2 – scientific and technological dynamism. The argument for this scenario tends to be based on the free spirit, open competition and dynamic character of American society, which it is thought will help the United States to reinvigorate its innovative and inventive capacity.

In my view, this scenario has a fairly high feasibility if the present predicament is managed well. For that purpose two policies are essential: first, close Japan–US macroeconomic policy co-operation and, secondly, the full-scale interlinking of the US economy with the Asian Pacific economies under US leadership. Whether the United States can achieve this without igniting Asian nationalism against it remains to be seen.

'Bigemony'

The feasibility of 'bigemony' depends critically on factor 3 – the debt of history. In other words, it is still an open question whether Japanese pacifist feeling can be overcome and whether the East Asian neighbours can be at ease with Japanese leadership in regional and global security matters, even a leadership based on co-operation with the Americans. To be feasible, therefore, this scenario requires very close friendship between the United States and Japan as a precondition for overcoming the debt-of-history problem. The argument against this scenario is that the steady progress of Japan–US economic integration and defence co-operation has been accompanied by recurrent and at times almost explosive friction between the two countries, which augurs ill for the future.

In my view, the 'bigemony' scenario can progress only slowly and steadily, in a moderate manner, as technological progress and economic dynamism push Japan and the United States closer together.

Pax Consortis

The feasibility of Pax Consortis depends critically on factor 1 – nuclear neutralisation. This is conceivable in the distant future, but certainly not in the foreseeable future. For the two superpowers to relinquish superpower status and revert to less important roles will take time, even assuming that their decline has already begun. One may recall Edward Gibbon's remark that it took another 300 years for the Roman empire to disappear after its inevitable decline and demise were declared by Tacitus. It is utterly beyond speculation whether and how an unknown perfect anti-nuclear defensive weapon system might be developed and deployed. The weaker form of Pax Consortis, one could argue, is more feasible. One may cite the inability of the superpowers to have much influence on the course of events in Nicaragua and Afghanistan, for example; the increasing importance of monetary and economic policy co-ordination and consultation among the major powers; increasing international collaboration in research and development; and the very frequent formation of consortia in manufacturing and financial activities. Needless to say, conventional forces will become more important when nuclear weapons are neutralised. Thus arms control – a kind of consortium – in conventional forces will become an important focus under Pax Consortis.

Pax Nipponica

The feasibility of Pax Nipponica depends critically on factors 1 and 2 – neutralisation of nuclear weapons and scientific and technological dynamism. If both factors are realised together, the historical factor may become less important. But the difficulty of neutralising nuclear weapons has already been mentioned. It must also be emphasised that the obstacles to Japan taking security leadership will not be easy to surmount. First, it will not be easy to persuade the overwhelmingly pacifist Japanese public. Second, it is not easy to see Japan shouldering the burden of the level of overseas armed forces the United States currently possesses for a prolonged period of time. It could easily lead Japan to suffer the kind of inefficiency that the Soviet Union has been so painfully experiencing. Thus estimates of Japan's likely scientific and technological dynamism will also affect the likelihood of Pax Nipponica.

In my view, Japan's innovative and inventive capacity for the next 10–20 years should not be underestimated. But beyond that period, the expected fall in demographic dynamism and associated social malaises that are bound to arise, such as the overburdening of the small productive working population for extensive social welfare expenditure and for Japan's increased contributions for international public goods, seem to augur ill for this scenario.

To sum up, it seems to me that scenarios one and two – Pax Americana, Phase II and bigemony – are more likely than scenarios three and four in the intermediate term of 25 years, while in the longer term of 50 years a mixture of Pax Americana, Phase II and Pax Consortis seems more feasible. Of the two scenarios feasible in the medium term, Pax Americana, Phase II is the more desirable because it entails fewer risks to the United States as well as to the rest of the world. The effort necessary to sustain the US hegemonic position in its fullest form, whether alone or jointly with Japan or other allies, may cause more stresses than benefits. In the longer term, a soft landing on a Pax Consortis seems desirable.

CONCLUSION

These four scenarios are, admittedly, incomplete. Yet their delineation is useful in order to know better what kind of futures the Japanese have in mind in their assiduous yet uncertain search for their place in the world. Some readers may be struck by the fact that these scenarios reflect peculiarly Japanese aspirations and apprehensions. The weight of the past not only lingers on, but fundamentally constrains the Japanese conception of the world. Any drastic restructuring of Japan's foreign relations away from the ties with the United States seems virtually impossible to the majority of Japanese. It is instructive to learn that in Japan only 7.2 per cent of the population are neutralists, who want to abrogate the country's security treaty with the United States, while in West Germany as many as 44 per cent are neutralists.[27]

The same thing can be said of the three major factors. First, the debt of history to the Pacific Asian neighbours has been deeply felt as a major constraining factor in our scenarios. It is as if an anti-Japanese alliance in Pacific Asia were always ready to be forged, despite that near half-century since the war, just because Japan once crossed a certain threshold of misconduct. Secondly, the neutralisation of nuclear weapons has been the dream of most Japanese since 1945, when two nuclear bombs were dropped on two Japanese cities. Thirdly, the innovative and inventive capacity of nations is one of those things many Japanese have long felt lacking within themselves. Perhaps reflecting that, they waver between unnaturally timid and exceedingly bold estimates of their own scientific and technological capacity.

Some may argue that my overall scenario – a soft-landing scenario proceeding from Pax Americana, Phase II to the Pax Consortis – is more than mildly optimistic. This may be true. It is arguable that this optimism is somewhat unfounded when the United States, the architect of the post-war order, is beset by severe problems. The point is that a large majority of responsible Japanese leaders have found it virtually impossible to think beyond a world where the United States is of primary importance to Japan and where the Japan–US friendship is a major pillar of global stability. My delineation of four scenarios, including the Pax Nipponica and bigemony, should not be understood as a disclosure of non-existent plans for Japan to become a world supremo, or co-supremo. Rather, it should be interpreted as a manifestation of the kind of independent impulse long suppressed, yet only recently allowed to appear on a very small scale in tander with Japan's rise as a global economic power. The Japanese are perplexed as they continue to rise in influence. Under what combination of the four scenarios Japan will stand up on the world stage remains a matter for our common interest.

Notes and References

Some of the material in this article is drawn from an earlier paper by the author, entitled 'Japan's global roles in a multipolar world' and presented to the Council on Foreign Relations, New York, in 1988. Professor Inoguchi gratefully acknowledges the constructive comments on that article by Shafiqul Islam and Brian Woodall, as well as the contributions of members of the Council's study group on Japan's role in development finance.

1. T. Inoguchi, *Tadanori to Ikkoku Hanei Shugi o Koete* (Beyond free-ride and prosperity-in-one-country-ism) (Tokyo: Toyo Keizai Shimposha, 1987); T. Inoguchi, 'Tenkanki Nihon no Kadai' (Japan's Tasks at a Time of Transition), *Nihon Keizai Shimbun* (1, 8, 15, 22 and 29 November 1989).

2. T. Inoguchi, 'The Ideas and Structures of Foreign Policy: Looking ahead with Caution', in T. Inoguchi and D. I. Okimoto (eds), *The Political Economy of Japan, Vol. 2: The Changing International Context* (Stanford, CA: Stanford University Press, 1988) pp. 23–63, 490–500; T. Inoguchi, 'Japan's Images and Options: Not a Challenger but a Supporter', *Journal of Japanese Studies*, 12(1) (Winter 1986) pp. 95–119; T. Inoguchi, 'Japan's Foreign Policy Background', in H. J. Ellison (ed.), *Japan and the Pacific Quadrille* (Boulder, CO: Westview, 1987) pp. 81–105.

3. M. Sayle, 'The Powers that Might Be: Japan is no sure bet as the next global top dog', *Far Eastern Economic Review* (4 August 1988) pp. 38–43.

4. Department of Public Relations, Office of the Prime Minister, *Gaiko ni Kansuru Yoron Chosa* (Opinion Poll on Diplomacy) (Tokyo: Office of the Prime Minister, April 1988).
5. Joji Watanuki *et al.*, *Nihonjin no Senkyo Kodo* (Japanese Electoral Behaviour) (Tokyo: University of Tokyo Press, 1986).
6. T. Inoguchi, 'Trade, Technology and Security: Implications for East Asia and the West', *Adelphi Papers*, 218 (Spring 1987) pp. 39–55; T. Inoguchi, 'The Legacy of a Weathercock Prime Minister', *Japan Quarterly*, 34(4) (October–December 1987) pp. 363–70.
7. When the 1987 fiscal budget draft was revealed early in 1987, it surpassed the 1 per cent limit. But because in 1987 GNP increased much more vigorously, defence expenditure became less than 1 per cent of GNP at the end of the 1987 fiscal year. On the opinion polls, see Nisihira Sigeki, *Yoron ni Miru Dosedai Shi* (Contemporary History through Opinion Polls) (Tokyo: Brain Shuppan, 1987) p. 295.
8. *Asahi Shimbun* (30 October 1987); see also K. Chuma, 'Nihon no Yukue o Kangaeru' (Thinking about Japan's Future Direction), *Sekai* (December 1987) pp. 85–98.
9. T. Inoguchi, 'Tenkanki Nihon no Kadai', *Nihon Keizai Shimbun* (15 November 1987).
10. Stephen Krasner (ed.), *International Regimes* (Ithaca, NY: Cornell University Press, 1983); Robert O. Keohane, *After Hegemony: Cooperation and Discord in the World Political Economy* (Princeton, NJ: Princeton University Press, 1984); Kenneth A. Oye (ed.), *Cooperation Under Anarchy* (Princeton NJ: Princeton University Press, 1985).
11. B. Russett, 'The Mysterious Case of Vanishing Hegemony: or, Is Mark Twain Really Dead?', *International Organization*, 39(2) (Spring 1985) pp. 207–31; S. Strange, 'The Persistent Myth of Lost Hegemony', *International Organization*, 41(4) (Autumn 1987) pp. 551–74; P. Kennedy, *The Rise and Fall of the Great Powers* (New York: Random House, 1987).
12. N. Amaya, *Nihon wa Doko e Ikunoka* (Whither Japan?) (Tokyo: PHP Institute, 1987); Y. Murakami, 'After Hegemony', *Chuo Koron* (November 1985).
13. C. I. Bradford and W. H. Branson (eds), *Structural Change in Pacific Asia* (Chicago, IL: University of Chicago Press, 1987); P. Drysdale, *International Economic Pluralism: Economic Policy in East Asia and the Pacific* (Sydney: George Allen & Unwin, 1988).
14. R. Gilpin, *War and Change in World Politics* (Cambridge: Cambridge University Press, 1981); R. Gilpin, *The Political Economy of International Relations* (Princeton, NJ: Princeton University Press, 1987).
15. T. Inoguchi, 'The Legacy of a Weathercock Prime Minister'.
16. Kennedy, *The Rise and Fall of the Great Powers*.
17. T. Inoguchi, 'Shaping and Sharing the Pacific Dynamism', paper presented at a symposium on 'Japan's Growing External Assets: A medium for growth?', Centre for Asian Pacific Studies, Lingnan College, Hong Kong (22–4 June 1988).
18. I. Wallerstein, 'Friends as Foes', *Foreign Policy* (Fall 1980) pp. 119–31.
19. K. Inoguchi, *Posuto Haken Sisutemu to Nihon no Sentaku* (An Emerging

Post-hegemonic System: Choices for Japan) (Tokyo: Chikuma Shobo, 1987).

20. T. Inoguchi, *Tadanori to Ikkoku Hanei Shugi o Koete.*

21. T. Inoguchi, 'Shaping and Sharing the Pacific Dynamism'.

22. E. Vogel, *Japan as Number One* (Cambridge, MA: Harvard University Press, 1979); E. Vogel, 'Pax Nipponica?', *Foreign Affairs*, 64(4) (Spring 1986) pp. 752–67; R. A. Morse, 'Japan's Drive to Pre-eminence', *Foreign Policy*, 69 (Winter 1987–88) pp. 3–21.

23. On the CDI pushed by the US Congress see D. C. Morrison, 'Earth Wars', *National Journal* (1 August 1987) pp. 1972–5; R. L. Kerber and D. N. Frederiksen, 'The Conventional Defense Initiative/Balanced Technology Initiative', *Defense Issues*, 2(36) pp. 1–5. I am grateful to Jefferson Seabright for enabling me to read these and other related materials.

24. *Nihon Keizai Shimbun* (26 March 1988).

25. *Ashai Shimbun* (evening edn, 24 March 1988).

26. P. Katzenstein, 'Supporter States in the International System: Japan and West Germany', paper prepared for the conference on 'Globalized Business Activities and the International Economy', Research Institute of International Trade and Industry, Tokyo (23–4 June 1988).

27. On the West German figure, see 'Disarmament is a Long Word and Takes a Long Time to Say', *The Economist* (30 July 1988); on the Japanese figure see Sayle, 'The Powers that Might Be'.

Index

Abe, Shintaro, Foreign Minister, 83
Afghanistan, 96, 103, 155
Africa, 89–94
    Japanese aid to, 113
African National Congress, 92
alliance, US–Japan, 149, 152
Amaya, Naohiro, 211
Amazon Basin, 94
apartheid, 90
Aquino, Corazon, President, 103,
    108
Aquino, Benigno, 108
Arafat, Yasser, PLO Chairman, 87
Argentina, 96
arms control, 221
    in Northeast Asia, 199
arms sales, Japan's policy on, 162
arms sales, US, 156
ASEAN (Association of Southeast
    Asian Nations), 74, 80–4
    Japanese aid to, 108
Asian Development Bank, 32, 80,
    131, 216

Baikal–Amur Railway, 192
Baker–Miyazawa Agreement, 18
Baldrige, Malcolm, Commerce
    Secretary, 59, 164
Bank of Japan, 31, 35
Baoshan Steel Complex, 127, 136,
    139
Bergsten, C. Fred, 213
Bertram, Christoph, 218
bigemony, 213–14, 220
Blanchard, James, 61
bond market, Tokyo, 36
Bonin Islands, 150
Brazil, 95
Bryant, John, Congressman, 49
Brzezinski, Zbigniew, 102, 213
burden-sharing (Japan–US), 148,
    152, 158–60, 207
Burma, 83–4
Bush, George, President, 29, 64, 163,
    165

Cairo Declaration, 181, 182
Cambodia, 83, 106
capital flows, 11
    controls on, 34
    from Japan, 24
    Japan to US, 18, 29
Carter, Jimmy, President, 152
CFIUS, *see under* US
Chernotsky, Harry, 75
Chiang Kai-shek, 181
Chile, 96
China, 78–9, 106, 107, 121–46
    passim, 189
    Japan's relations with, 3
    Japanese technology transfer to,
    13
    Japanese direct investment in,
    128–30, 137
    Japanese aid to, 11
    textbook crisis with Japan, 133–4
    trade with Japan, 126–8, 136–7
Churchill, Winston, 181
COCOM, 138, 215
Cold War, 176, 179, 182
Colombia, 96
comprehensive security, 72, 77, 96,
    102, 103, 113, 118, 153, 161
    role of ODA in, 123
Conventional Defense Initiative, 217
creditor nation
    Japan as, 6, 7, 13, 19, 23–7, 216
    Saudi Arabia as, 25–7
    US as, 25–32
cultural diplomacy, 82

Daiwa Securities, 29
Davidson, James Dale, 12
de Gaulle, Charles, 10
debtor nation, US as, 15, 17
defence, maritime, 160–1
defence industry, Japan, 163
defence spending
    Japan, 155, 159, 165, 167
    US, 148
Deng Xiaoping, 135, 139

Diamond-Star Motors, 61
dollar, 10, 37, 38
  fall in value of, 28, 29, 30
Doyukai, 92
Drucker, Peter, 17, 18
Dulles, John Foster, Secretary of
  State, 180, 186

East Asia, 20
  Japanese investment in, 16
economic influence effect, theory of,
  122–3
Egypt, 89
Eichelberger, Robert, General, 187
Emmott, Bill, 26
equities markets, Japanese, 36
Etorofu, 175
Exon–Florio Provisions, *see under*
  US, 1988 Trade Act

Fairchild Semiconductor, 56, 164
foreign direct investment (FDI), 11,
  12, 45–67, 50–1
foreign direct investment, British in
  US, 47
foreign direct investment, Dutch in
  US, 47
foreign direct investment, Japanese,
  2, 24
  in China, 121, 128–30, 137
  in South Africa, 91
  in South Korea, 85
  in Third World, 73, 75
  in US, 2, 50, 51–4, 53
  increase of 1987–8, 123
foreign direct investment, US, 55
  compared with Japanese, 16
fishing rights, 175, 191–2
Foreign Ministry, Japan, 91, 103,
  215
Formosa, 179
free-trade regime, 214
FSX jet fighter project, 58–9, 67,
  163–4
Fujio, Masayuki, Minister of
  Education, 133
Fujitsu, 56, 16
Fukuda, Takeo, Prime Minister, 81
Fukukawa, Shinji, 215

fumie diplomacy, 79

Gabon, 93
Galenson, Walter and David W.,
  165
Garn, Jake, Senator, 63
General Ceramics, 164
Germany, as an economic power, 7
Ghana, 90
Gilpin, Robert, 23, 25, 28, 213
Gorbachev, Mikhail, General
  Secretary, 157, 190, 194, 195,
  197, 198
Great Britain
  direct investment in US, 47
  as an economic power, 6, 8, 9–15,
  216
Gu Mu, Vice Premier, 139

Habomai Islands, 175, 179, 180, 181,
  185, 189
Harris, Anthony, 66
Hatoyama, Prime Minister, 185,
  186, 189
hegemonic decline, of US, 147–8,
  149, 153–4, 211–13, 215
Hills, Carla, 66
Hirschman, Albert O., 122–3, 130–1,
  140–1, 143
Hokkaido, 176
Hollerman, Leon, 95
Hormuz, Straits of, 88
Hu Yaobang, General Secretary,
  China, 135, 219
Hume, David, 7
Huntington, Samuel P., 46

Ikeda, Hayato, Prime Minister, 184
IMF (International Monetary
  Fund), 12, 34, 131
India, 96
Indonesia, 76, 81, 106, 109
Inman, Bobby, Admiral, 64
Inoguchi, Kuniko, 215
International Cooperation Initiative,
  154
International Banking Facilities,
  Japan, 35
International Court of Justice, 180

internationalisation
    of Japanese business, 48
    of Japanese finance, 2, 39
    of Japanese manufacturing, 54
Iran–Iraq war, 88
Israel, 87, 89

Jamaica, 105
Japan Communist Party, 186
Japan Defense Agency, 163
Japan Economic Institute, 52
Japan Foundation, 155
Japan–Palestinian Parliamentary
    League, 87
Johnson, Chalmers, 74, 79, 157
Jordan, 89, 113

Kampuchea, *see* Cambodia
Karafuto, *see* Sakhalin
Keidanren, 60, 92
Kennedy, Paul, 154, 211
Kenya, 93
Kimura, Foreign Minister, 90
Kissinger, Henry, 102
Kojima, Kiyoshi, Foreign Minister,
    15
kokaryo case, 134
Korea, 84–6, 152
Korea, Democratic Republic of, 188
Korea, Republic of, 103, 106, 109,
    111, 152
Korean War, 150
Krause, Lawrence B., 18
Kunashiri, 175
Kuranari, Tadashi, Foreign
    Minister, 90
Kurile Islands, 175–6, 178–82, 184,
    185
    definition of, 183
Kyocera Ceramics, 55
Kyoto dormitory controversy
    (Sino–Japanese), 134

Lamm, Richard, Governor, 45
Laos, 107, 108
Latin America, 94–6
    recycling of Japanese surplus to,
    113

Liberal Democratic Party, Japan
    (LDP), 47, 150, 151, 166, 167
Lewis, W. Arthur, 7
Liberia, 93
Lincoln, Eric, 30
Long-Term Trade Agreement
    (LTTA), Sino–Japanese, 3, 121,
    126, 132, 139
Louvre Agreement, 18

Maekawa Report, 15
Mahathir, Mohamed, Prime
    Minister, 82
Malaysia, 106
Mandela, Nelson, 90
maquiladora assembly plants, 95
Marshall Plan, 9
Mauritania, 93
McNamara, Robert, 118
McGrath, Paul, 64
Mexico, 95
Middle East, 86–9
Miki, Takeo, Prime Minister, 190
military balance, US–Soviet, 152–3
military spending, Japanese, 1, 102
Minebea, 164
MITI, 38, 48–9, 75, 91–2, 107, 137,
    215
    involvement in aid policy-making,
    115
MOF, Ministry of Finance, Japan,
    28, 38
money market, Japan, 37–8
Morse, Ronald, 88, 216
Mosbacher, Robert, 59
Multilateral Assistance Initiative
    (US–Philippines), 162
multipolar world system, 214–16,
    222
Murakami, Yasusuke, 211
Murkowski, Frank, Senator, 50
Mutual Defense Assistance
    (US–Japan), 162
Mutual Security Treaty (US–Japan),
    125

Nakasone, Yasuhiro, Prime
    Minister, 29, 88, 90, 112, 134,

Nakasone, Yasukiro – *cont.*
  135, 152, 162, 165, 182, 189–90,
  213
neomercantilism, 72, 73
Netherlands, direct investment in
  US, 47
Neutrality Act (Soviet–Japan), 184
Nichibei economy, 17
Niger, 93
Nigeria, 90, 93
Nippon Steel, 55
Nixon Doctrine, 151, 155
Nomura Research Institute, 20
Nomura Securities, 29
North, Douglass, 24
Northeast Asia, 124–6, 141–2, 176
  arms control in, 199
Northern Territories, 178–90, 191–2,
  193–7
  Soviet forces in, 187–8
  see also Kurile Islands
nuclear weapons, 6, 188, 217
Nyrere, Julius, President, 94

official development assistance
  (ODA), Japanese, 3, 32, 73, 77,
  100–20 *passim*, 168
  aid friction, 117
  as part of defence burden, 161
  distribution by country, 105–7,
    110
  policy-making process for, 111–13
  to Africa, 94
  to Asian countries, 100–10
  to China, 128, 139
  US influence on, 103
Ohira, Masayoshi, Prime Minister,
  112, 153
oil crisis, 35, 158
oil imports, Japanese, 87
Okinawa, 150, 186
Okita, Saburo, Foreign Miniter, 137,
  139
Oman, 113
omiyage diplomacy, 73, 81, 82
Onda, Takashi, 92
OPEC, 26, 87
Organski, A. F. K., 5

Pacific region, Japan's role in, 20
Pakistan, 96, 103, 104, 106, 107
Panama, 96
Payne, Richard J., 91
Peace and Friendship Treaty
  (Sino–Japanese), 125, 132, 187,
  189
Perry, Commodore, 176, 177
Persian Gulf, 113, 155
Peru, 96
Pescadore Islands, 179
Philippines, 100, 103, 104, 106, 110,
  116, 156, 162
PLO, 87, 89
portfolio investment, 24, 46
Potsdam Conference, 183
power-sharing (US–Japan), 207
Prestowitz, Clyde V., 45
protectionism, 6
  in US, 6, 67
public opinion, Japanese
  on Japan's international role,
    208–10
  on neutrality, 222
  on Soviet Union, 193–4
Putiatin, Admiral, 176

Reagan, Ronald, President, 45, 59,
  152, 165, 190, 213, 219
Recruit scandal, 166
Rees-Mogg, William, 12
Reich, Robert, 66
relational power, 23, 38
Rodger, Ian, 29
Roosevelt, Franklin Delano,
  President, 181
Russett, Bruce, 211

Sakhalin, 175, 176, 179, 185
Sakonjo, Naotoshi, Vice Admiral,
  164
Sato, Eisaku, Prime Minister, 80
Saudi Arabia, 25–7, 87
Scowcroft, Brent, US National
  Security Advisor, 148
SDI (Strategic Defense Initiative),
  157, 162, 217
security cooperation, US–Japan,
  159

Security Treaty, US–Japan, 150, 186
Self-Defence Forces, Japan, 150, 151, 188
Sematech, 64
Semiconductor Research Corporation, 64
Sen, Gautam, 7
Senegal, 93
Senkaku Islands, 195–6
Shevardnadze, Eduard A., Foreign Minister, 194
Shigemitsu, Mamoru, Foreign Minister, 186
Shikotan, 175, 179, 180, 181, 185, 189
Shultz, George, 59
Siberia, 175, 192, 193
Single European Act, 8
Somalia, 105, 106
South Africa, 89–93
South Asia, 94, 96
Southeast Asia, 78–84
Soviet Union, 4, 175–205 *passim*
  military presence in Asia, 156–7
Sri Lanka, 96
Stalin, Joseph, 179, 182
Strange, Susan, 23, 211
structural power, 23, 36–9
Sudan, 93, 106
Sudo, Sueo, 82
Suzuki, Zenko, Prime Minister, 87, 160
Syria, 89

Taiwan, 78–9, 109
takeovers, Japanese of US companies, 53
Takeshima Islands, 196
Takeshita, Noboru, Prime Minister, 74, 80, 82, 137, 154, 166, 207
Tambo, Oliver, 90
Tamura, Hajime, Education Minister, 92
Tanaka, Kakuei, Prime Minister, 81
Tanzania, 90, 94
Tazawa, Kichiro, Japan Defense Agency Director, 163
technology transfer, 137–8, 162

textbook crisis, Sino–Japanese, 133–4
Thailand, 81, 103, 106, 126
Third World, 3, 71–99 *passim*
  Japanese direct investment in, 75, 76
  Japanese trade with, 75
Toshiba Machine Tools, 63–4, 157, 192, 215
Toyota, 91
trade, Japanese with Third World, 75
trade surplus, Japan's, 6
trade, China–Japan, 126–8
trade, Japanese–Soviet, 191
Treaty of Mutual Cooperation and Security, US–Japan, 150
Treaty of St Petersburg, 176, 183
Treaty of San Francisco, 181–2, 183
Treaty of Shimoda, 175, 176, 180
Truman, Harry, 179, 181
Turkey, 103, 105, 106, 107, 112

UNESCO, 155
United Nations, 1, 74, 93
  peacekeeping forces, 83, 155
Uno, Sosuke, Prime Minister, 77, 89, 166
uranium, Japanese imports of, 92
US, 3, 4, 100
  1988 Trade Act, 55, 57–8, 63
  Agency for International Development, 116
  alliance with Japan, 16, 189
  arms sales in Asia, 156
  as an economic power, 7, 8, 9–15
  bases in Japan, 150
  budget deficit, 17–18, 152, 166
  Commerce Department, 49, 65
  Committee on Foreign Investment in the US (CFIUS), 55, 56–8
  Comprehensive Anti-Apartheid Act, 90
  decline of, *see* hegemonic decline of US
  defence build-up, 152
  Defense Department, 49, 59, 64, 65

UNESCO – *cont.*
Export Administration
   Regulations, 60
forces in Japan, 159
foreign control of industry in, 49
Foreign Exchange and Foreign
   Trade Control Law, 34
Foreign Ownership Disclosure
   Bill, 49
House of Representatives,
   Committee on Government
   Operations, 58
influence on Japanese ODA, 103
Japanese investment in, 25, 28–31
Justice Department, 65
National Cooperative Research
   Act, 64
National Security Council, 59
position on Kurile Islands, 179
rapprochement with China, 152
relations with Soviet Union, 189
State Department, 49, 58
stock market crash, 29
strategic interests in Asia, 150
Trade Representative, 58
Treasury Department, 49, 57, 58,
   62
troop reductions in Asia, 156

US–Japan economic relations, 17–20
US–Japan strategic co-operation,
   214

Venezuela, 96
Vietnam, 82–3, 106
Vogel, Ezra, 216

Weinberger, Caspar, Defense
   Secretary, 165
Western Europe, 7, 8, 14
World Bank, 12, 131

Yalta Conference, 178, 179, 180,
   181, 183
Yamazaki, Tokoyo, 219
Yasukuni Shrine, 134
Yasutomo, Dennis, 118
yen, 16, 54, 37, 216
   revaluation of, 6, 10
Yen–Dollar Agreement, 34
Yen–Dollar Committee, 17
Yoshida Doctrine, 150
Yoshida, Shigeru, Prime Minister,
   183, 186, 187

Zaire, 90, 93
Zambia, 93